THE DAILY STUDY BIBLE

(OLD TESTAMENT)

General Editor: John C.L. Gibson

JOB

JOB

JOHN C.L. GIBSON

THE WESTMINSTER PRESS
PHILADELPHIA

Published by
The Saint Andrew Press
Edinburgh, Scotland
and
The Westminster Press ®
Philadelphia, Pennsylvania

PRINTED IN THE UNITED STATES OF AMERICA
2   4   6   8   9   7   5   3

Library of Congress Cataloging-in-Publication Data

Gibson, John C. L.
  Job.

  (The Daily study Bible series)
  Bibliography: p.
  1. Bible. O.T. Job—Commentaries. I. Title.
II. Series: Daily study Bible series (Westminster Press)
BS1415.3.G52 1985   223'.1077   85-13652
ISBN 0-664-21815-6
ISBN 0-664-24584-6 (pbk.)

GENERAL PREFACE

This series of commentaries on the Old Testament, to which the present volume on *Job* belongs, has been planned as a companion series to the much-acclaimed New Testament series of the late Professor William Barclay. As with that series, each volume is arranged in successive headed portions suitable for daily study. The Biblical text followed is that of the Revised Standard Version or Common Bible. Eleven contributors share the work, each being responsible for from one to three volumes. The series is issued in the hope that it will do for the Old Testament what Professor Barclay's series succeeded so splendidly in doing for the New Testament—make it come alive for the Christian believer in the twentieth century.

Its two-fold aim is the same as his. Firstly, it is intended to introduce the reader to some of the more important results and fascinating insights of modern Old Testament scholarship. Most of the contributors are already established experts in the field with many publications to their credit. Some are younger scholars who have yet to make their names but who in my judgment as General Editor are now ready to be tested. I can assure those who use these commentaries that they are in the hands of competent teachers who know what is of real consequence in their subject and are able to present it in a form that will appeal to the general public.

The primary purpose of the series, however, is *not* an academic one. Professor Barclay summed it up for his New Testament series in the words of Richard of Chichester's prayer—to enable men and women "to know Jesus Christ more clearly, to love Him more dearly, and to follow Him more nearly." In the case of the Old Testament we have to be a little more circumspect than that. The Old Testament was completed long before the time of Our Lord, and it was (as it still is) the sole Bible of the Jews, God's first people, before it became part of the Christian Bible. We must take this fact seriously.

Yet in its strangely compelling way, sometimes dimly and sometimes directly, sometimes charmingly and sometimes embarrassingly, it holds up before us the things of Christ. It should not be forgotten that Jesus Himself was raised on this Book, that He based His whole ministry on what it says, and that He approached His death with its words on His lips. Christian men and women have in this ancient collection of Jewish writings a uniquely illuminating avenue not only into the will and purposes of God the Father, but into the mind and heart of Him who is named God's Son, who was Himself born a Jew but went on through the Cross and Resurrection to become the Saviour of the world. Read reverently and imaginatively the Old Testament can become a living and relevant force in their everyday lives.

It is the prayer of myself and my colleagues that this series may be used by its readers and blessed by God to that end.

New College   JOHN C.L. GIBSON
Edinburgh   General Editor

CONTENTS

INTRODUCTION

I do not intend to eulogize the Book of Job in this introduction. I am writing it after I have finished the commentary, and I have long since run out of superlatives. I am also left with feelings of utter inadequacy and dissatisfaction. I have lost count of the number of times I have turned back to emend this sentence, recast that paragraph, or even rewrite a whole section. And if the publishers were not at this moment breathing down my neck to get my manuscript onto their desk, I should doubtless be chopping and changing for months, if not years, to come. I have taught this book at New College now for more than two decades, and I thought with this commentary I would have an opportunity to get my conclusions on what it is saying down on paper in some sort of organized form. I was deluding myself. Try to pin this book down and it slips like sand through your fingers.

What I offer the readers of this commentary is not, therefore, in any way a definitive statement of what the Book of Job is about and what lessons it has to teach the Christian believer in the twentieth century. It is not even, for reasons I have outlined, a definitive statement of what it means to me, although it is a strongly worded statement. Every reader must work out his or her own interpretation of the book as it speaks to him or her in his or her own life; and I can only help. But there is one warning I must issue right at the start. You must not be tempted to tone down or spiritualize or sentimentalize its language, even where it offends (as it often does) with its stridency and impropriety and, yes, blasphemy. Job is a real sufferer, and his complaints against both God and the three friends who come to counsel him, are real and bitter. If we get into the habit of saying, "What Job really means is this", and of coming up with a substitute of some pious and balanced generality, out of which all bite and emotion have been squeezed, we will almost certainly be missing the point. Of that at least I am sure. This book, in short, is not for the faint-hearted. As President Harry Truman is reputed to have said, "If you can't stand the heat, get out of the kitchen".

The author takes as his starting-point an old folk story about a righteous patriarch called Job, who remained faithful under the severest trials which God could visit upon him, and who received God's approval for his constancy. But this tale, with its rather simplistic moral, is very soon left behind. Into the middle of it, between the sending of the trials and the pronouncement of the favourable verdict, the author inserts a long series of confrontations between Job and his friends, and between Job and God, where the message is anything but uncomplicated.

The patient Job of the folk tale quickly loses his patience and goes on the offensive. He attacks the friends for advising him to confess his guilt and turn to God for forgiveness. He had done nothing of which he need be ashamed. And what in any case did they, with their traditional religion, know about the real God and his dealings with men? Then Job attacks God for treating him as though he were a sinner, for refusing to give him the vindication that was his right, for being deaf to his cries and, his logic making him ever bolder, of also being deaf to the cries of all the world's oppressed and suffering people and making a sorry mess of governing his creation. Eventually God speaks to Job out of the whirlwind, peremptorily puts him in his place, and extracts from him a submission. But there is a sting in the tail! At no point does God impugn Job's integrity, something the friends were constantly doing; and the author allows the happy ending of the old folk tale to stand. Even though the lengthy disputations of which I spoke have intervened, Job is still praised for saying of God "what is right" (42:7), and the friends are angrily dismissed for not doing so. And Job is restored to his former health and prosperity.

Whatever else this is, it is not a gospel of "none is righteous, no, not one" nor of "saved only by faith". Job has to submit before God, but the submission is not the kind commended in our evangelical hymns. He has to abhor himself and repent in dust and ashes, but he does not have to say that he is a miserable sinner, incapable of good. We are miles away, in the Book of Job, from the Epistle to the Romans. And there are other places where it is obvious that the Book of Job is pre-Christian. There is not in the Book of Job, despite the famous passage in Chapter 19, "I know that my Redeemer lives", any real belief in a meaningful life after death. Nor is there any notion that Job's sufferings have a positive function as, in the light of the Cross, a Christian's sufferings may.

There are many other things of which I could inform the reader or prepare him for: the fact that the book belongs, along with the Books of Proverbs and Ecclesiastes, to the "Wisdom" literature of the Old Testament; its surface arrangement in the form of a debate in which various positions are advanced and rejected in formal speeches; the fact, nevertheless, that most of it is in poetry, which is not doctrine (there is, for instance, considerable use of pagan imagery); the even more important fact of the human situation behind the debate which, as far as Job and the friends are concerned, is of a sick man being comforted and counselled and, as far as Job and God are concerned, is of a troubled soul wrestling in prayer with its Maker; the question whether because of this book, protest against God should be given a larger place in Christian piety than it usually gets; the pervasive presence, throughout, of the language of worship and the author's obvious indebtedness to the laments and hymns of praise in the Psalter; the quite widespread recourse to humour, often macabre, and to irony and sarcasm; the possibility that two substantial sections in the book's second half (chapters 24–28 and chapters 32–37) may not be original to it; the question of its date (I would place it in the period just before the Babylonian Exile around the same time as Jeremiah, say 600 B.C., but I would not object if it were dated a little later). But we can pick these matters up as we come to them.

As for the book's purpose, it clearly wishes to discover a solution to the age-long problem of unmerited suffering. For all their "wisdom", the philosophers of Israel had in their most representative product—the Book of Proverbs—found little or nothing to say either on this or on the wider issues of God's providence which it raises. The author of the Book of Job therefore is intent on plugging a gap in the teaching of the Wisdom schools. But as, in the speeches he puts into the mouths of Job and his three friends, he probes this way and that, the gap only seems to grow larger. It will be for us to judge—if we can—whether, when in the final chapters, the author daringly puts words in the mouth of God, he succeeds in coming up with a solution that can be called satisfactory, or whether he fails and has to allow the argument to be swallowed up in mystery. I believe the truth lies somewhere between these two assessments.

But of one thing we will be certain. When we reach the end of this unique and scarifying and excoriating book, we will know that we have had an exceedingly uncomfortable and tempestuous ride. No book before or since has so remorselessly peeled away the layers of piety and hypocrisy, of self-pity and self-deceit, of meretricious grovelling and heaven-defying arrogance with which, down the ages, humankind has tried to cover over the truth about itself. And no book before or since has so pitilessly confronted men with the claims of the One in whom alone their soiled and burdened lives can find meaning and peace. To read and study the Book of Job is to grow up in the faith with a vengeance; and that is worth all the theology in the world.

THE GREATEST OF ALL THE
PEOPLE OF THE EAST

Job 1:1–5

¹There was a man in the land of Uz, whose name was Job; and that man
was blameless and upright, one who feared God, and turned away
from evil. ²There were born to him seven sons and three daughters.
³He had seven thousand sheep, three thousand camels, five hundred
yoke of oxen, and five hundred she-asses, and very many servants; so
that this man was the greatest of all the people of the east. ⁴His sons
used to go and hold a feast in the house of each on his day; and they
would send and invite their three sisters to eat and drink with them.
⁵And when the days of the feast had run their course, Job would send
and sanctify them, and he would rise early in the morning and offer
burnt offerings according to the number of them all; for Job said, "It
may be that my sons have sinned, and cursed God in their hearts."
Thus Job did continually.

These opening verses describe Job's character in glowing terms
and follow it up with a list of his numerous offspring, his vast
material wealth and his hordes of servants. Not only did he lead a
blameless life and scrupulously attend to the duties of his religion
(that is probably what the phrase "feared God" means in this
context), but he was also abundantly supplied with this world's
goods. And, as if we had not yet understood how upright and
pious he was, we are told that it was his custom to offer sacrifices
on the day after various family festivities in case his sons had
inadvertently been guilty of what we would call swearing, as the
wine flowed.

(i)

It is all a bit overdone for our taste. And it jars with its undoubted
implication that Job's prosperity was a reward for his virtue.

5

Christian religious language is usually more circumspect. We do not readily ascribe sainthood to anybody, and, when we do, we demand that our saints have as few of this world's goods as possible. We are too ingrained with St Paul's teaching—that human beings cannot earn God's approval by their own good works—to be impressed by a character reference like the one here given to Job.

Modern commentators usually try to mitigate our unease by suggesting that the verses are not as simplistic as they seem. In particular they argue that the Hebrew word translated as "blameless" in the RSV and, more crudely still, "perfect" in the Authorized Version, might be more accurately rendered by adjectives or phrases denoting wholeness or soundness or honesty or integrity. The commentators have a point, especially when we find the equivalent Hebrew noun translated as "integrity" twice in the next chapter; once when God is praising Job (v. 3), and once when Job's wife is remonstrating with him (v. 9). Other examples of the noun in this broader sense are to be found in Genesis 20:5–6 (where it is combined with the word, "innocence"), Judges 9:16 (where it is translated "honour" and combined with a word meaning truth or good faith), and Proverbs 28:6 (where the integrity of a poor man is contrasted with the perversity of a rich man).

The commentators also have a point when they insist that Job himself, later on, does not claim to be sinless or devoid of defects: see, for example, Job 13:26 and 14:16–17. In 9:20, therefore, when he says "I am blameless", he cannot be arrogating unqualified purity to himself, but is instead drawing attention to the sincerity of his efforts to live a good life.

It would, however, be quite misleading to pretend that these introductory verses are describing Job's integrity *rather* than his good works, or that later, when disaster strikes him, he takes his stand on that integrity *rather* than on his behaviour. Taking the book as a whole, Job does not often confess his faults and when he says he is blameless, he means—whatever else he means—that his conduct has been such that he deserves his riches and large family and good health. We are, in the Book of Job, light years away from a Pauline suspicion of good works, and in touch with a culture where, for a good man to claim to be good, was not deprecated but expected. It was indeed that claim which, as much as anything else, constituted Job's integrity.

(ii)

The Book of Job belongs to what we call the Wisdom literature of the Old Testament. The *hakamim*, or "wise men", were a class of philosophers or teachers who believed that by studying the world of nature and the workings of human society, a man could discern the inner harmony of the universe and tease out the principles of behaviour which would bring him into contact with that harmony and ensure his happiness and success in life. Religion was important to them and, in a real sense, the basis of all their study: "The fear of the Lord is the beginning of knowledge" is how their enduring memorial, the Book of Proverbs, puts it in its first chapter (v. 7)—and there the phrase means a lot more than punctilious attendance at worship. But it was a broadly conceived religion, more concerned with the God who had created the universe and made it as it was, than with the God who had specially revealed himself to Israel and chosen them to be the means whereby he would save the rest of mankind.

That kind of concern, the wise men left to the priests and prophets and psalmists, and, by choosing a non-Israelite like Job as his hero, the author of the Book of Job shows, in a quite forcible way, that he sides with them. This does not imply that he was not himself a good Israelite who kept the law of Moses and attended the Temple as prescribed, nor indeed that the God of whom he writes was any other than *Yahweh*, the God of Israel. Naturally, foreigners like Job and his friends, could not be expected to use the special name of Israel's God, and, except for the odd occasion, they do not. But we, the readers, know that it is *Yahweh* who is behind all Job's experiences, and so the name *Yahweh* can be used in the prologue which sets the scene. It is a bit of a fiction, but it is nonetheless a valuable fiction. It emphasizes that the knowledge of God and his ways, which Job and his friends have (or claim to have) is on the whole the kind that is available to man, as man. It is not the revealed kind dispensed by priests and prophets, but the kind to be won by reflection on human life in general and its background in nature and society.

For reasons that will become clearer as we proceed, the theology that underpins the Wisdom movement plays a large part in the Book of Job. It was, however, the practical corollaries of such a theology on which the *hakamim* of Israel generally placed most weight. Many of them seem to have been employed as teachers of the young, and the Book of Proverbs is, for much of its length, a record of the everyday lessons that were the mainstay of their classroom work. It is a veritable compendium of wise and foolish actions and attitudes: the *first* being the ones that tended to the welfare of society and held out before their youthful charges the prospect of success and esteem in life; the *second* which led to society's disruption and which must at all costs be avoided by their pupils.

No-one can fail to be charmed by the wit and shrewdness of the pithy sayings which abound in the Book of Proverbs, but it is a utilitarian ethic that they enshrine. Virtue is good because it brings rewards, and wickedness is as much folly as it is sin because it lands those who commit it in avoidable trouble. There is hardly ever any doubt expressed that a man can choose whether to join the righteous or to throw in his lot with the wicked, and therefore he is, to that extent, master of his own fate. Why then should he not feel pleased with himself if he chooses rightly, and why should he not say so out loud when circumstances make it necessary? Above all, surely he is entitled to look to God to bless him, for surely it was God who had brought the established order of things into being and whose providence maintained it?

(iii)

The Book of Job is, as everyone knows, an attack on this traditional equation between goodness and prosperity. But it cannot be stressed too often that it is an attack from *within* the Wisdom movement, and by a thinker who wishes fervently to reinstate it on a more mature and less naïve basis.

Israel's wise men were tellers of moral tales as well as teachers of proverbial wisdom, and the author chooses one of these tales with which to begin his book. It was indeed from this tale that he got the name of his hero. In the part which he reproduces, it is plainly a tale for popular consumption, and in the manner of such tales everything is painted in black and white. Thus Job is the epitome of goodness, almost as though he were the best man who had ever lived; and he is mightily blessed, the greatest among the great men in his eastern patriarchal society. This very good and great man is about to experience an equally great fall into the blackest tragedy, and in the folk tale it is clear that through his piety he emerges with glorious credit. Not so, however, in the book as a whole. There he becomes less than ideal and is cut down to human size; there he has a lot to learn before the happy ending is reached. He is still a heroic figure, but his heroism is a realistic and not an idealized one. But even in the book as a whole, his essential goodness and sincerity, his integrity if you like, is, although impugned by his friends, never doubted by himself nor, more importantly, overturned by God. A coming to terms with "grace" in the Pauline sense and a giving up of belief in the effectiveness of good works, are not among the lessons he has to learn.

It is hard for the Christian reader of this book to cast his mind back to a time before the great New Testament apostle existed, and think himself into an age when a man could be proud of his righteousness. But it is vital that we do so, otherwise Job's tragedy loses its cutting edge. Perhaps the best way for us to capture the atmosphere of Israel's Wisdom literature—in this regard at least—is to imagine the Pharisee in Our Lord's parable saying his—as far as we are concerned—dreadful words, "God, I thank thee that I am not like other men" (Luke 18:11), with utter honesty and without the slightest trace of hypocrisy. That is the kind of man Job was.

DOES JOB FEAR GOD FOR NAUGHT?

Job 1:6–12

> [6]Now there was a day when the sons of God came to present themselves before the Lord, and Satan also came among them. [7]The Lord said to Satan, "Whence have you come?" Satan answered the Lord, "From going to and fro on the earth, and from walking up and down on it." [8]And the Lord said to Satan, "Have you considered my servant Job, that there is none like him on the earth, a blameless and upright man, who fears God and turns away from evil?" [9]Then Satan answered the Lord, "Does Job fear God for naught?" [10]Hast thou not put a hedge about him and his house and all that he has, on every side? Thou has blessed the work of his hands, and his possessions have increased in the land. [11]But put forth thy hand now, and touch all that he has, and he will curse thee to thy face." [12]And the Lord said to Satan, "Behold, all that he has is in your power; only upon himself do not put forth your hand." So Satan went forth from the presence of the Lord.

(i)

There are quite a few passages in the Old Testament where we have pictured for us the heavenly court with *Yahweh* (the "Lord") sitting on his throne surrounded by the "sons of God", or, as they are also frequently called, *angels*. Such pictures should not be regarded as detracting from Old Testament monotheism. They may survive from the days when the Hebrews were polytheists, but they survive because of their usefulness in preserving God's majesty and holiness. The angels stand between God and mankind and prevent too close a contact between them. See in particular Psalms 29:1–2,10; 89:5–7.

In a number of passages, however, the members of the court are not simply present, but take on some measure of individuality. In 1 Kings 22:19ff., for instance, the "host of heaven", as they are there called, all give their opinion on how best to get King Ahab to the place where he is to meet his fate. Such scenes are frequent in the myths of surrounding peoples, as in the Babylonian Flood story where, in the divine assembly at the beginning, some of the gods and goddesses want to be rid of mankind, and others oppose them. In retaining this polytheistic motif the Old Testament writers were being rather more daring, but they knew what they were doing; nor were their audiences or readers, as far as we can judge, ever perturbed. It was no more than a device, a colourful way of showing the one God making up his mind on a matter to hand. It is a sign of the Old Testament's sturdy attachment to monotheism, rather than the opposite, that it could use such picture language and remain unconcerned about it.

(ii)

The scene before us is of the type mentioned in the paragraph above, although only one divine being, other than Yahweh ("the Lord") himself, speaks and he is rather a special divine being. He is called *the* Satan and, although it is not reproduced in the RSV, the definite article is important. For it denotes what is, strictly speaking, a title meaning "the adversary" (*sc* in court) rather than a personal name for the Devil as, without the definite article, it becomes in New Testament times. Reading between the lines we may describe his rôle as a kind of divine prosecutor. It seems he had a roving commission to investigate affairs on earth and report anything amiss to Yahweh. Then when the case came up for trial, if we may so put it, he was expected to place as bad a light as possible on the accused's actions. Finally when a decision was reached, he was the officer deputed to carry it out. But there is never any suggestion that he made the decision. That was for God alone.

What we have in the present scene, however, is not quite a court case, presumably because Job was not guilty of anything that could be made the occasion of a trial. But the Satan has obviously had him under surveillance and knows all about him; for whenever God mentions that he is pleased with Job, the Satan is ready with his answer. He cunningly suggests that it has been easy for Job to be good because he has been blessed and protected by God. Remove this divine "hedge" around him, he tells Yahweh, and we will see a very different Job, one you will have to put on trial like any of the other cases I bring before you. His piety will give way to blasphemy and it will not be long before he will be raising his fist defiantly at heaven. Yahweh immediately accepts the challenge. He invites the Satan to do what he likes with "all that he [Job] has" which, as the sequel shows, includes Job's family as well as his possessions; but he is not to touch Job's own person. Happy with what he is sure will, in the outcome, be tantamount to a court sentence, the Satan goes off on his nefarious mission.

What are we to make of this sinister and busy figure? The Satan is a nasty piece of work, brazen and impertinent towards God, and cynical and sneering about men. These are traits he carries with him into his subsequent career as God's enemy or opposite when as Satan, rather than *the Satan*, he will have his own "kingdom" as opposed to God's, and his own army of lesser devils to carry out his commands. But here, he is patently not yet God's enemy in that full sense, but still very much his subordinate, although a rather difficult one to keep in check. Nor is he yet the tempter *par excellence* whispering things in men's ears; a rôle that he may have taken over from the serpent in the Garden of Eden story. All through the book, Job knows nothing about him and is completely unaware of the Satan's involvement in his fate. So there is only one possible conclusion: the Satan is, in this story, just like the other "sons of God", *still* an extension of God. He represents an aspect of God's providence: that side of him which, for whatever reason, visits suffering upon human beings; that side of him which is responsible for the evil and tragedy which afflict the lives of men.

Or rather, the pictures we are given in the story of *both* God *and* the Satan represent together that darker side of the divine providence as it operates on human lives. For God hardly emerges from it all any better than the Satan. He rises to his challenge like a fish to the bait and almost lays a bet on Job's

virtue. But much worse, he stands aside while his minion destroys
not only Job's cattle and sheep, but his servants and finally his
sons and daughters—all fair game, it seems, as long as he can win
his wager.

(iii)

It is not at all easy for us today to speak in a way like this which,
however obliquely, makes God the sole cause of the evil that can
occur in individual lives. Our most natural reaction is to skip the
centuries to a time when *the Satan* becomes *Satan* and is no longer
there simply to do God's bidding. So we are tempted to argue that
God here merely permits Job's misfortunes and that the Satan is
their chief cause. But not only is such an interpretation one
which, as emphasized, no "true blue" Old Testament monotheist
would dream of adopting, it is one which flies in the face of the
facts of this particular book. Not only does Job himself never
mention the Satan, but neither do his friends. In the debate about
to begin, the problem at issue is not *whether* God is the originator
of Job's misery, but *why*. We are up against another basic Old
Testament belief which, however contrary it may be to our ways
of doing theology, we must honestly acknowledge if we are to
make sense of this ancient and disturbing book.

There is one point, however, which we can in fairness make:
the naïve and distasteful, if dramatic, manner in which this
passage presents God planning Job's downfall, is due more to the
popular story, than to the author of the book. He uses the story as
his starting point because it sets forth initially Job's surpassing
virtue and *then* God's responsibility for what happens to him in
what is, at least to the Hebrew mind, a quite unambiguous way.
But he does not necessarily approve of the crudity of its language
about God any more than he did of the fulsomeness of its
language about Job. Certainly he himself does not put such naïve
language into the mouths of Job and his friends when they begin
later to argue about Job's fate. Let us then try hard to do what he
wanted his first readers to do, to let this unsophisticated story set
the scene for the sophisticated debate to follow, and no more. In

that debate it is not the childish and rather petty God of these verses whose providence will relentlessly be probed, but the God who, just as bluntly but rather more refinedly, lets us all know in Isaiah 45:7—

I form light and create darkness,
I make weal and create woe,
I am the Lord, who do all these things.

(iv)

A final thought: we may not shudder quite so violently at Isaiah's way of putting it, but we still find it exceedingly difficult to sanction the Old Testament's habitually robust habit of attributing evil to God's direct will. We prefer to avoid the issue by having the Devil, or even some impersonal force, perform the evil, and God simply permit it. But that is in theory only. What do we do in practice? When trouble comes our way we do not usually wonder what the Devil, or the principalities and powers, have to do with it, but in pain and perplexity we ask what God is up to. As in so many other spheres, our practice is perhaps more revealing than our theory. It shows that we are not so far removed from Job's world as we might suppose.

BLESSED BE THE NAME OF THE LORD

Job 1:13–22

[13]Now there was a day when his sons and daughters were eating and drinking wine in their eldest brother's house; [14]and there came a messenger to Job, and said, "The oxen were ploughing and the asses feeding beside them; [15]and the Sabeans fell upon them and took them, and slew the servants with the edge of the sword; and I alone have escaped to tell you." [16]While he was yet speaking, there came another, and said, "The fire of God fell from heaven and burned up the sheep and the servants, and consumed them; and I alone have escaped to tell

you." [17]While he was yet speaking, there came another, and said, "The Chaldeans formed three companies, and made a raid upon the camels and took them, and slew the servants with the edge of the sword; and I alone have escaped to tell you." [18]While he was yet speaking, there came another, and said, "Your sons and daughters were eating and drinking wine in their eldest brother's house; [19]and behold, a great wind came across the wilderness, and struck the four corners of the house, and it fell upon the young people, and they are dead; and I alone have escaped to tell you."

[20]Then Job arose, and rent his robe, and shaved his head, and fell upon the ground, and worshipped. [21]And he said, "Naked I came from my mother's womb, and naked shall I return; the Lord gave, and the Lord has taken away; blessed be the name of the Lord."

[22]In all this Job did not sin or charge God with wrong.

(i)

The Satan does his work well. Calamity follows calamity as, without a break, messengers arrive to tell Job—*first*, that his cattle and asses have been stolen in a Bedouin (Sabean) raid and the servants tending them slain; *second*, that a bolt of lightning has destroyed his sheep and their shepherds; *third*, that bands of Aramaean (Chaldean) marauders have carried off his camels and killed their guards; and *fourth*, and most tragic of all, that the dreaded sirocco wind from the desert has brought down the house of his eldest son when all his sons and daughters were there for a celebration, and that all of them are dead. The formula style of the story—"there came a messenger", "I alone have escaped to tell you", "while he was yet speaking there came another"— serves to increase the horror. So do the links with the beginning of the chapter—notably the huge numbers of animals which we learned therein that Job possessed, and which we are now told were destroyed. There is also the ironic circumstance that the last disaster happened when his family were present at the kind of feast at which, immediately following, Job used to offer sacrifices in case his sons had unknowingly taken God's name in vain. We cannot but ask whether Job, having lost so much, will not now knowingly do the same.

Three of the calamities—the two raids by Arab and Aramaean nomads, and the sudden insweep of the sirocco—are the kind to which a farming and pastoral community on the eastern side of the Jordan (like the one to which Job belonged) would regularly be exposed. But that all three should happen in a single day is hardly credible. Did the two groups of invading clansmen not encounter each other, and were they not affected by the violent sandstorm? The *fourth* calamity—the lightning—is of a more general nature, but its presence in the list is not calculated to increase our respect for the story's feasibility either. Do lightning and sandstorms go together? But probably we should not be asking such questions. The story-teller is trying to match the disasters to Job's exemplary character, and to do this he must also make them larger than life.

(ii)

But might he be making a hidden point by using the poetic phrase "fire of God" instead of the straightforward Hebrew noun for lightning? If he is, it can only be to remind us that, although the Satan is the agent, it is really God who is bringing all this about.

Certainly it never occurs to Job, either in the first two chapters, or later in the book, to implicate the Satan in what had happened to him. It is God, and God alone, who fills his mind. He receives the messengers seated, and when the last has reported, he says nothing, but rises up and first performs the ritual actions of rending his robe and shaving his head. To do the latter, he must have gone to fetch a razor. His subsequent falling to the ground is not then an involuntary reaction of shock but a deliberate act of obeisance before God in the age-long Oriental manner. Only after this does he speak, uttering the first of the two noble sentiments about God's providence which have made his name famous as the exemplar of acquiescence in the divine will. The economy of the tiny scene, encompassing only a couple of verses, is breathtaking, beautifully balancing the rather long-winded and repetitive account of the bringing of the dire news.

The *first* part of Job's statement is paralleled in 1 Timothy 6:7, where the apostle reminds Timothy and through him the faithful: "we brought nothing into the world, and [it is certain that] we cannot take anything out of the world." But we should beware of comparing the two passages too closely. The apostle is commending "godliness with contentment" (Tim. v. 6) and warning against the allure of riches, whereas in the folk tale, Job is accepting with fortitude, the loss of the riches he had once possessed, and of much else besides. The apostle is suspicious of riches, Job is not. But at least, the apostle and patriarch agree that when death comes, possessions are of no further use. Compare also Ecclesiastes 5:13–17, where the same thought is characteristically given a sceptical twist.

In the *second* part of his statement, Job admits that all his material possessions, and all his sons and daughters, had come to him from God, and that, although they may have been a reward for his goodness, they belonged first to God. His point seems to be that God had for reasons of his own taken them back to himself before he—Job—was inevitably parted from them at death. This God had a perfect right to do, and it in no way cancelled out his—Job's—duty to worship and praise him.

(iii)

Note that in making his statement, Job uses the name *Yahweh* or "the Lord". The story-teller may have momentarily forgotten that Job was not an Israelite, but it is more likely that he is quoting and that the verse was already so well-known that he felt he could not change it. Did he get it from a Hebrew burial service? We cannot say, but so poignant and cruelly evocative are the words, that they are often used at Christian funerals, especially in circumstances of great distress. Or should I say that, in sturdier times, they *were* thus used? This remark is prompted by the fact that the words appear in a burial prayer in the 1940 *Book of Common Order* of the Church of Scotland, but are not to be found in its successor of 1979. They are, it seems, too strong meat for the modern Scottish faithful.

And strong meat they indubitably are, piercing remorselessly and in characteristic Old Testament manner behind natural accident and man-made disaster, to the direct will of God. Was the Church of Scotland right to drop them? Theoretically few Christians will, as I have already suggested, be able to stomach them. Yet the same Christians, when they are in trouble, are rather more inclined to ascribe evil to God, than when they are on their best behaviour doing Bible study. At such moments there may be more resentment in their voices than resignation, but they are at least at such moments on Job's wavelength and, who knows, ready to be both challenged and comforted by Job's words. Let us then ask ourselves as honestly as we can whether, in the event of the death of one of our loved ones—and I am thinking not so much of a normal death in old age, but of a tragic death, like the death of a child, or a mother with cancer, or a young man in a motor-cycle accident—we could bring ourselves to utter such words in faith. And if not, why not?

(iv)

The last verse of the chapter gives the story-teller's laconic verdict. Job has taken all that the Satan, with God's connivance, could throw at him. No blasphemy and no word of anger or complaint against God has escaped his lips.

The phrase translated "did not . . . charge God with wrong" (v.22) in the RSV is a tricky one. The Authorized Version understands the "wrong" to be Job's, and renders the phrase as "nor charged God foolishly". The Jerusalem Bible follows the same line with "[nor] offered any insult to God". But most versions understand the phrase to refer to Job's refusal to impute fault to God, and this fits much better with the Satan's sinister assumption earlier that, when disaster struck him, he would curse God. The same noun, (*ie* "wrong") or its adjective, is rendered "that which is tasteless" (of food) in 6:6, "an unsavoury thing" (of what other prophets were doing) in Jeremiah 23:13, and "deceptive" (of the visions of false prophets) in Lamentations 2:14. In later Hebrew, the adjective is used of "unsalted" fish. The movement of meaning is clearly from food which lacks taste or relish, to advice or actions which are pointless or unseemly.

Job then refuses in his agony to accuse God of having done anything remiss or out of character. There is nothing to suggest that he has changed his view of his own integrity, but he has obviously been compelled to move away from an easy attachment to the traditional belief that good works and material happiness must always go together. For a Wisdom story to admit this, is quite something.

CURSE GOD, AND DIE

Job 2:1–10

[1]Again there was a day when the sons of God came to present themselves before the Lord, and Satan also came among them to present himself before the Lord. [2]And the Lord said to Satan, "Whence have you come?" Satan answered the Lord, "From going to and fro on the earth, and from walking up and down on it." [3]And the Lord said to Satan, "Have you considered my servant Job, that there is none like him on the earth, a blameless and upright man, who fears God and turns away from evil? He still holds fast his integrity, although you moved me against him, to destroy him without cause." [4]Then Satan answered the Lord, "Skin for skin! All that a man has he will give for his life. [5]But put forth thy hand now, and touch his bone and his flesh, and he will curse thee to thy face." [6]And the Lord said to Satan, "Behold, he is in your power; only spare his life."

[7]So Satan went forth from the presence of the Lord, and afflicted Job with loathsome sores from the sole of his foot to the crown of his head. [8]And he took a potsherd with which to scrape himself, and sat among the ashes.

[9]Then his wife said to him, "Do you still hold fast your integrity? Curse God, and die." [10]But he said to her, "You speak as one of the foolish women would speak. Shall we receive good at the hand of God, and shall we not receive evil?" In all this Job did not sin with his lips.

(i)

Undeterred by being proved wrong and still convinced that Job is too good to be true, the Satan fastens onto the proviso laid down by God in the first test: namely that the Satan should not touch Job's own person. He insinuates that if Job were struck down by disease, the hedge around him would finally be removed and the integrity which God had so highly prized, would finally collapse and vanish.

"Skin for skin!" (2:4) is obviously a proverb, but it is an enigmatic one to us who do not know its background. It can hardly refer to the simple exchange of one pelt for another in trade or barter; a meaning which would lack bite. We should expand the phrase: "[A man, if he has to, will surrender someone else's] skin [life] for [to save] [his own] skin [life]." It will be remembered that the phrase "all that he has" in 1:11 included Job's servants and his sons and daughters as well as his vast animal possessions. The Satan's jibe is then insolently worthy of him. The death of his nearest and dearest had not moved Job to blaspheme, but the prospect of his own death would.

Again the Satan is nothing if not thorough. We, reading the story, are aware that God had insisted that Job be not allowed to die but, as his acquaintances saw his pitiful state, they did not have the benefit of knowing that. Nor, of course, did Job himself. Not enough information is given for us to be able to diagnose Job's disease, but it was patently of an acuteness that, in these far-off days, would more often than not have resulted in death. Leprosy comes first to mind, especially since we are told that Job "sat among the ashes" (v.8), *ie* on the rubbish dump outside the village, away from contact with other human beings. But from the descriptions which Job himself gives of his suffering later on (*eg*, 7:5; 30:28–30), it is more probable that he was afflicted with some kind of virulent dermatitis covering his whole body and breaking out continually in malignant ulcers and eczema. People would be bound to shun him if only in fear of contagion.

But, in that age, they would have done so for another reason as well. It was an age when ill-health, especially a serious disorder, was not only almost universally thought of as a scourge from God, but also widely considered as a punishment for sin. Job's agony of body can scarcely be imagined by us who live in today's medicine-orientated society; his agony of mind and spirit, with such views being so prevalent, must far surpass our comprehension, as he broods upon his fate.

(ii)

In Psalm 38 we are allowed to listen in to the private distress of a man grievously ill, who succumbed to these prevailing views and confessed his guilt before asking God to restore him. In this story—and indeed, throughout the book until the very end—Job refuses to repent of anything, but holds fast to his integrity. It has been remarked upon before that this is a trait to which we cannot easily warm and, even although we are insistently reminded that Job is suffering undeservedly, we would prefer it if he himself did not make so much of it but used more of the language of Psalm 38. Apparently Job's wife also preferred this, and we cannot but have a sneaking sympathy for her as she tries to communicate with a husband so sure of himself. It is hard for us to have to admit that in the Old Testament, Job's attitude to his integrity is just as likely to be the one adopted by a believer faced with misfortune as that of the author of Psalm 38. But there it is. Perhaps the very strength of the popular equation—between ill-health and God's anger—had something to do with it.

But also involved in Job's integrity, it will be recalled, was a belief in a harmonious world order sustained by a consistent providence. It is more to our liking that Job did not abandon this belief at his wife's prompting. He had learned the hard way that God could, and sometimes did, send evil on a good man. He had no idea why, and it placed a fearful strain on the confident teaching on which he had been raised, but humbly he acquiesced.

And that is as far as the Wisdom story goes. It tells how a saintly man long ago had, with his head held high, and without a murmur against God, courageously borne the most horrendous suffering. Its purpose is clearly to encourage those listening to have patience in their lesser troubles. It assumes no doubt that they were not as virtuous as Job, but it also takes for granted that they knew where they stood and that they had not, in the words of Psalm 1:1, walked "in the counsel of the wicked." This being so, it directs their attention to the attitude they ought to adopt when misfortune comes their way. And having done that succinctly, it says no more.

If there is any further theology to be gleaned from the story, it is that God, by letting a good man suffer, is testing his mettle, satisfying himself that he is not in the game of religion, as it were, for what he can get out of it. But whether it quite commends disinterested goodness is doubtful. Job says: "Shall we receive good at the hand of God, and shall we not receive evil?" (2:10), which is, on the face of it, as good a definition of disinterestedness in the religious sphere as one could wish for. Nevertheless, a due reward is still there at the end. Job is eventually restored to health, he is given another family to replace the one that had perished, all his possessions are miraculously restored, and he resumes his status as a great man admired and respected far and wide. An Old Testament audience could take only one lesson from that: adversity is, for the one who reacts to it like Job, a temporary trial, and will, when in due course a pass mark in humble acceptance has been achieved, be replaced by prosperity.

(iii)

The story, in effect, shows Wisdom teaching taking serious account, as the Book of Proverbs had not, of the possibility of unmerited suffering but, at the same time, keeping its underlying theology intact. It is because this story depicts Job's wife in an unenviable rôle of challenging the consistency and benevolence of the divine providence that she is so harshly treated. She is introduced without ceremony and immediately speaks her despairing and embittered words. We are not allowed to have a fellow feeling with *her* dilemma of faith but are bluntly left in no doubt that what she advises Job to do we must never do. We must not join the wicked either in practice or in thought by concluding that when trouble comes we might as well hang for a sheep as for a lamb, or, worse, by suggesting that God is being unfair and has it in for us.

Israel's wise men had often met these typical human reactions, and the story stamps on them savagely by having Job upbraid his wife with what is one of the strongest Hebrew words for a fool. Her kind of folly is the kind that in Deuteronomy 32:4–6 responds to God's graciousness with ingratitude, or that in Isaiah 32:5–6 practises ungodliness and utters error concerning the Lord, or that in Psalm 74:18 pagan-like reviles God's name or, horror of horrors, that in Psalm 14:1 says there is no God. The word denotes arrogance and impiety as well as stupidity.

(iv)

At the level of theory, the idea of misfortune as a test sent by God will not bear close scrutiny, especially if, as here, other people, who are not being tested, have to share in the misery; and especially if, as again here, the thought of a prize for passing the test is present. Yet in spite of these and other objections, it is in practice an idea that has strengthened faith and brought out the best in men since the day when Abraham was commanded to sacrifice his son to God and prove that he put God even before God's promises. The fact that we can still say today, whether jokingly or not, that such and such has been sent "to try us", shows how deep an influence it has always exerted on the ordinary believer's interpretation of his duty to God.

The same applies to the attitude adopted by Job in this story, as has been emphasized a number of times. Take away the aspects of it that worry us, because they do not accord with St Paul and the New Testament in general, and there remains Job's marvellous patience in adversity and his resolute refusal to criticize God. We are shortly going to leave the simplistic folk tale of the patient Job behind and find ourselves encountering a loudly complaining Job who will seem to us to have followed his wife's advice only too well. It will become obvious that the author of the Book of Job considers that the folk tale does not go far enough, and that its answer to the problem of innocent suffering is too naïve to account for the enormity of evil's power, and for the stranglehold it exerts on the lives of men. And when we have thought harder about it, I hope we will agree.

But this in no way justifies us in denigrating the central lesson of this story or sneering at its simplicity. Job's attitude in it may be too ingenuous and childlike for the realities of life in a complicated adult world. But for those uncluttered souls who have been able to embrace it, the important thing is that it works. We call them saints and, although we are ourselves rarely made of the stuff to emulate them, we cannot but be humbled by them. In the last analysis, and when we have made full allowance for its penchant for exaggeration and oversimplifying, we may wish to conclude that the old folk tale of the good man Job has its heart in the right place. Many simple believers down the ages will echo that verdict. See James 5:11.

A Note On Job's Wife

In the massive debate to come, between Job and his three friends, the author of the Book of Job will make full use of the dramatic possibilities latent in their simple confrontation in the old folk tale. It has sometimes been thought a weakness that he ignores the even more dramatic possibilities latent in the short but exceedingly sharp clash between husband and wife, especially since it is Job's wife who, in what survives of the tale, is the chief, although unwitting, counterpart on earth of the Satan in the heavenly court. There is no doubt that she is treated abominably by Job, and this cannot but cast aspersions on his celebrated "perfection", even within the context of the folk tale. His savage dismissal of her is one of several hints, both in the folk tale and in the ensuing debate, that there is something not altogether healthy about Job's obsession with his own integrity and the speed with which he takes offence when anyone impugns it. As the author develops these themes later, there will be many occasions when a further intervention by her, or at least a backward allusion to her, either by Job or one of the friends, would seem to be called for. But she is hardly mentioned again until the Epilogue in chapter 42 (and, even there, not directly). Perhaps in the age in which this book is set it was not considered proper for women to engage in theological controversy, or even for their status or opinion to be considered germane to the kind of issues which it raises.

Nevertheless, Job's wife remains a powerful hidden presence throughout and, if the patriarchs who do all the talking will not think of her, that is no reason why we should forget her. Job's angry rejection of her pleas will be an unspoken reproach to him when he too begins to lose his faith and to say wild things about God. And his total lack of sympathy with her predicament will not dispose us to be over-indulgent with him when he cries out to the friends to have pity on him and they do not hear. We will be apprized from time to time of a larger circle of onlookers in the shadows around Job, and we can take it as certain that she will be among them. It is appropriate that we remember her and listen for her silent tears in the background.

The reader may like to know that Archibald MacLeish gives a prominent place to Job's wife in his play *J.B.*, a modern version of the Book of Job. She is called Sarah, and her single sentence in the Prologue is, in the play, made the starting-point of many embittered and poignant utterances, as when, at the very end of Act I, she screams in anguish "Oh, my babies! My poor babies!" It is also revealing that in William Blake's magnificent woodcuts (which everyone who reads the Book of Job ought to see and ponder) Job's wife remains his loyal companion throughout. And there is the beautiful and haunting painting by Georges de La Tour, *Job Visited by his Wife*, now in a museum in Epinal, France. (It is reproduced on the back cover of the hardback edition of Muriel Spark's novel *The Only Problem*, itself based on the Book of Job). We should welcome these attempts to give belated justice to a much maligned lady.

THEY RAISED THEIR VOICES AND WEPT

Job 2:11–13

[11]Now when Job's three friends heard of all this evil that had come upon him, they came each from his own place, Eliphaz the Temanite, Bildad the Shuhite, and Zophar the Naamathite. They made an appointment together to come to condole with him and comfort him. [12]And when they saw him from afar, they did not recognize him; and they raised their voices and wept; and they rent their robes and sprinkled dust upon their heads toward heaven. [13]And they sat with him on the ground seven days and seven nights, and no one spoke a word to him, for they saw that his suffering was very great.

In contrast to Job's wife the story-teller lingers upon the discomfiture of Job's friends, all eastern patriarchs like himself.

Great play is made of their sympathy for him as, risking contagion and even public censure, they made a concerted decision to visit one who had so obviously become an offence to society. But having come to comfort him, they found they had nothing to say. So appalled were they at the change in their friend, that they could only have recourse to the well-known rites of mourning as though he were as good as dead, and sit beside him in the solidarity of silence.

(i)

It is a touching picture, but it does not necessarily mean that the folk tale was more favourably disposed towards them than it was towards Job's wife. The traditional story breaks off at this point and does not resume until the last chapter, where we find God condemning the friends for not having spoken of him "what is right" as his servant Job had done (42:7). It seems that the part of the prose story dealing, presumably quite crisply, with the confrontation between Job and his friends, has been omitted and in its place the author of the book has inserted the long and sophisticated dialogue or debate of chapters 3ff., in which the four of them set forth their respective positions in formal poetic speeches. In this, as far as Job is concerned, we notice a quick turning away from simplistic acceptance of, towards a searching attack upon, divine providence. By leaving the folk tale's verdict unchanged at the end, the author is thus, and with considerable irony, implying that God approved of the second Job of the debate more than he did of the first Job of the folk tale.

Logic would seem to demand that the author performed a similar ironic hatchet job upon the friends, and changed them from critics of God into the defenders of orthodoxy that they are in the debate. If that is so, then we may assume that in the folk tale they played a supporting rôle to Job's wife and, like her, tried to get him to abandon his rigidly courageous stance. The story-teller, therefore, in these last sentences before the gap, must merely be building up the tension before the friends eventually speak, and before what they say is as curtly dismissed by Job as his wife's advice had been.

(ii)

There is support for this reconstruction of the missing part of the folk tale in a much later apocryphal work called the *Testament of Job*; the Hebrew original of this has perished, but it survives in a Greek translation discovered only a century ago.

It is pious and turgid to a fault and may simply be a rewriting of the Biblical book, omitting the debate between Job and his friends and substituting something which its orthodox Jewish author thought was more acceptable and fitting. He would not be the only one, in either the Jewish or Christian communities, to disapprove of the debate which we are now going on to study, or to wish that the first two chapters and the last were all that we had. Bishop Theodore of Mopsuestia, who lived in the fifth century A.D., is on record as having accepted the popular story of Job as the genuine account and dismissing the rest of the biblical book as the product of a clever man who thought more of parading his learning than of coming to terms with true wisdom. The temptation to rewrite must often have been strong.

Nevertheless, it is not impossible that the author of the *Testament of Job* was in touch with the old story through the same oral tradition from which the author of the biblical book received it, and got from it some guidance for the portrait he gives of the friends. In his work, they first lament Job's state and then raise doubts about God's intentions, suggesting that their own physicians would be better able to cure him. They also accuse Job of overweening pride in his own worthiness. (They do not go quite as far as Job's wife who, in the *Testament*, is explicitly stated to have lost her faith.) But Job roundly rejects their advice, defending God's justice at all times and saying things like "My cure and restoration come from God, the Maker of physicians"; and in the end the friends are also roundly condemned by God himself.

(iii)

Two thoughts before we leave the popular tale of Job. The *first* is that in the book as we now have it, the tension is also built up in the concluding paragraph of chapter 2, but it is in preparation for

Job's outburst in chapter 3, not for a sermon by the friends. We
are meant to assume that, in the perhaps lengthy period it took
them to hear of his predicament and to make arrangements to
come to visit him, Job became more and more depressed and
began to regret his staunch defence of the divine providence.
Their seven days of silence was the last straw and, able to stand it
no longer, he gave vent to the black despair in his heart.

The *second* is that we should take warning from what the
Testament of Job has done, and what good Bishop Theodore
would have liked to have done with the scarifying debate which is
about to commence. Orthodoxy, while not always at ease with
them, has on the whole tended to nod assent to the book's first
two chapters and to start squirming only when chapter 3 is
reached. If when we dip our toe into the water of that chapter, we
discover that it is too hot for us, then perhaps we should stop
reading right now and hurry off to a more comfortable part of
Scripture for our daily study. From this point on, the Book of Job
is not for the timid .

WHY DID I NOT DIE AT BIRTH?

Job 3:1–19

[1]After this Job opened his mouth and cursed the day of his birth.
[2]And Job said:
[3]"Let the day perish wherein I was born,
    and the night which said,
      'A man-child is conceived.'
[4]Let that day be darkness!
    May God above not seek it,
      nor light shine upon it.
[5]Let gloom and deep darkness claim it.
    Let clouds dwell upon it;
      let the blackness of the day terrify it.
[6]That night—let thick darkness seize it!
    let it not rejoice among the days of the year,
      let it not come into the number of the months.
[7]Yea, let that night be barren;

[8]Let those curse it who curse the day,
    who are skilled to rouse up Leviathan.
[9]Let the stars of its dawn be dark;
    let it hope for light, but have none,
    nor see the eyelids of the morning;
[10]because it did not shut the doors of my mother's womb,
    nor hide trouble from my eyes.

[11]"Why did I not die at birth,
    come forth from the womb and expire?
[12]Why did the knees receive me?
    Or why the breasts, that I should suck?
[13]For then I should have lain down and been quiet;
    I should have slept; then I should have been at rest,
[14]with kings and counsellors of the earth
    who rebuilt ruins for themselves,
[15]or with princes who had gold,
    who filled their houses with silver.
[16]Or why was I not as a hidden untimely birth,
    as infants that never see the light
[17]There the wicked cease from troubling,
    and there the weary are at rest.
[18]There the prisoners are at ease together;
    they hear not the voice of the taskmaster.
[19]The small and the great are there,
    and the slave is free from his master."

The opening speech of the author's new Job is, above all, a desperate cry for relief by a man for whom life has ceased to have meaning. He is not yet in the mood for theology. Rather, stricken with bodily and mental anguish, he wishes simply that he were dead. He curses the day of his birth (vv. 3, 4–5) and the night of his conception (vv. 3, 6–10). Why, he asks, was he not still-born (vv. 11–12), for then he could immediately have found peace among the shades in *Sheol* (vv. 13–15)? Or, better, why was he not aborted before his term (v. 16), for then he would have been at rest even sooner in the underworld (vv. 17–19)? It is only after this forlorn and bitter lament that (verse 20) Job introduces a modicum of argument into his words, although even then it is tentative and indirect.

(i)

There are parallels in other places in the Old Testament, both to Job's cursing of the day he was born and to his picture of life's pale counterpart in *Sheol*, but they do not match the forlorn pessimism of this poem.

The prophet Jeremiah, in one of his more desolate moments, also wishes that he had not been born. In Jeremiah 20:14–18 he too curses the day his mother bore him, but his next curse is on the man who brought the glad news to his father:

> Let that man be like the cities
>   which the Lord overthrew without pity;
> let him hear a cry in the morning
>   and an alarm at noon,
> because he did not kill me in the womb;
>   so that my mother would have been my grave,
>   and her womb for ever great.
>
>   (vv. 16–17)

These are savage and extravagant words, almost a cursing of his parents for having him (and thereby a breaking of the Fifth Commandment—Exod. 20:12). He just manages to avoid that irreverence by concentrating his venom on the unknown and innocent man who made the birth announcement. But Jeremiah is not, like Job, at death's door. His words have to be judged in the context of his ongoing spiritual struggle with a God who had commissioned him to announce his people's doom. As he knows well, it was a doom that the people richly deserved. He is therefore really protesting at the unpopularity and ignominy that his God-given task had brought upon him, as a previous lament in Jeremiah 15:10 makes clear: "Woe is me, my mother, that you bore me, a man of strife and contention to the whole land!" But he does not doubt that God was right, and when he recovers his courage and composure he will be able to return to his ministry and eventually, once the blow of judgment has fallen, to look ahead in faith to his people's restoration.

Job's curse on his day of birth is altogether more radical. What he is wishing for is little less than a reversal of the process of creation. God's good light, which had once pierced the original darkness and made room for the world's first day, should have been withheld from that day. An eclipse with black scudding clouds shutting out the sun would have been a more fitting fate for it; an eclipse which, to the fearful eyes of ancient man, would indeed have been a sign of chaos come again (cf. Joel 2:30–31).

He follows that curse with an even longer and more intense curse on the night of his conception; for it was from it, rather than from his day of birth, that his miserable existence began its true ascent. It ought to have been excised from the calendar. No joyful lovemaking ought to have taken place in it, implanting the future Job in his mother's womb. It deserved to be damned by those whose magic skills brought them into contact with the ancient and baleful powers of chaos; powers which, Israel's faith told her, had long ago been vanquished by her God. Would that such a night had not been succeeded by the next day's dawn! An even blacker darkness than its own should have enveloped it; a darkness like the one that covered the primaeval waters when, as yet, the divine Spirit had breathed no life anywhere, and the monstrous Leviathan was untamed, and only disorder reigned. See Genesis 1:1–5 and Psalm 74:12–16 as examples of what, in the Bible's vivid and imaginative language, happened at the world's beginning; and of what Job now so ardently wishes had not happened at his beginning.

(ii)

Next Job goes on to wish that he had been still-born and carried straight to *Sheol*. This is the name given in the Old Testament to the underworld abode where it was believed that the souls of the dead had a temporary wraith-like existence as they waited for their bodies to decompose; at which time, they too would disappear for ever, and the return to the dust so sombrely described in Genesis 3:19 would be complete. The Psalms are full of pleas to God from sick and distressed people to be saved from death's approaching power, and praise to him when in his mercy he drew them back from its embrace. See, for example, Psalm

116:1–9, and Hezekiah's psalm preserved in Isaiah 38:10–20. But once Sheol's portals were crossed, God's writ no longer ran and hope was gone, as Isaiah 38:18–19 and, even more trenchantly, Psalm 88, that bleakest of all the lamentation psalms, make obvious:

> Dost thou work wonders for the dead?
> Do the shades rise up to praise thee?
> Is thy steadfast love declared in the grave,
> or thy faithfulness in Abaddon?
> Are thy wonders known in the darkness,
> or thy saving help in the land of forgetfulness?

(vv. 10–12)

There are many centuries still to go before St Paul will make the mighty affirmation of 1 Corinthians 15:19–20: "If in this life only we have hope in Christ, we are of all men most miserable. But now is Christ risen from the dead . . ." (AV). It was precisely *in this life only* that Old Testament man had hope. He could, if he had descendants (and Job now did not), look forward to his name being held in honour among them. But if he were ill or persecuted or unjustly treated, any cure or redress had to come in this life. Once again the Christian reader of the Old Testament, with his belief in personal immortality, has constantly to be on his guard. There was for Old Testament man no happy land beyond the skies where this life's problems could be unravelled and this life's unfairnesses put right or, for that matter, where the rewards and punishments held out by Israel's Wisdom teachers could be meted out if they were not won or suffered on earth.

As they thought on death, poor or oppressed people in Israel might squeeze a little ironic satisfaction from the thought that the rich and powerful of this world would, like them, one day die and come to dust. Thus in a magnificent taunt song, Isaiah could picture the shades of other great men welcoming the king of Babylon to their company with these words:

> "You too have become as weak as we!
> You have become like us!"

(Isa. 14:10)

And later in the same chapter he could make the denizens of Sheol marvel:

> "Is this the man who made the earth tremble,
>   who shook kingdoms,
> who made the world like a desert
>   and overthrew its cities,
>   who did not let his prisoners go home?"
>
> (Isa. 14:16–17)

But Job's irony in this passage is quite unique. It is not death, "the Great Leveller", that attracts him, but the quietness and stillness of a place that other men dreaded. The kings and counsellors and princes in Job's Sheol have willingly surrendered their earthly responsibilities and are glad to be quit of the quest for power and riches. Even the wicked are at rest. Criminals need no longer fear arrest, nor is the prisoner awakened by the gaoler's cry. The slave can turn a deaf ear to his master's summons and all earth's weary people find at last a blessed peace.

WHY IS LIGHT GIVEN TO HIM THAT IS IN MISERY?

Job 3:20–26

> ²⁰"Why is light given to him that is in misery,
>   and life to the bitter in soul,
> ²¹who long for death, but it comes not,
>   and dig for it more than for hid treasures;
> ²²who rejoice exceedingly,
>   and are glad, when they find the grave?
> ²³Why is light given to a man whose way is hid,
>   whom God has hedged in?
> ²⁴For my sighing comes as my bread,
>   and my groanings are poured out like water,
> ²⁵For the thing that I fear comes upon me,
>   and what I dread befalls me.
> ²⁶I am not at ease, nor am I quiet;
>   I have no rest; but trouble comes."

(iii)

The attentive listener to Job's lament so far—and we can presume his three friends were such—may well have glimpsed behind its poignancy and pathos, the most disturbing implications for the state of mind of the man who uttered it. Was there more to it than despair and hopelessness? In wishing that chaos had returned momentarily at the two points in time when he was conceived and then born, was he cynically hinting that it had in reality returned on not a few occasions with the connivance of the so-called creator of cosmos? And in longing for death, and dwelling so unusually on the restfulness of Sheol, was he angrily hinting at his own imprisonment on earth, and his desire to escape the attentions of a divine gaoler in the only place where he could be sure he would not pursue him? In view of the fact that the third section of Job's opening speech contains some slightly more audible insinuations in that direction, I think we may answer yes. Certainly the atmosphere is becoming more charged as pessimism gives way to an indictment of the God whose name has so far hardly been heard on the new Job's lips.

(iv)

God's name has in fact only been mentioned once in the first 19 verses of the chapter—in verse 4, in the middle of a list of imprecations on Job's day of birth, where it is hardly noticed among the impersonal constructions which begin with, "Let . . . !" Verse 20 also has an impersonal form, "Why is [the] light [of life] given to him that is in misery?" But this time no-one in the original audience would have been fooled. Only God could give life. Job is now indirectly, but unmistakably, implicating God in his fate; not only in his fate, but also in the fate of many more people besides himself.

There follows an image whose daring is quite breathtaking. The other embittered humans, of whose existence Job has reminded us, are pictured digging for death like graverobbers digging for treasure, who raise a cry of triumph when they break through to the burial chamber where the loot has been deposited.

The despoiling of tombs, especially of great men's tombs, where valuables were laid beside the corpse to enable them to buy a privileged position in the netherworld (or, taking into account our recent descriptions of Sheol, let us say, a relatively privileged position), was widespread in antiquity and is the bane of archaeologists. The discovery of an unrifled tomb, like that of Tutankhamun, the boy Pharaoh, is a rare event indeed.

That Israel was not exempt from such depredations is shown by a plaintive three-line Hebrew inscription on an official's tombstone found near Siloam. It dates to about the same period (700 B.C.) as the famous Siloam tunnel inscription, and is now in the British Museum. It reads (the words in square brackets being very plausible restorations):

(a) This is [the tomb of Sheban]iah who is over the household.
There is no silver or gold here,

(b) only [his bones] and the bones of his maidservant with him.
Cursed be the man who

(c) opens this!

If I were a graverobber, I think such a warning would have me reaching for my tools rather than the opposite! And as an Old Testament scholar, I cannot help wondering how such sentiments were reconciled with Israel's faith. But what an apt illustration it supplies of Job's powerful metaphor!

(v)

Verse 23 finally brings in God's name, although only in a subordinate clause. Job's complaint seems to be that he, and those like him, had been given no advance warning that they were destined to be hedged in by a hostile divinity. The verse's real cutting edge, however, is to be found in an ironic wordplay. The verb "to hedge" is the same as the one used by the Satan in 1:10 in his insinuation that it was easy for Job to be a paragon of virtue because God had put a protective hedge around him and his. Job of course knew nothing of what had transpired in the heavenly court, and his irony is unconscious. But how effectively it underscores his change of mood! A God who once had enclosed him in his love, was now boxing him in and suffocating him.

And there (after a few more lines describing his agitation and dread) we leave, for the time being, a man who as his troubles began was keen to defend the divine justice but who, following some weeks of lonely and painful brooding, is on the verge of mounting a frontal assault upon it. The instincts of a lifetime of orthodox piety are inexorably losing their power to restrain him.

WHO THAT WAS INNOCENT EVER PERISHED?

Job 4:1–11

¹Then Eliphaz the Temanite answered:
²"If one ventures a word with you, will you be offended?
    Yet who can keep from speaking?
³Behold, you have instructed many,
    and you have strengthened the weak hands.
⁴Your words have upheld him who was stumbling,
    and you have made firm the feeble knees.
⁵But now it has come to you, and you are impatient;
    it touches you, and you are dismayed.
⁶Is not your fear of God your confidence,
    and the integrity of your ways your hope?

⁷"Think now, who that was innocent ever perished?
    Or where were the upright cut off?
⁸As I have seen, those who plough iniquity
    and sow trouble reap the same.
⁹By the breath of God they perish,
    and by the blast of his anger they are consumed.
¹⁰The roar of the lion, the voice of the fierce lion,
    the teeth of the young lions, are broken.
¹¹The strong lion perishes for lack of prey,
    and the whelps of the lioness are scattered."

The first of the friends to speak, presumably because he was the eldest of the three, is Eliphaz the Temanite. He is—at least at this early stage in the debate—an urbane and far-seeing exponent of

orthodox Wisdom who is well aware of its weaknesses and who
indeed seems to share some of the scepticism which Job has so
recently made his own. And he seems, too, to have a genuine
sympathy for his old friend's tragic plight. Yet his well-meaning
attempt to counsel the man on the ash heap fails utterly. Let us,
by our study of his remarkable speech in chapters 4 and 5, see if
we can find out why.

(i)

He begins with a generous acknowledgment of Job's former piety
and neighbourly concern, and follows this with a rebuke: "now it
has come to you, and you are impatient", or, rendering the verb
more forcefully, *you collapse* (v. 5). It is sharply put but, in the
circumstances, hardly undeserved. He has only recently arrived
at Job's side and has just listened to his immoderate and agitated
moans of chapter 3. It is easy to see why he should conclude that
the physician who had in the past healed so many, now seemed
incapable of healing himself. Where was his vaunted "fear of
God"? Ought not his knowledge of the divine ways and of his own
innocence sustain him through what could only be a temporary
crisis?

For this is what it had to be. Eliphaz reminds Job of the
traditional insight of Hebrew Wisdom, backing it up from his own
observation of life ("as I have seen", v. 8). This, he wants us to
believe, has convinced him of the insight's general truth, in much
the same way as the venerable author of Psalm 37 could declare
(v. 25):

> I have been young, and now am old;
>> yet I have not seen the righteous forsaken
>> or his children begging bread.

It was the same with the punishment of "those who plough
iniquity and sow trouble." The image of verse 9 is of the sirocco,
the hot wind of the desert, rising in a moment and sweeping in to
destroy the harvest, and verses 10–11 show a sudden attack on a
lion's den and the dispersal of the pride: in the same way and just
as instantaneously the wicked perished.

(ii)

In his first argument, then, we have Eliphaz, the upholder of the
Wisdom teaching of the Book of Proverbs, speaking—or, as it
may be truer to say, the upholder of the teaching of the folk tale
we have just been studying; for the issue confronting Eliphaz, as
he himself admits, is that of an innocent man suffering the kind of
thing only wicked men should. Job had shown himself to be a
good and god-fearing man. He must not give way to self-pity or
resentment at the first sign of trouble in his life—however
extreme and however hard to bear—but persevere in faith. It was
only those who ploughed evil who reaped its full and permanent
harvest, and Job was not of their number—yet.

We need not question the sincerity of Eliphaz's initial approach
to Job. But, just as perturbing undertones could be detected in
Job's lament in chapter 3, so here too there are hints of menace
behind the kind words. Eliphaz enlarges more on the fate of the
wicked than he does on the rewards of goodness. And why does
he have to use the notorious desert wind as an image of the fate of
the wicked, when it was that same sirocco which had destroyed
the house in which Job's family had met their end (1:19)?

CAN MORTAL MAN BE RIGHTEOUS BEFORE GOD?

Job 4:12–21

12"Now a word was brought to me stealthily,
   my ear received the whisper of it.
13Amid thoughts from visions of the night,
   when deep sleep falls on men,
14dread came upon me, and trembling,
   which made all my bones shake.
15A spirit glided past my face;
   the hair of my flesh stood up.
16It stood still,
   but I could not discern its appearance,

A form was before my eyes;
    there was silence, then I heard a voice:
[17]'Can mortal man be righteous before God?
    Can a man be pure before his Maker?
[18]Even in his servants he puts no trust,
    and his angels he charges with error;
[19]how much more those who dwell in houses of clay,
    whose foundation is in the dust,
    who are crushed before the moth.
[20]Between morning and evening they are destroyed;
    they perish for ever without any regarding it.
[21]If their tent-cord is plucked up within them,
    do they not die, and that without wisdom?'"

(iii)

To his argument from experience Eliphaz adds some thoughts on God's relations with men, which he claims came to him through a special revelation. The eeriness and solemnity of the occasion are powerfully described in words that recall the "deep sleep" of Adam in the Garden of Eden (Gen. 2:21) and the "still small voice" heard by Elijah at Horeb (1 Kings 19:12). It is almost like hearing an Isaiah or a Jeremiah speak. But Eliphaz is a practitioner of Wisdom, and the Wisdom movement did not usually resort to revelation. It studied and deduced and observed, and did not need, or so it thought, to look for guidance from on high. Eliphaz must clearly have something very vital to say if it comes to him that way.

What then did the voice out of the silence tell him? It told him that no man on earth could be righteous or pure in God's eyes. It seems to us a platitude. But there is more. It transpires that God could not trust the angels, who shared his life of eternity, to refrain from error. (Probably in mind here are stories of angelic misbehaviour like the one recorded in Genesis 6:1–2; see also Psalm 82:1–2, 6–7.) How much less could he trust his human creatures, who were made of dust and lived hardly longer than a moth! In so short a span they had no chance to achieve wisdom.

It is important to emphasize that Eliphaz is recounting a vision he saw before, and perhaps well before, he heard of Job's calamity. He will apply it to Job's case presently, but it is not so that he may impress Job that he claims divine sanction for its message. We must look at the vision first, not in the context of what Job has been saying, but in the wider context of the orthodox Wisdom movement, which he and the other two friends represent. Eliphaz is, it seems, rather less than satisfied with the old orthodoxy and wishes to introduce a new dimension into its teaching.

If we recall the difficulty we ourselves had with the fulsome description of Job's "perfection" at the beginning of the folk story, we may be able to guess why. Eliphaz too is uncomfortable with the easy distinction traditional Wisdom made between the righteous and the wicked, and with its easy assumption that a man could both discern and control his way through life. As he grows older, it all sounds too neat and too optimistic for him to swallow. He has just told Job that, in his long life, he had never come across good men who suffered, or bad men who prospered, except temporarily. But it now appears that in his heart of hearts he doubts whether there is such a thing as a truly good or innocent man.

(iv)

On the face of it, the two positions Eliphaz espouses in chapter 4 are contradictory. It is not consistent to be stressing, as the chapter opens, that a man like Job is a good man who deserves to be restored; and to be denying, as it ends, that any man can be justified in God's sight. Christian readers of the Book of Job must, however, be very careful not to read too much into Eliphaz's shift of stance. We may be glad to see it, but we are not entitled to take Eliphaz's vision as indicative of a change of life which is anything like as fundamental as that experienced by St Paul when he surrendered a total reliance on the Jewish law for an equally total reliance on faith in Christ. That would be to transport him from the world of Old Testament Wisdom into the world of the Epistle to the Romans. Certainly he has taken a few steps along that road, but he is far from formulating a hard doctrine of original or universal sin that would cut out any reliance on good works.

Rather he presents us with a picture of a Wisdom teacher who has lost his nerve. He is no longer as sure as he was that God's world is a good place, or that God's will for men is clear and accessible to those who apply themselves to finding it. The old distinctions between good and bad men have not ceased to be relevant for him, but they have become blurred by a new appreciation of God's holiness and hiddenness, and of men's frailty and corruption and ignorance. If we may so put it, Eliphaz the Wisdom teacher had been paying more attention than his kind normally did, to Israel's prophets and priests and psalmists. It is from them and not from St Paul that he gets his more pessimistic, and at the same time more realistic, insight into human nature and the human condition.

For the sake of comparison it may help to cite a few verses from such sources:

The Lord saw that the wickedness of man was great in the earth, and that every imagination of the thoughts of his heart was only evil continually. And the Lord was sorry that he had made man on the earth, and it grieved him to his heart.

(Gen. 6:5–6)

The sacrifice acceptable to God is a broken spirit; a broken and contrite heart, O God, thou wilt not despise.

(Ps. 51:17)

Of old thou didst lay the foundation of the earth, and the heavens are the work of thy hands. They will perish, but thou dost endure; they will all wear out like a garment. Thou changest them like raiment, and they pass away; but thou art the same, and thy years have no end.

(Ps. 102:25–27)

The Egyptians are men, and not God; and their horses are flesh, and not spirit

(Isa. 31:3)

> All flesh is grass,
>   and all its beauty is like the flower of the field.
> . . . .
> The grass withers, the flower fades;
>   but the word of our God will stand for ever.

(Isa. 40:6,8)

> Can the Ethiopian change his skin
>   or the leopard his spots?
> Then also you can do good
>   who are accustomed to do evil.

(Jer. 13:23)

> The heart is deceitful above all things,
>   and desperately corrupt;
>   who can understand it?

(Jer. 17:9)

To these quotes many could be added from the Book of Ecclesiastes ("Vanity of vanity, says the Preacher") which, like the Book of Job, belongs within the Wisdom movement; but it is probably later than the Book of Job, so I choose instead one from the Book of Proverbs to show that the cast of mind of an Eliphaz was not entirely lacking even among the older Wisdom's thinkers:

> A man's steps are ordered by the Lord;
>   how then can man understand his way?

(Prov. 20:24)

It is, I believe, because pessimistic thoughts of the kind Eliphaz is propounding were relatively rare in Wisdom circles that he speaks of receiving them in a vision. But, as the above citations show, they are neither new nor rare in the Old Testament as a whole. Eliphaz through his vision is in effect directing a plea to his colleagues to be less rigid and more open in their teaching. They claimed to study life, but he is suggesting to them that there were areas of life which they were surprisingly ignorant and that it was time this imbalance was corrected.

(v)

It could be fairly argued that not only Eliphaz, but Job (who is also in a sense a representative of Wisdom) has lost his nerve and been forced to abandon the confident outlook on life on which he had been raised. Chapter 3 makes this clear. It will become clearer later on when we find Job drawing deeply on the same abundant reservoir of wider Old Testament teaching on the human condition which Eliphaz is drawing upon here. Indeed, if the truth were told, Eliphaz and Job are at this point in the dialogue not very far from each other. There exists a real opportunity for counsellor and counselled to come together in a common recognition of life's mysteries and enigmas, and to work out together a therapy that would comfort wounded sufferers like Job without, of necessity, either disparaging the divine providence or doing violence to human dignity. The ingredients are there on both sides for such a therapy.

Sadly the opportunity is not seized and two friends who might have learned from each other quickly drift apart. Both are, in their different ways, responsible for the breakdown in communication that is about to occur.

MAN IS BORN TO TROUBLE

Job 5:1–7

> [1]"Call now; is there any one who will answer you?
> 　　To which of the holy ones will you turn?
> [2]Surely vexation kills the fool,
> 　　and jealousy slays the simple.
> [3]I have seen the fool taking root,
> 　　but suddenly I cursed his dwelling.
> [4]His sons are far from safety,
> 　　they are crushed in the gate,
> 　　and there is no one to deliver them.

⁵His harvest the hungry eat,
　　and he takes it even out of thorns;
　　and the thirsty pant after his wealth.
⁶For affliction does not come from the dust,
　　nor does trouble sprout from the ground;
⁷but man is born to trouble
　　as the sparks fly upward."

(vi)

The crunch between the two men comes, I believe, in the first paragraph of chapter 5. Job must have been taken aback by Eliphaz's vision and therefore quite confused. His old friend had been sharp with him earlier but he had been generous as well. But what could this divine revelation with all its talk of God's holiness and human impurity have to do with his present predicament? Was Eliphaz going on to condemn him or comfort him?

When Eliphaz began to address him again I do not think it can have taken him long to make up his mind. His questions in verse 1 clearly expected the answer, *no*. It would be futile for Job to cry out in his anguish to heaven, for not even the "holy ones"—those angelic beings with whom in Eliphaz's vision God had been finding fault—would listen to him. Although there is a brief reference to an interceding angel in 33:23ff. (a passage from the speeches of Elihu, which most scholars think are a later addition to the book), it cannot seriously be argued that Eliphaz is here advising Job to seek help in such a quarter. The question had to be a rhetorical one. And to a man in Job's state of mind the obvious implication had to be that *God* would not hear his prayers.

No doubt the reason was that if he continued in the strain of chapter 3 his prayers would be resentful ones. If that was how Job took verse 1, he could hardly avoid concluding that in verse 2, Eliphaz was already all but categorizing him as a "fool" about to be slain by "vexation". The word he uses for "fool" is certainly a strong one, if not quite as strong as the one Job had himself applied to his wife (2:10). It denotes the kind of person who in Proverbs 12:16 is quick to lose his temper, or who in Proverbs 20:3 is incessantly quarrelsome but, perhaps most significantly, it denotes the kind of person who in Proverbs 1:7 has rejected the way of wisdom and given up that fear of God which is the beginning of knowledge.

Hardly less strong is the word translated as "vexation" by the RSV. That this word in particular needled Job is plain from the fact that he employs it himself as soon as he begins his next speech (6:2). The way Job uses this word is paralleled in 1 Samuel 1:16 where, on Hannah's lips, it expresses a deep sense of grievance that God has left her childless. But as Eliphaz uses it, Job must have detected the nastier nuance of Proverbs 21:19—"It is better to live in a desert land than with a contentious and fretful woman [literally, a woman of vexation]." It implied discontent and peevishness on his part, rather than genuine grievance, just as in the next line (5:2) the words translated as "jealousy" and "simple" must have suggested to Job that Eliphaz was accusing him of envy of others, and of witlessness.

It would be hard to think of a more tactlessly cruel set of words to use in counselling a man in despair. The cruelty and insensitivity appear to mount as Eliphaz describes the fate of such fools. He had once personally known such a man, and so much had his prosperity ("taking root") offended him that he had taken it upon himself to call down God's curse upon him and his own—with devastating effect. His sons had been "crushed in the gate", *ie* refused justice in the square inside the gate where the town or village elders held court (see Amos 5:12), and he himself had suddenly lost all his possessions to wandering vagrants. Job must have bridled in astonishment. Had this man who called himself a friend completely forgotten what had happened to Job?

Then he hears Eliphaz's final words, contained in the famous couplet of verses 6 and 7. Just as infallibly as a campfire gives off sparks (the Hebrew is literally and colourfully "sons of flame") so do troubles leap out on men. Eliphaz was back with his vision again. "Man is born to trouble". Job could have said that himself. But coming immediately after his curse on the fool, it looked as though Eliphaz was implying that all men, himself included, were fools from birth and deserved any suffering that came to them.

(vii)

By a very small change in the Hebrew vocalization of verse 7, this vicious meaning can be unambiguously imparted to the couplet. The change has the effect of turning a passive "is born" into an active "causes to be born". The Good News Bible adopts it and renders verses 6–7 thus:

> Evil does not grow in the soil;
>   nor does trouble grow out of the ground.
> No! Man brings trouble on himself,
>   as surely as sparks fly up from a fire.

The Jerusalem Bible also accepts the emendation, but most other modern versions follow the AV in resisting it. I am sure that they are right. The emended meaning has the attraction of logic—disasters do not simply come out of the blue, but men (Job included) create their own. But such a sense is too straightforwardly orthodox. It merely repeats in different words the thrust of Eliphaz's curse. It does not really evoke the querulousness and scepticism of the vision.

At the conclusion to this part of Eliphaz's speech we are back then with imperfection and decay and suffering as the ineluctable human condition. And we ought in fairness to ask, not simply how Job may have taken the couplet, but how Eliphaz meant it to be taken. It seems to me that he cannot be speaking about trouble arising involuntarily out of the ground in order to contrast that thought with the thought of man being born inevitably to trouble. If there is one idea that, even more than man's impurity and man's ignorance, dominates Eliphaz's heavenly message, it is precisely that *man* comes from the ground. He inhabits a house (body) of clay which has its foundation in the dust (4:19) and he is doomed because of that to a life that is nasty, brutish and short (4:19, 20–21).

We cannot but be reminded of the story of the Garden of Eden. There God first forms man "of dust from the ground" (Gen. 2:7), and later, after his fall, he utters the curse (Gen. 3:17–19):

. . . .
cursed is the ground because of you;
  in toil you shall eat of it all the days of your life;
thorns and thistles it shall bring forth to you;
  and you shall eat the plants of the field.
In the sweat of your face
  you shall eat bread
till you return to the ground,
  for out of it you were taken;
you are dust,
  and to dust you shall return.

Not only are the words *man*, *ground* and *dust* common to the couplet and to Genesis, but the verb *sprout* recalls Genesis' *shall bring forth* (literally, shall make to *sprout*); nor is there a great difference in the ranges of meaning of the nouns *affliction* and *trouble* and Genesis' *toil*.

It is a pity that Hebrew does not possess a question mark; it has an interrogative particle which is placed at the beginning of a question, but it does not always use this and in such cases only the context tells the translator that a question is intended. There is thus no proof that Professor Pope and others are correct in their proposal that verse 6 should be regarded as a question. But I am inclined to accept it, for it would make the parallels between Genesis and Eliphaz's new found pessimistic outlook on life very close indeed. The couplet would then read:

Does not affliction come forth from the ground
  and trouble sprout from the dust?
Surely man is born to trouble
  as the sparks fly upward.

Man's origin in the dust and his speedy return to it, his life of unremitting toil and misery, his tampering with a knowledge that is beyond him, his disobedience of and thus his alienation from God, his desire to be master of his own fate—these are the kind of notes that are sounded in Genesis. And many of them are sounded in Eliphaz's vision and in the splendidly morose couplet which sums it up. The couplet in effect directs Job's thoughts beyond the trouble that arises out of the individual man's own foolishness to a trouble which God has ordained for all men. This trouble, far from being easily traced to a particular person's behaviour, is part and parcel of the mystery of a holy God's dealings with the general mass of wayward, weak and untrustworthy humanity.

(viii)

What if the intended meaning of verse 1 was not to deny Job the consolation of prayer but to persuade him that to pray to God was the only thing he could do? Verses 2–5 in that case become not a shrill condemnation of Job but a sincere, if indelicately worded, warning to him to draw back from the brink of blasphemy before it is too late. And verses 6–7 become a genuine attempt to sympathize with Job's growing pessimism and to suggest a means of coming to terms with it. Eliphaz, in other words, is still convinced that Job is a good man as good men go. But he points out to him that even good men are inextricably embroiled in the struggle for existence in an evil world. They cannot expect in such a world to enjoy the rewards of virtue all the time. They share the common guilt of humanity and for that reason they should not complain if, some of the time, some of the common suffering of humanity comes their way. Let Job take comfort in the thought that he is not alone either in his suffering or in his bewilderment. Then let him plead in prayer his own real but relative innocence and see if a holy God will not become to him a loving Father and acknowledge his faithful servant and bind up his painful wounds.

That is, as I see it, the message Eliphaz means Job to take from his words at the beginning of chapter 5. That Job does not comprehend it thus is partly and perhaps largely due to Eliphaz's maladroitness in presenting it. It is nothing less than amazing that so talented and urbane a theologian should be at the same time so thoughtless and insensitive a counsellor. But has Job been entirely fair in his sour and suspicious response to a case which, in its content if not its presentation, ought to have received his close attention—as it ought to receive ours today? I do not think he has. But let us postpone that issue until Job next speaks, and for the moment stay with Eliphaz for the gentler peroration of his discourse.

AS FOR ME, I WOULD SEEK GOD

Job 5:8–27

[8]"As for me, I would seek God,
and to God would I commit my cause;
[9]who does great things and unsearchable,
marvellous things without number:
[10]he gives rain upon the earth
and sends waters upon the fields;
[11]he sets on high those who are lowly,
and those who mourn are lifted to safety.
[12]He frustrates the devices of the crafty,
so that their hands achieve no success.
[13]He takes the wise in their own craftiness;
and the schemes of the wily are brought to a quick end.
[14]They meet with darkness in the daytime,
and grope at noonday as in the night.
[15]But he saves the fatherless from their mouth,
the needy from the hand of the mighty.
[16]So the poor have hope,
and injustice shuts her mouth.

[17]"Behold, happy is the man whom God reproves;
therefore despise not the chastening of the Almighty.
[18]For he wounds, but he binds up;
he smites, but his hands heal.
[19]He will deliver you from six troubles;
in seven there shall no evil touch you.
[20]In famine he will redeem you from death,
and in war from the power of the sword.
[21]You shall be hid from the scourge of the tongue,
and shall not fear destruction when it comes.
[22]At destruction and famine you shall laugh,
and shall not fear the beasts of the earth.
[23]For you shall be in league with the stones of the field,
and the beasts of the field shall be at peace with you.
[24]You shall know that your tent is safe,
and you shall inspect your fold and miss nothing.
[25]You shall know also that your descendants shall be many,
and your offspring as the grass of the earth.
[26]You shall come to your grave in ripe old age,

as a shock of grain comes up to the threshing floor in its season.
²⁷Lo, this we have searched out; it is true.
Hear, and know it for your good."

(ix)

Sympathetic or tactless—and he can be both!—Eliphaz is a master of words. The exquisite poem in verses 8–16 in which he describes the God who will answer the innocent man's prayer could have come straight out of the Psalter. The cut and thrust of argument are laid aside and the more sombre parts of Scripture, for which Eliphaz has so obviously developed a fellow feeling, are for the moment disregarded as he tries to lift a despairing man's eyes to see the positive and kindlier attributes of the God of whom he is in peril of harbouring negative thoughts. It is as though he were berating Job for speaking only the language of lament and forgetting those other psalms of praise and thanksgiving with which the Psalter is also replete—psalms in which God's generous provision in nature and his merciful providence in the lives of men are celebrated, and in which, so often, the humbling of the wicked and the elevation of those whom the world despises are emphasized. See among others Psalms 9, 53, 65, 103, 104, 107, 113, 147; compare also the Song of Hannah in 1 Samuel 2 and Mary's *Magnificat* in Luke 1, which are modelled on such psalms.

"As for me" (or "If I were you") says Eliphaz. Is this simply another case, like those in 4:8 ("As I have seen") and 5:3 ("but suddenly I cursed"), of an egotistical old professor intruding himself into the dialogue? Quite likely—but there is probably again a reason. In the former cases he was calling upon his own experience (or perhaps what he would have liked his own experience to be) to back up his arguments. Here the noteworthy feature is his choosing, as examples of the wicked and powerful who are dethroned, the "crafty" and the "wise" and the "wily" (vv. 12–13). The *first* of these words (translated "prudent") is always a good word in the book of Proverbs (*eg* 13:16; 14:8) and, of course, the *second* (*hakamim*) is, as a title, the designation of the "wise men" among whom he counts himself. Only the *third* invariably has an approbrious sense (cf. Prov. 8:8 where it is translated "twisted").

Surely there is more than a hint in the use of these words of Eliphaz's growing distaste for the confident pretensions of his own class? If that is so, then he must in this lyrical outburst be rather forlornly addressing himself as well as Job. His vision had taught him that not only is no man pure in God's sight, but that no man is wise. Like another clever scholar who saw the light he has become suspicious of "the wisdom of this world"; see 1 Corinthians 3:18–19 where St Paul cites Eliphaz's verse 13. To Eliphaz, the exponent of Wisdom, the only true wisdom in the final analysis is to turn humbly in prayer to him who alone can save the poor and needy and shut the mouth of injustice; and he invites Job to join him.

Did even Job, who has inexorably been coming to the conclusion that Eliphaz has nothing to say to him, unfreeze a little as he heard these poignantly beautiful words? In his final paragraph (vv. 17ff.) Eliphaz suggests, on the whole kindly, that Job's sufferings may be a blessing in disguise, if only he will accept them in the proper spirit. Verse 17 should not be read as implying that Job was being punished for his sins, although Job may well have taken it that way. It is much more likely that Eliphaz is again identifying Job as a good man caught up in the general guilt and pain of human existence. The kind of disasters from which he will be saved, if he is sensible enough to recognize this, are not, like those visited on the fool in 5:3ff., the kind appropriate to individual correction but those which afflict mankind as a whole and swallow up both the innocent and the guilty.

In numerical sayings like the one in verses 19–22, the significant number is the second one (cf. Prov. 30:18–19). So the *seven* calamities are:

verse 20 *famine*
　　　　　war
verse 21 *fire* (RSV "tongue", *ie* of flame)
　　　　　flood (by a slight emendation; RSV "destruction")
verse 22 *plunder* (RSV again "destruction")
　　　　　dearth (a different word from "famine" in v. 20)
　　　　　wild beasts

Verses 23–26 then describe the happy and protected life which Job will have amid, and in spite of, these natural and ever threatening disasters. He will make his peace with a recalcitrant soil and no wild beast will attack him. His house ("tent" is poetic licence, since Job was not a Bedouin) will be safe from attack, and his flocks and herds will not be plundered. And he himself will live to a ripe old age surrounded by his numerous family.

Perhaps this time Eliphaz is intentionally thinking of the restoration by a kindly God of what Job had in fact lost, although Job himself must have been again horrified by the crass insensitivity of his so-called friend. How sad that this should be the last impression he carries away from Eliphaz's speech! For, of the three counsellors, this old man is not only the warmest in admitting Job's integrity but also the one who best understands Job's state of mind. He feels, as Job feels, the shaking of the foundations and the passing of an order where certainty and confidence reigned, and he has succeeded in enlarging his theology to take account of this. Life has become for him anything but simple and its enigmas perturb him greatly. But when the bit begins to chafe, he will not surrender his basic belief in the essential justice and consistency of the divine economy. This above all is where he parts company with Job. It is because he suspects Job of being about to take that dangerous route that he assails him with a mixture of approbation and warning, and of caution and lyrical appeal.

We may sense, in several places during Eliphaz's long speech, menace seething just beneath the surface; but it has not yet boiled over. So in his final powerful and indeed extravagant entreaty, he briefly but tellingly admonishes Job to suffer in silence and indeed count himself fortunate to be laid low by a fatherly God who wishes thereby only to promote his greater well-being. But his main purpose is to paint a glowing picture of the God he himself so passionately longs to know; a God who in troublesome times will not abandon those who trust in him but will protect and restore them and gently overshadow them until they reach their journey's end in peace. This is the ultimate lesson he has learned over a long life of thought and experience and worry, and he desperately wants his old friend also to make it his own.

Alas! the next time he will speak, it will be an Eliphaz we will hardly recognize. The menace will have surfaced. But several bitter speeches by Job will have intervened to turn his tactlessness into violent anger, and his sharp warnings into vicious censoriousness. We may, when that stage is reached, conclude that the real Eliphaz has emerged from his shell but, if that is our conclusion *then*, we should not let it prevent us from giving credit where credit is due *now*. He did try hard in a speech of no mean theological accomplishment and of quite ravishing literary beauty to give his old friend the benefit of the doubt for as long as he felt he could.

A NOTE ON SUFFERING AS DIVINE DISCIPLINE

We have in our study so far come across several ideas and emphases which are alien to Christian sentiment or which have been superseded in the centuries between the Old Testament and the New. It may be helpful to remind ourselves of the three most important of these at this stage:

(a) a man in Old Testament times who sincerely tried to live a good life was not ashamed to say so or to look to God to bless and reward him;

(b) such a man had to experience the blessing due to him in this life, for there was in Old Testament times no expectation of a meaningful existence after death to which his reward could be postponed; and

(c) if such a man encountered mishap or tragedy in his life he knew it could only come from God, for there was in Old Testament times no belief in a power independent of God (such as the Devil, or Satan, in the New Testament period) who could be blamed for it. (In addition to the Satan of the Prologue to this book, who operates—under divine licence, of course—in the lives of individuals, the Old Testament knows of a wider-ranging, or cosmic, power of chaos or evil, which it often pictures under the guise of Leviathan or some other monstrous beast, and which is in fact given a vital rôle to play in God's government of the universe as this is portrayed in the speeches of the Lord at the close of the Book of Job; but it, no less than the Satan, is a creature of God. See further in the commentary to chapters 40 and 41.)

It is against the background of these typical Old Testament beliefs that the battle of words between Job and his friends to find an explanation for his particular plight is conducted, and to obtrude beliefs from a later period would be to deprive the debate both of its agonies and its glories. It is only after we have considered the Book of Job in its own setting and on its own terms that we will be able honestly to enquire how it measures up to the Christian understanding of evil and suffering, and whether it has a genuine supplementary message for us in our modern predicaments.

It is for a similar reason that I did not press the brief, but passing, reference made towards the end of Eliphaz's speech to the idea of suffering as something sent by God on men with a *positive* end in view. He speaks in 5:17 of the man whom God "reproves" (AV *correcteth*) being blessed; but it is clear from the rest of the passage that the blessing comes afterwards, and that his suffering is not part of it. Only in so far as it teaches him to trust more urgently in God and to appeal more contritely to him, does it take on even a partially positive function. Indeed it could be argued that Eliphaz uses the idea of suffering as a discipline more as a counselling device to get Job to turn humbly to God than as, in any way, a satisfactory explanation of his condition. Certainly compared to the passion he invests in the theology of his visionary experience, it carries the stamp of an afterthought, and he does not come back to it later. Nor does it figure in the discourses of Bildad or Zophar. The idea does get a further airing in the speeches of Elihu, notably in 33:19ff., but these probably do not belong to the original Book of Job (see the Appendix). And it is found elsewhere in the Old Testament, in a number of places, notably Deuteronomy 8:1–10; Psalm 94:12–15; and Proverb 3:11–12. But it is not developed as a main argument in the wider contexts of these passages either. One gets the impression that, as with the related idea of suffering as a test of faith (which, it will be recalled, was implied in the folk story of Job), it is advanced as a mitigation of the harsh doctrine of suffering as a punishment for sin rather than as a theory in its own right. Almost universally, the Old Testament regards suffering as a hostile and evil thing. Its characteristic response is, as in the lamentation psalms, an agonized *why*? But if it has to look suffering straight in the eye, it much prefers to see in it a mark of divine displeasure and judgment, than to see in it an avenue of divine grace. If we may so put it, grace can conquer it, but does not make use of it.

The New Testament also believes that suffering, like evil itself, is something that should not be there and is doomed to disappear in God's new age. But because of the Cross of Christ the New Testament is able to invest it with a rich, warm glow, and sometimes almost to welcome it as the martyr's badge of faith or as a means whereby the humblest Christian may imitate or be united with his Lord. See, among many relevant passages, Matthew 10:32–39; 16:24–26; Romans 5:3–5; 2 Corinthians 1:3–7; Philippians 3:7–11; 2 Timothy 2:3; Hebrews 13:12–13; 1 Peter 2:21; 4:12–13. This *is* positive teaching about suffering. We never get anything like this in the Old Testament (unless it is in Isaiah chapter 53), and insights derived from it should not therefore be read by Christian readers into the Book of Job.

THE ARROWS OF THE ALMIGHTY ARE IN ME

Job 6:1–13

¹Then Job answered:
²"O that my vexation were weighed,
    and all my calamity laid in the balances!
³For then it would be heavier than the sand of the sea;
    therefore my words have been rash.
⁴For the arrows of the Almighty are in me;
    my spirit drinks their poison;
    the terrors of God are arrayed against me.
⁵Does the wild ass bray when he has grass,
    or the ox low over his fodder?
⁶Can that which is tasteless be eaten without salt,
    or is there any taste in the slime of the purslane?
⁷My appetite refuses to touch them;
    they are as food that is loathsome to me.

⁸"O that I might have my request,
    and that God would grant my desire;
⁹that it would please God to crush me,
    that he would let loose his hand and cut me off!
¹⁰This would be my consolation;
    I would even exult in pain unsparing;
    for I have not denied the words of the Holy One.

¹¹What is my strength, that I should wait?
    And what is my end, that I should be patient?
¹²Is my strength the strength of stones,
    or is my flesh bronze?
¹³In truth I have no help in me,
    and any resource is driven from me."

Job's second speech is as abandoned and terrible as his first was
forlorn and bitter. In the middle section (6:14–30) he makes it
abundantly clear that he will have no further dealing with
anything his three friends may say. Eliphaz is the only one of them
to have spoken, but his speech has so goaded Job that he feels no
compunction about turning in fury on all three and savagely
accusing them of disloyalty and betrayal. In chapter 7 he ignores
them completely and with equal savagery addresses directly the
one he regards as his real opponent—namely God. But before
these two intense and frightening passages, he tries in 6:1–13 to
convince his friends that if his words have been extreme, it is
because he had good cause; and for the first time he brings into
the open what it is that is driving him to distraction—not the
change in himself, but the change in him whom he had been
taught to see as his Maker and Preserver. It too is a taut and highly
charged passage.

(i)

Not until his next speech (see 9:2) will Job grapple with Eliphaz's
central theological assertion (4:17): that no man can be justified
in God's eyes. It is Eliphaz's appeal to him to place his case
humbly before God that occupies Job for the moment, and
especially his implication that "vexation", or resentment, is by
definition a bad thing (5:2). Why should he not, like Hannah, "a
woman sorely troubled", express his deep anxiety and sense of
grievance at the way he has been treated (see 1 Sam. 1:15–16)?
Indeed, why should he not, like the psalmist, accuse God of
hiding his face from him, and complain at the incessant pain in his
soul and the unrelieved sorrow in his heart (see Ps. 13:1–2)? If his
protestations and the disasters that were causing them were put in

the scales against all the sand in the sea, the former, not the latter, would be the heavier. It is for that reason that his words in chapter 3 were so impetuous.

Job then states openly what there he had only hinted at. It is not simply that his afflictions come from God—everyone knew that—but that God has become his enemy. And so that his friends may be in no doubt about what he is saying, he employs, like Hamlet with his "slings and arrows of outrageous fortune", metaphors derived from military combat. His physical pains and disease are the Almighty's arrows, whose poisoned tips send venom into his innermost being. And his mental terrors are an army of soldiers sent by God to besiege him.

There follow two proverbial sayings of the kind beloved by all Wisdom teachers. No animal, wild or tame, makes a noise when it has food. And no human being eats what is unsalted or tasteless. (For RSV's "slime of the purslane", a plant with a sticky but tasteless juice, the AV has the much more effectively nauseating "white of an egg" (to our ears at least); but it seems that such a rendering only goes back to the Jewish rabbis. The phrase is still argued over.)

The force of the *first* proverb is clear: Job has a reason for crying out. But the *second* is more enigmatic. Does it refer to Eliphaz's advice, which Job finds flat and insipid and cannot stomach? Or, since the adjective "tasteless" is related to the noun which the RSV translated "wrong" in 1:22, is there a sharper edge to it? In the folk tale, Job was praised for not accusing God of doing anything "tasteless" in the sense of doing anything unfitting or out of character. Is he now, under the guise of a proverb, doing just that? The only hesitation, in my opinion, about accepting the more pointed meaning is that the metaphor of a tasteless diet seems a weak one to use to describe afflictions which Job has just said were causing him the severest physical and mental torture. Perhaps the primary allusion is to the speech of Eliphaz, and the other is slipped in by the author, in an ironic word play, for the audience to savour. Where now, we are meant to ask, is God's doughty defender of these early days of tragedy?

The final line of the paragraph (v. 7) is obscure; but the New

International Version catches the probable sense better than the RSV: "such food makes me ill" ("vomit" would be even better).

(ii)

The military metaphors employed by Job to describe God's treatment of him are bold ones but not unparalleled in other passages of Scripture where faithful souls reel under life's blows; see Psalms 38:1–2; 139:5; Lamentations 2:4–5. But in such passages there is always (or nearly always) a countervailing plea to God for help; *ie* a prayer of the very kind that Eliphaz had appealed to Job to make: see Psalm 38:15, 21–22; Lamentations 2:18–20. (It is these pleas, and the expressions of trust that so often accompany them, that turn so many of the "lamentation" psalms into warm and positive religious poems.) But Job is not yet, by a long chalk, ready for this stratagem of combining reproach with faith. He had already tried the way of humble submission, and it had not worked. Did his friends not know that?

There was nevertheless one request that he could with a clear conscience make (v. 8). In chapter 3 he had wished for death. Now he would ask God outright to finish him off, and see if that pleased Eliphaz. In keeping with the bitter irony of the context, verse 10 should be rendered:

> For that at last would bring me comfort
>   and I would leap for joy in spite of unsparing pain,
>   though I have never betrayed the Holy One's commands.

The prospect of death at his great enemy's hands would afford him a perverse satisfaction and enable him happily to forget his present agony. He had lived a blameless life and kept God's laws punctiliously, but even that seemed hardly to matter any more. There would be no public vindication for him, but at least he himself knew that he had done nothing to deserve his fate and others could draw the conclusion, if they dared, that the "Holy One" had been less than holy in what he had done to him. Job does not use this divine title again and is probably thinking back caustically to Eliphaz's vision and his taunt in 5:1.

Job has by these words patently and irrevocably thrown caution to the wind and is beginning a climb to a level of sustained invective against the divine purposes that no lamentation psalm, however rancorous, could approach. It is not, however, arrogance or bravery that makes him do this, but the weakness of desolation. He has no strength left and none of that patience which Eliphaz had urged him to display. Hounded mercilessly by a divine foe, he can only beg his heavenly tormentor to administer the *coup de grâce*.

MY BRETHREN ARE TREACHEROUS
AS A TORRENT-BED

Job 6:14–30

¹⁴"He who withholds kindness from a friend
    forsakes the fear of the Almighty.
¹⁵My brethren are treacherous as a torrent-bed,
    as freshets that pass away,
¹⁶which are dark with ice,
    and where the snow hides itself.
¹⁷In time of heat they disappear;
    when it is hot, they vanish from their place.
¹⁸The caravans turn aside from their course;
    they go up into the waste, and perish.
¹⁹The caravans of Tema look,
    the travellers of Sheba hope.
²⁰They are disappointed because they were confident;
    they come thither and are confounded.
²¹Such you have now become to me;
    you see my calamity, and are afraid.
²²Have I said, 'Make me a gift'?
    Or, 'From your wealth offer a bribe for me'?
²³Or, 'Deliver me from the adversary's hand'?
    Or, 'Ransom me from the hand of oppressors'?

²⁴"Teach me, and I will be silent;
    make me understand how I have erred.
²⁵How forceful are honest words!
    But what does reproof from you reprove?

²⁶Do you think that you can reprove words,
    when the speech of a despairing man is wind?
²⁷You would even cast lots over the fatherless,
    and bargain over your friend.

²⁸"But now, be pleased to look at me;
    for I will not lie to your face.
²⁹Turn, I pray, let no wrong be done.
    Turn now, my vindication is at stake.
³⁰Is there any wrong on my tongue?
    Cannot my taste discern calamity?"

(iii)

The RSV, basing itself not on the Hebrew, but on the ancient
Syriac and Latin versions, places a little sermon in Job's mouth at
this point, as he turns to confront his friends. A man who is
unkind (or better, *disloyal*) to his friends, is not a truly religious
man. This is, in effect, what the sermon is saying. It is a stern
rebuke, but it is not so brutal (or so audacious) as the Hebrew
original. The first word in the Hebrew text of verse 14 is very
unusual and the syntax is staccato, giving literally "to someone
melting—loyalty—from his friend." But, although ancient
translators may have been misled by an unusual word and an
abrupt rhythm, these are no reasons for us to question the text.
On the contrary, we ought to be arguing that they exactly match
Job's mood which, from the beginning of this speech, has been
growing more and more agitated. The second line then
introduces the audacious element, giving for the whole;

A man in despair is owed loyalty by his friend,
    even though he forsakes the fear of the Almighty.

Yes, he was, as Eliphaz had insinuated, in danger of losing his
faith in God—or, as he would prefer to put it, he could no longer
bring himself to worship or respect the God whom he had once
known. But even in such a case, a true friend ought to be able to
remain faithful to him.

Instead, his three friends had betrayed his expectations and
they too had become his enemies. In a simile of almost Homeric

proportions (long similes are very rare in Hebrew) he compares them to one of the many wadis (dry river-beds) or brooks, of the Transjordanian highlands, which run down into the Jordan basin, or join one of the few perennial rivers of the region like the *Yarmuk* or the *Jabbok*. In winter, when nobody needs them, they are in spate, their surface chequered with ice and snow as they thunder past. But in the summer, when the caravans are on the move again (the great King's Highway from Arabia to Damascus passed through this area; see Num. 20:14–21; 21:21–23), they dry up and only stony beds await the thirsty merchants; and not even detours along their empty courses bring the tiniest trace of water as they vanish into the desert sands. (In a similar passage, 15:18, Jeremiah—for once more caustic than Job—compares God to a "deceitful brook" whose waters fail.)

So were Job's friends to him when he had most need of them, cringing as though they had seen a ghost. It was not as if he had been asking them for money! He had not been begging them for a loan or for help to cross an important person's palm (then as even now, it seems, the way to get things done in the East: see Isa. 1:23; Mic. 3:11). Nor had he been imprisoned for debt, or kidnapped and a large redemption price or ransom slapped on his head which he wanted them to pay for him. All he was asking for was a little human sympathy, and they didn't want to know him.

(iv)

But was that all he was asking for? Not according to verses 24–30. There Job's sarcasm becomes even more biting as he makes it obvious that his integrity, his desire to be vindicated, was the only thing that mattered to him. He longed intensely for death to end his agony, but it was a moment of weakness that had led him (see 6:10) to place that blessed belief above his all-consuming desire to know why God was misusing him so. In short, the only loyalty he looked for was that his friends should agree with him. Anything less and they were no friends of his.

I would import considerably more vitriol into the paragraph than the RSV and render verses 24–30 as follows:

So continue as my teachers and I must be silenced,
   keep showing me where I have gone wrong.
How sickening is the advice of righteous people,
   how to the point your criticisms!
You think you are arguing about words,
   but are the desperate man's words mere wind?
Would you cast lots for an orphan?
   Yet you haggle over your friend.
Please for once consider my side of it;
   I am not lying to your faces.
Think about it, and have done with injustice!
   Think about it again; my integrity is at stake!
Is what I am saying perverse?
   Have I not sense enough to know disaster for what it is?

There is despair, but precious little decency, in these words. Was it in any way fair of Job to accuse the friends of "bargaining" over him as though he were an orphaned child waiting to see which hard-faced creditor would be lucky enough to win him at cards and sell him into slavery to pay off his dead father's debts? Had they given him any cause to suppose that they thought he was lying to them? Had he any right to say that they were not listening to his side of the case when Eliphaz had admitted (however hypocritical he thought he was being) that he was a good man suffering undeservedly? Honesty compels us to answer *no* to these questions. Nor is it reasonable to point out that when Bildad and Zophar speak for the first time, and Eliphaz for the second, Job will in fact be seen to be almost accurate in his judgment. Surely there is no place for a "pre-emptive strike" in a war of words. Is it not tantamount to himself willing the end he wanted them to avoid?

There can be no escaping the verdict that Job is being unforgivably malicious towards three men who, we are told, had come long distances to "condole with him" and who had then sat silently by him for a week because "they saw that his suffering was very great" (2:13). Why should we believe the folk tale when it spoke of Job's integrity and not believe it when it described the friends' costly and caring concern for him?

The plain fact is that Job, in his present mood, is beyond the reach of any human compassion and any human help. Not even a saint—and saints the friends were not—could have turned him from his frenzied aim of standing religious propriety on its head and arguing from his own innocence to God's malevolence. Desolate and alone, he feels himself locked in combat with a divine foe who is infinitely stronger than he, but whom he must somehow make to yield if justice was to have any meaning. And in that sense he is also perhaps beyond any human blame. His vindictiveness towards his friends is deeply reprehensible; but might it not be kinder to say that it is directed not so much at them personally, but at anyone and everyone who was not suffering what he was suffering, and who, because of that, could have no conception of what he was going through? His assault on them has the effect of slamming a door in their faces; but was it ever open? Was it not inevitable that anything they said should have the blackest interpretation put upon it?

I believe that only a defence of Job on such lines can be made to hold water. He was not, item by item, justified in condemning them so virulently. Rather we have a man, like Lear, half-mad with grief, recognizing with utter melancholy and supreme contempt that there could be no meeting of minds between them. It is a truly appalling moment as a dialogue, which on paper has still a long way to go, grinds in reality to a dismal halt. From this moment on, neither Job nor the friends will give, or indeed expect, to receive a fair hearing.

"The wretched have no friends," said John Dryden; and it is well said. But the fault does not invariably lie with the friends.

WHAT IS MAN, THAT THOU DOST MAKE SO MUCH OF HIM?

Job 7:1–21

[1]"Has not man a hard service upon earth,
    and are not his days like the days of a hireling?
[2]Like a slave who longs for the shadow,
    and like a hireling who looks for his wages,

³so I am allotted months of emptiness,
  and nights of misery are apportioned to me.
⁴When I lie down I say, 'When shall I arise?'
    But the night is long,
    and I am full of tossing till the dawn.
⁵My flesh is clothed with worms and dirt;
    my skin hardens, then breaks out afresh.
⁶My days are swifter than a weaver's shuttle,
    and come to their end without hope.

⁷"Remember that my life is a breath;
    my eye will never again see good.
⁸The eye of him who sees me will behold me no more;
    while thy eyes are upon me, I shall be gone.
⁹As the cloud fades and vanishes,
    so he who goes down to Sheol does not come up;
¹⁰he returns no more to his house,
    nor does his place know him any more.

¹¹"Therefore I will not restrain my mouth;
    I will speak in the anguish of my spirit;
    I will complain in the bitterness of my soul.
¹²Am I the sea, or a sea monster,
    that thou settest a guard over me?
¹³When I say, 'My bed will comfort me,
    my couch will ease my complaint,'
¹⁴then thou dost scare me with dreams
    and terrify me with visions,
¹⁵so that I would choose strangling
    and death rather than my bones.
¹⁶I loathe my life; I would not live for ever.
    Let me alone, for my days are a breath.
¹⁷What is man, that thou dost make so much of him,
    and that thou dost set thy mind upon him,
¹⁸dost visit him every morning,
    and test him every moment?
¹⁹How long wilt thou not look away from me,
    nor let me alone till I swallow my spittle?
²⁰If I sin, what do I do to thee, thou watcher of men?
    Why hast thou made me thy mark?
    Why have I become a burden to thee?

²¹Why dost thou not pardon my transgression
   and take away my iniquity?
For now I shall lie in the earth;
   thou wilt seek me, but I shall not be."

(v)

His friends disdainfully dismissed to where they belong, outside
as spectators and not inside his prison as sharers of his misery, Job
gives vent to another poignant lament. He begins with a general
statement on the human condition that Eliphaz might almost
have made were it not for its implication of another's arbitrary
will behind it. Man, like a conscripted soldier, is marked down by
a superior's command to a life of "hard service" on earth. His
"warfare" (the same word in Hebrew) does not end, as a more
optimistic Old Testament voice once prophesied to Jerusalem
that hers would: see Isaiah 40:2. And, like a hired labourer, he is
allotted by a stern taskmaster only the shortest span of unceasing
toil. Compare Our Lord's use of the same metaphor in Matthew
20:1–16.

But almost immediately it is his own special experience of a
common fate that fills Job's thoughts. *He* is a slave longing for the
cool and shade of evening; he too is a hired labourer waiting for
his shift to end so that he can collect his day's pay. But what
happens then? Each futile day for months on end is succeeded by
a night of restless tossing as, kept awake by his festering malady,
he craves the dawn: see Deuteronomy 28:67. Yet how quickly, in
spite of the long days of vain expectancy and the longer nights of
itching distress, his life speeds past! In verse 6, where he
compares his days to a piece of cloth being woven by the fast
to-ing and fro-ing of the shuttle, there is a play on the Hebrew
word *tiqwah*, which means both "thread" and "hope". The
second line of the verse may thus be rendered; "they [my days]
stop for lack of hope's thread."

Then suddenly, without title of majesty or greatness, he
addresses God (vv. 7–10): "must I remind you, my life is but a
puff of wind." He shall never again see good times, and indeed
before long not even God's watching eye will be able to follow

him. Like a cloud dispersing he will be there one moment, and the next in *Sheol*, the place from which there can be no return. Again, as at the close of chapter 3, irony is taking over from pathos.

(vi)

And with the irony there comes a fierce anger as urgently—for he has little time left (v. 11)—he presses God to answer three questions. Each of the questions is heavy with remonstrance; each is more impudent, if that is possible, than the one before; and each, as though expecting no answer, closes with a wish to be quit of life or of God, or both.

First Job asks (vv. 12–16) whether he is a threat to God. Does he endanger the order and stability of the universe like the great deep of chaos which (according to Gen. 1:2, 6–10) God had to bring under control at creation (see also Ps. 104:6–9), or like the monster Leviathan of Hebrew folk lore who is a personification of the deep and whom (according to Psalm 74:14) God had to engage in battle and defeat? Another Hebrew name for this monster is *Rahab* whom (in Psalm 89:10) God had to crush, and whom, in a later allusion by Job (26:12) he had to smite (see also Job 9:13). The same monster is called *Prince Sea* in the Canaanite myths from Ras Shamra (Ugarit), and we should probably therefore translate "Am I Sea or Dragon?" with capitals.

Is he, Job asks God, a chaos-come-again, that he has to be kept in chains in case he should escape and ruin God's fair earth with his floods, as in the time of Noah? Is he a Leviathan reborn, that he has to be placed under constant surveillance, even at night, so that instead of rest he is haunted by nightmares, and longs to be suffocated as he sleeps rather than awake to another day of emaciated existence ("my bones")? Of course he is not, is the answer to his pained but audacious question. Then please let the God who plagues him so and gives him no reason leave him be. Let God afford him a little respite before the life he has come to hate hastens soon to its close.

Second Job asks (vv. 17–19) whether puny man could be such a slight threat to God that he should need to bother with him at all. It is almost the opposite question, but since the answer this time is in the affirmative—yes, he is as puny as that—the condemnation of God is essentially the same. The eighth Psalm says (vv. 4–5, AV):

> What is man, that thou are mindful of him?
>   and the son of man, that thou visitest him?
> For thou hast made him a little lower than the angels,
>   and hast crowned him with glory and honour.

Although only one verb is exactly the same, Job's words are so similar that he must have that Psalm in mind as he says (translated literally);

> What is man, that thou exaltest him,
>   that thou settest thy heart upon him,
> that thou visitest him every morning
>   . . . . . . ?

But there the resemblance ceases; for Job's next phrase is "that thou triest him every moment" (see RSV "test").

It is a parody that Job is giving; and the parody centres on the verb "to visit". It is one of the Bible's loveliest words when the thought is of God drawing near with his aid and consolation (see Exod. 4:31; Ruth 1:6; Ps. 65:9; Luke 1:68), and one of its harshest when the thought is of him coming in judgment (see Exod. 20:5 and, translated as "punish" in Isa. 13:11; Jer. 5:9; Amos 3:2). But the verb also has a military use: to "review" or "muster" troops (see 1 Sam. 11:8); or "to number", "take a census of" the people for army service (used, frequently, in the Book of Numbers). It is this use Job is thinking of. Translating his words then with negative nuances as he meant them to be taken, we get (vv. 17–18);

> What is man that you make so much of him,
>   that you pay such heed to him,
> have him on parade every morning,
>   try every single moment to catch him out?

The psalmist looks at the starry heavens in wonder that the great God who made them should so condescend as to heap such

honour upon puny mankind as he does. Job in his blasphemous
parody (and it is splitting hairs to say that it is not) wonders that
such a great God should attach such importance to men that he
cannot put them out of his mind but has to hector them every day,
every moment even, like a sergeant-major on the parade ground.
Oh that he would avert his critical gaze just long enough for one
poor soldier to clear his throat!

Thirdly (vv. 20–21) Job asks a question that I am sure even he
would rather not have asked when irony is in the air; but he is
driven to it by the perverse thrust of his satire. Suppose he has
sinned—and it is a supposition—how does that harm God? God's
actions make no sense to him. He, who as Creator is supposed to
be independent of his creatures, has turned himself into the
"watcher" or *keeper* of men (a warm concept elsewhere, speaking
of the preservation of the faithful; see Deut. 32:10; Ps. 31:23; Isa.
49:8), engaged in "constant espionage" (A. B. Davidson) to
uncover their faults. And the Creator has chosen him, Job, in
particular to be the butt for his target practice, so that Job must by
now have become a burden and a weariness to him. So God has at
last found Job out! Then, why does God not forgive him?

Can sarcasm and ridicule of the divine go further than this? It is
devastatingly brilliant. And it is archetypally Jewish. Think of
Topol's request in the *Fiddler on the Roof*:

> Would it spoil some vast, eternal plan
> If I were a wealthy man?

But while we laugh at Topol, we do not find Job so amusing.
There is about his request something of the scurrilous impiety of
the philosopher Heine who, when advised on his death-bed to
make his peace with God, is credited with saying;

> Le bon Dieu me pardonnera. C'est son métier.
> ("The good God will pardon me. That's his trade").

And there is still a mordant little twist to come in the tail as Job
abandons, for the present, his relentless pursuit of his enemy and

contemplates again (v. 21*b*) his fast approaching death. Any moment now he will be in *Sheol* and God will look for him in vain, because he will no longer be around for him to torment.

The atmosphere crackles with both venom and desperation throughout this first speech proper of Job's, but he has more—much more—to say to God, and we must wait for his next speech before we can hope to begin to understand this most wretched of men, and make even a provisional appraisal of his attitude. But at least we can see why a reasoned debate with the friends is simply not on. They and Job are on entirely different wavelengths.

INQUIRE, I PRAY YOU, OF BYGONE AGES

Job 8:1–22

[1]Then Bildad the Shuhite answered:
[2]"How long will you say these things,
   and the words of your mouth be a great wind?
[3]Does God pervert justice?
   Or does the Almighty pervert the right?
[4]If your children have sinned against him,
   he has delivered them into the power of their transgression.
[5]If you will seek God
   and make supplication to the Almighty,
[6]if you are pure and upright,
   surely then he will rouse himself for you
   and reward you with a rightful habitation.
[7]And though your beginning was small,
   your latter days will be very great.

[8]"For inquire, I pray you, of bygone ages,
   and consider what the fathers have found;
[9]for we are but of yesterday, and know nothing,
   for our days on earth are a shadow.
[10]Will they not teach you, and tell you,
   and utter words out of their understanding?

[11]"Can papyrus grow where there is no marsh?
   Can reeds flourish where there is no water?

¹²While yet in flower and not cut down,
    they wither before any other plant.
¹³Such are the paths of all who forget God;
    the hope of the godless man shall perish.
¹⁴His confidence breaks in sunder,
    and his trust is a spider's web.
¹⁵He leans against his house, but it does not stand;
    he lays hold of it, but it does not endure.
¹⁶He thrives before the sun,
    and his shoots spread over his garden.
¹⁷His roots twine about the stoneheap;
    he lives among the rocks.
¹⁸If he is destroyed from his place,
    then it will deny him, saying, 'I have never seen you.'
¹⁹Behold, this is the joy of his way;
    and out of the earth others will spring.

²⁰"Behold, God will not reject a blameless man,
    nor take the hand of evildoers.
²¹He will yet fill your mouth with laughter,
    and your lips with shouting.
²²Those who hate you will be clothed with shame,
    and the tent of the wicked will be no more."

In Dickens' novel, *Dombey and Son*, it is said of a certain Mr. Feeder, B.A., that "he was a kind of human barrel-organ, with a little list of tunes at which he was constantly working, over and over again, without any variation." That is almost true of all three friends from this point on, as the chasm between them and the sufferer before them grows ever wider. But it is particularly true of Bildad who is brought in here as the perfect dramatic foil to Job's blasphemies. No two men could have been more different. As if aware that his readers will have been shocked to the core by Job's audacity in chapter 7, the author decides to confront them immediately, and at its stiffest and most uncompromising, with the orthodoxy which has been moving him to such violent protest. I am sure that he intends them to be just as shocked by Bildad's heartless—but, as usual in this book, beautifully expressed—certainties, as they were by Job's insolent questions.

(i)

Bildad's *first* tune is the simple one that, by definition, God can do no wrong. And his *second* one is equally simple: God rewards the good and punishes the bad. But there is no tune in his repertoire for the problem of unmerited suffering. It just does not exist for him, nor does the larger problem of evil and tragedy in God's world. The catastrophes that so perplex and sadden people of feeling in every generation, and which, as I write these words, are exemplified daily on television by the shrunken heads and distended bellies of starving children in Ethiopia, cause not a furrow to dent the smooth brow of this purblind dogmatist.

The only concession Bildad will make to reality before he passes sentence on the human beings of his acquaintance, is one of timescale: there is sometimes a delay in the awarding of the appropriate prizes. And it is there that he finds a loophole for Job. He is deeply perturbed at the implications of the questions which Job has been hurling at heaven (by calling them "a great wind", he probably means not simply their empty rhetoric, but the destructive threat they pose to old and cherished beliefs) and he is sorely tempted to classify Job on that score with the wicked. But *if* indeed he is pure and upright as his former life has suggested, and *if* he drops immediately his insane attacks on God's providence, and *if* instead he makes humble supplication to him, then there may still be hope for Job. His children have died and must therefore have sinned. No other explanation is possible; for God is just to his enemies. But Job is still alive and has not been suffering all that long. God may yet judge that his previous goodness outweighs his present rebellion and, if asked nicely enough, God may even bring forward the day of expected blessing; for he is also kind to his own.

(ii)

It is instructive to contrast Bildad's grudging admission (within an "if" clause, v. 6*a*) with Eliphaz's warm acknowledgment of Job's exemplary character before his illness. It is also instructive to note how Bildad argues straight from the early deaths of Job's sons and daughters, to their guilt. He makes, without a qualm, that profoundly inhuman error of judgment which our Lord so unequivocally condemns, both in the case of the accident in the tower of Siloam (Luke 13:4) and that of the boy born blind (John 9:2–3). It is finally instructive to see how Bildad avoids raising the possibility that Job was being tested or disciplined by God; the solutions to the problem of innocent suffering that were implied in the folk tale, and toyed with by Eliphaz towards the end of his speech in chapter 5. Bildad much prefers to have his categories cut and dried. To him, as in the Book of Proverbs, mankind divides itself into two groups: the wise and the foolish, or—the same thing—the righteous and the wicked. And dogma dictates that their fates should be commensurate. Exceptions may occur from time to time—wicked men who prosper, and righteous folk who suffer—and these worry him; but he is content to put them down to a God who postpones, for a temporary period, the inevitable working out of his own rules. To ask why he allows such exceptions is, to Bildad, impious; it is enough for him that the general pattern is maintained.

This, in a nutshell, is the traditional doctrine of the *two ways* which is so succinctly set forth in the first Psalm, and which Bildad now pronounces (vv. 8–10) to be the sum of received wisdom. Far better, he concludes, to rely on the teaching of our fathers handed down over many generations, than to argue perversely, as Job has been doing, on the basis of our own short and single experiences—or for that matter to talk, as Eliphaz had done, of being granted private visions of new truth. Men in the world's golden age (in Hebrew tradition, patriarchs like Noah or Abraham) had lived long and rich lives, and they had already worked out the principles of human behaviour. All that remained for sensible people to do in the few years allotted to them in this punier age, was to listen and ponder, and to make that ancient wisdom their own.

In his lengthy peroration, Bildad changes tack a little, although in fact he is merely restating his basic position. He describes first (vv. 11–19) the sudden fading of the lusty vigour of all who forget God. They are like the papyrus of Egypt, and the rushes that grow by the bank of the Nile (see Gen. 41:2) which thrive when they have plenty of water but which, when this is denied them, dry up and perish quicker than any other grass. The thread of hope (he uses the same word-play as Job in 7:6) sustaining them snaps. Their confidence is a "spider's web" (*house* in Hebrew); and so too their own house will collapse when they lean on it. They are a sturdy plant deeply embedded among the rocks but, when the gardener grubs it up, it lies rotting on the path and is replaced by others. Such is the "joy" of their way.

But God will not cast out a blameless man thus (v. 20). It is here that we notice the change. The grudging tones of earlier are muted, and the provisos have disappeared. It is assumed that Job is blameless and that, being such, he can look forward to laughter after tears (cf. Ps. 126:2) and to the discomfiting of those who hate him.

(iii)

It seems a generous ending to a speech which had opened so ungraciously. But which part shows us the real Bildad? Considering that he had himself been so harshly judged by Job before he had spoken at all, it is to Bildad's credit that he succeeds in softening his language as in his final phrases, he holds out the hope of restoration to his old colleague. Yet the strong and strident "ifs" with which he began cannot but leave a nasty taste in our mouth. There was nothing like this in Eliphaz's speech. And Bildad's dastardly verdict on Job's unfortunate family speaks volumes as to the true state of his soul. My own lasting impression of Bildad's speech is not of a man who is convinced at heart of Job's goodness, but of a man who has all but concluded the opposite and is making one last despairing effort to save his erstwhile friend from perdition.

The velvet glove conceals the fist of a hidebound conservative who cannot abide the whiff of heresy. This word means in the original Greek, "choice"; in other words, having one's own opinion on religious matters, and men like Bildad find that almost impossible to concede. I find it significant that he, unlike Eliphaz, makes no intellectual move towards Job whatsoever, but takes his stand on an interpretation of orthodoxy that is even narrower than that espoused in the folk tale. Where the lines are laid down so rigidly, it is only a matter of time before a suffering and a complaining Job is assigned the only slot allowed for his kind. One senses that the axe of judgment is already raised high and is about to come down on him with all that ferocity which in religious communities, where men like Bildad are in charge, seems to be reserved for those who backslide.

HE WHO REMOVES MOUNTAINS,
AND THEY KNOW IT NOT

Job 9:1–10

¹Then Job answered:
²"Truly I know that it is so:
  But how can a man be just before God?
³If one wished to contend with him,
    one could not answer him once in a thousand times.
⁴He is wise in heart, and mighty in strength
    —who has hardened himself against him, and succeeded?—
⁵he who removes mountains, and they know it not,
    when he overturns them in his anger;
⁶who shakes the earth out of its place,
    and its pillars tremble;
⁷who commands the sun, and it does not rise;
    who seals up the stars;
⁸who alone stretched out the heavens,
    and trampled the waves of the sea;
⁹who made the Bear and Orion,
    the Pleiades and the chambers of the south;
¹⁰who does great things beyond understanding,
    and marvellous things without number."

Even those of us with a sympathy for Bildad's unswerving loyalty to the "good old-time religion" can see that his tactics were almost bound to fail. And so it turns out. Job is in no mood to grovel before Bildad's forgiving God when he can see no reason

in his own conduct why he should. And so, almost as though
Bildad had not spoken, Job resumes in chapter 9 the same wild
and abandoned stance he had adopted in chapter 7.

(i)

Job begins with an admission that what Bildad and Eliphaz have
been saying may be true enough. But there is heavy sarcasm in
the words, since they are followed by a "but". They are spouting
general truths which, by their very nature, can only apply to most
people most of the time. What he wants, however, is an
explanation of his *particular* case. Why, having enjoyed so many
years of blessing, was he now suffering so acutely? It was as
simple as that and, come hell or high water, he must know the
answer; not the answer that would account for this or that man's
good or ill fortune, but the answer that would account, at one and
the same time, for his own personal previous good fortune and his
own personal present ill fortune.

So once again Job is forced to turn from the theologians who
only spoke about God, to the living God himself, and, once
again, not in the spirit of submission which they advised and
which had hitherto got him nowhere, but demandingly and
urgently, with the question on his lips which they could not
answer and that hitherto God had disdained to answer. And with
ironic contempt he phrases it in their words: "how can a man be
just before God?" This is almost, word for word, the message
Eliphaz received in his vision in 4:17, where it invites the answer,
"No man can." But Job uses the verb "be just" (or to be
"righteous") in its forensic or legal sense, *ie* "to receive justice, be
declared innocent, be acquitted." For examples of this usage see
Genesis 38:26 (where Judah confesses that Tamar is less guilty
than he) and Isaiah 43:26 (where God dares Israel to go to court
with him and argue her innocence). And most apposite of all,
there is Job 40:8, where God, having at last broken his long
silence, asks Job: "Will you condemn me [pronounce me guilty]
that you may be justified [be acquitted]?" But there is a long way
to go before that stage is reached. In chapter 9 Job is putting God
on trial.

Or rather, he wishes that he could. So he asks, "How can a man get God to acknowledge his innocence?" or, more curtly, "How can a man get justice from God?"

(ii)

But even as he asks this question, he is overwhelmed by a sense of his own hubris, and of the terrifying might and incomparable power of the one he is questioning. According to the RSV, verses 2–3 show "a man" wishing to argue his case with God, but quite incapable of answering any of the thousand questions which God would put to him. The New English Bible makes God the subject of the second clause of verse 3 and renders it thus:

If a man chooses to argue with him,
    God will not answer one question in a thousand.

But "wishes" and "chooses" do not sound right. I would rather, as in the New English Bible footnote, make God the subject of the first clause and "a man" the subject of the second. The sense then is that should God "deign" to come to court and debate a man's case with him, he (the man) would be unable to muster a single argument against him. This seems to me to fit best in the context which, in Job's imagination, has God turning up to listen to him, but which, in reality, has him (Job) throwing ever wilder questions into ever emptier space. There will be no answer from heaven for Job until chapter 38.

There follows a lyrical stretch (vv. 4–10) which, in its beauty, compares with Eliphaz's exquisite little hymn in 5:8–16 and indeed has one verse (9:10 and 5:9) in common with it. But whereas Eliphaz had praised the God who condescends to answer the poor man's prayer, Job is lost in dread before the God who, with irresistible force, could remove mountains, shift the earth from its place, black out the sun's light and whip up the waves of the sea—and Job is lost also in wonder before the God who stretched out the heavens and made the amazing constellations whose shape could be traced in the evening sky.

As with Eliphaz's hymn, many parallels in the Psalter come to mind, especially the great nature Psalms like 8 or 19 or 104 (vv. 10–35), which celebrate God's marvels in creation; or such Psalms as 18 (vv. 7–15) or 29 or 104 (vv. 1–9), where it is the violence and crash of storms and floods and earthquakes that catch the poet's imagination. But Job is not singing psalms in the Temple. There is more than the Creator's praise in his thoughts as he goes on to draw more sinister corollaries from his profusion of natural pictures than any psalmist ever did.

HE DESTROYS BOTH THE BLAMELESS AND THE WICKED

Job 9:11–24

> [11]"Lo, he passes by me, and I see him not;
>   he moves on, but I do not perceive him.
> [12]Behold, he snatches away; who can hinder him?
>   Who will say to him, 'What doest thou'?
>
> [13]"God will not turn back his anger;
>   beneath him bowed the helpers of Rahab.
> [14]How then can I answer him,
>   choosing my words with him?
> [15]Though I am innocent, I cannot answer him;
>   I must appeal for mercy to my accuser.
> [16]If I summoned him and he answered me,
>   I would not believe that he was listening to my voice.
> [17]For he crushes me with a tempest,
>   and multiplies my wounds without cause;
> [18]he will not let me get my breath,
>   but fills me with bitterness.
> [19]If it is a contest of strength, behold him!
>   If it is a matter of justice, who can summon him?
> [20]Though I am innocent, my own mouth would condemn me;
>   though I am blameless, he would prove me perverse.
> [21]I am blameless; I regard not myself;
>   I loathe my life.
> [22]It is all one; therefore I say,
>   he destroys both the blameless and the wicked.

²³When disaster brings sudden death,
  he mocks at the calamity of the innocent.
²⁴The earth is given into the hand of the wicked;
  he covers the faces of its judges—
  if it is not he, who then is it?"

(iii)

Job's little hymn closes with a verse (it is the one he borrows from Eliphaz) underlining how incomprehensible are God's ways in nature. He then turns to the human scene and, with himself as the exemplar, concludes that God's ways with men are equally incomprehensible and equally violent. God's power is omnipresent—felt but invisible—and menacingly so (for "moves on" in RSV, read "steals past", v. 11). It descends unheralded and irrationally ("he snatches away"), and challenging it is useless (v. 12). Its fury is relentless and unappeasable, as Rahab's cohorts had found out to their cost in the great primaeval battle so long ago (v. 12; cf. 26:12). How then can mankind—how then can he, Job—stand up to God?

All of a sudden we are back in the rhetoric of the courtroom, and with Job's burning certainty of his own innocence. A lyrical poem about God's mysterious dealings in the world of nature and the world of men, which in another context would have moved us to wonder and to a proper sense of our own helplessness before so great a Being, is made to serve as a backcloth to a portrait of pernicious and inconsistent divine dealing which, for gross irreverence, is unparalleled in the annals of literature. The fiercest atheist cannot hold a candle to this distraught believer when he gets going.

He imagines himself challenging this mighty God in court. But immediately he is lost for words, quite incapable of forming a reasoned case. The fact that he is innocent makes no difference. Job finds himself having to beg for mercy from the one who is wronging him. If God attends at all to his summons, he will not even listen to him. For God is the same enemy who has already crushed Job for a trifle (we should read this in v. 17, literally a "hair"; the word for "tempest", which the RSV prefers, has the same consonants, but different vowels); and the same enemy who has ceaselessly wounded him "without cause". Is there an ironic echo for our benefit here of God's own words in the folk tale, 2:3? God does not even let him catch his breath before burdening him with fresh bitterness. What chance has poor Job got?

Verse 19 is cryptic, reading literally: "If it is for strength of the mighty, behold! and if for justice, who shall appoint me a time?" I do not see any reason, however, for changing "me" to "him" (RSV), and would propose as a free translation;

> If it is a contest of strength, enough said!
> But if (as it is) it is a matter of justice, who is going to give me
>   my turn to speak?

Job then goes on (vv. 20–22), his language becoming more and more jagged and defiant;

> Though free of guilt, my own mouth would condemn me;
>   though blameless, it would prove me a crook.
> But I am blameless!
> I no longer care what happens to me.
> I renounce my life.
> Nothing matters any more,
> and so I say—
> Guilty or Not guilty,
> he pronounces doom on both.

Having begun with Eliphaz's question—"How can a man be in the right before God?"—and having concluded (although in a quite different sense than that which was intended by Eliphaz) that there is no way he can, Job is here giving his answer to Bildad's question in 8:3—"Can God twist right into wrong?" And the answer is: "Yes, he can—and does."

This elusive God, from whom he can get no answer, is far too strong for him. God has no intention of explaining why he is treating Job as guilty when he is innocent. Job can therefore only argue from his own agonized experience, and blame an absent and irresponsible deity not only for his own condition, but for the condition of the world around him where, through hurt eyes, he can now only see cruelty and suffering. God's habitual behaviour, he must conclude, is not benign but malign. In his divine economy, ordinary simple goodness gets no reward. God mocks (v. 23) when tragedy strikes down innocent men. The whole earth is delivered into the hands of the wicked; he even *blindfolds* (v. 24) its judges, making sure that the human dispensers of justice are as corrupt as he.

There is nothing of Cowper's "smiling face" behind this "frowning providence", no "fresh courage" for "fearful saints" to take because;

> The clouds ye so much dread
> Are big with mercy, and shall break
> In blessings on your head.

To Job at this moment, this is the voice of the friends. The time will come when he will learn Cowper's lesson:

> God is his own interpreter,
> And He will make it plain.

But, for the present, Job's God has removed himself from an earth where might alone is right and he is sitting laughing at the result in heaven.

(iv)

These rebellious and thoroughly blasphemous verses in which Job turns Wisdom orthodoxy on its head, mark the nadir of his alienation from God. Those who preached a God who brought harmony out of disorder and held the cosmos together by his wisdom, and a God who wished to see that harmony and wisdom reflected in human affairs, were deceiving both themselves and those to whom they preached. God did not distinguish between the good and the wicked, nor did he protect those who trusted in him. He had no interest in justice, far less in mercy, but only in exercising his irresistible power. This alone made him feel like God; and if he had a bias towards any on earth, it was towards those who there most resembled him, and who pursued advancement and riches and empire at the expense of all who stood in their way. From such a God, Job could never hope to receive recognition of his case; for God was both his tormentor and the one who turned a deaf ear to his cries.

It is an appalling indictment which quite overwhelms anyone daring to comment on it. How can we respond? Let me try this way: in a real sense there is a logic, although it is a mad logic, in what Job says. He is a good man being torn apart by a fate which he and every Old Testament contemporary of his were convinced belonged within the will of God. And he had been brought up to believe that this will held good and evil in equilibrium, both in the universe as a whole and in the daily lives of men. There was thus a right path and a wrong path for men to follow, and as long as God was in charge, one of these paths ought to lead to happiness and prosperity, and the other to misery and pain. Yet he who had chosen the right path was suffering as though he had chosen the wrong. Since Job had not changed, he had to conclude that God had. He, who was by definition all-powerful, had lost his desire to maintain a balanced providence, and had allowed naked and arbitrary force to get the better of harmony and justice. In the same way, and by a very similar perverse logic, Job's friends, who had been raised on the same cherished beliefs, were even as he was speaking, preparing to call good evil, include him (Job) among the wicked, and insist he was only getting what he deserved.

Those who today land themselves on Job's side of this logical impasse often take an escape route closed to Job and become atheists. If there is a God, he could not possibly allow all the pain and grief and crime and suffering that exist in the world to continue; therefore in logic there can be no God. Equally those who today hold onto belief in God have an escape route, which was closed to Job's friends, and are able to blame much of the world's distress on a Devil or some vaguer power of evil independent of God. This makes it slightly easier for them to defend God's goodness and justice without seeming to make him responsible for the suffering of today's Jobs. But only slightly; for they know that God is still ultimately in control and can overrule the Devil whenever he wants. So God's faithful are not absolved from confrontation with today's pessimists and complainers, not all of whom have become atheists. And alas! how often do they react with the spirit and logic of the friends. Think of the heretics and rebels and campaigners, nearly all of them good and honourable men, who have been drummed out of the Church's ranks with anathemas ringing in their ears as though they were the worst of sinners. And sadder still, think of the distressed and burdened souls in danger of losing their faith, who have been driven to go to that extreme by hard and rigid pastors who refused to understand their tears, and who told them peremptorily what they must do—and believe—to be saved.

Is it then the logic of the theology, from which both Job and his friends start, that is driving them in spite of themselves to the extremes of blasphemy and censoriousness which they are now encompassing? If we accept that it is, we may then be beginning to trace on the distant horizon the outline of a solution to Job's fearsome dilemma.

Perhaps a story will edge us a little further along the road towards that solution. A young father was on his way to hospital to visit his little daughter who was stricken with cancer. It was her birthday. He was carrying a cake for her. He passed by a church and, although never devout, he entered it to pray. Later, as he arrived at the hospital a block or two away, he was told his child had died. He did not say, "The Lord gave, and the Lord has taken away; blessed be the name of the Lord", but immediately returned to the church and flung the cake at the crucifix behind the altar. He scored a direct hit and the sticky icing trickled slowly down our Saviour's face and shoulders. This story was told on what we, in this country, call the "God slot" on the radio, and the commentator gave what was, on the surface, a strange verdict, calling the father's hurling of the cake a "profoundly religious action". Agree with that verdict and think of what Bildad might have said to that young man, and Job's terrible words in this chapter begin to glow with a new significance.

THERE IS NO UMPIRE BETWEEN US

Job 9:25–35

> 25"My days are swifter than a runner;
>   they flee away, they see no good.
> 26They go by like skiffs of reed,
>   like an eagle swooping on the prey.
> 27If I say, 'I will forget my complaint,
>   I will put off my sad countenance, and be of good cheer,'
> 28I become afraid of all my suffering,
>   for I know thou wilt not hold me innocent.
> 29I shall be condemned;
>   why then do I labour in vain?
> 30If I wash myself with snow,
>   and cleanse my hands with lye,
> 31yet thou wilt plunge me into a pit,
>   and my own clothes will abhor me.
> 32For he is not a man, as I am, that I might answer him,
>   that we should come to trial together.
> 33There is no umpire between us,
>   who might lay his hand upon us both.
> 34Let him take his rod away from me,
>   and let not dread of him terrify me.
> 35Then I would speak without fear of him,
>   for I am not so in myself."

(v)

We come in these verses to what I would claim is a real watershed
in Job's spiritual pilgrimage through the dark valley. It is as
though just as *in words* he is renouncing God and all but fulfilling
the Satan's prediction (do we even, reading verses 22–24 again,
need the *all but*?), the thought inserts itself in his mind that *in
faith* he is still holding onto God. And this causes a shift,
imperceptible at first, but gathering momentum as time goes on,
in his rhetoric. His anger at God still scalds, his sense of injustice
is still solid, his frustration at getting no answer from heaven still
rankles, his satirical antennae are still quivering. But from this
point forward I believe that the evidence of a genuine search on

Job's part not only for vindication from, but for reconciliation
with, God can be detected in and through his continuing protests.
His view of God as nothing more than sheer unbridled power is
on the turn and, concomitant with this, his view is of himself as
nothing less than perfect. Almost without realizing it,
Prometheus is beating a slow retreat.

Job's immediate reaction to his terrifying vision of a universe in
the grip of evil and chaos is to return as quickly as possible to his
own painful but smaller condition—that at least he knows about.
Again he uses the language of lament. Three figures of his life's
swift inexorable passage are added to that of the weaver's shuttle
in his last speech (7:6): those of a courier straining every muscle
to deliver his message (see 2 Sam. 18:19ff.); of a skiff or canoe
skimming on its urgent mission over the waters of the Nile (see
Isa. 18:2); and of a bird of prey swooping with deadly purpose on
its victim (see Hab. 1:8).

Then come two short but very revealing complaints against
God. In the *first* (vv. 27–28) Job speaks of resolving to be of good
cheer, to look (as his friends had urged him to) on the bright side
of things, and to wait for a kindly God to restore him. But his
pains remain to plague him and he knows therefore that God has
not acquitted him. In the *second* (vv. 29–31) he acknowledges
that he is guilty in God's eyes and that it is useless trying to justify
himself. On the contrary, even if he were to wash himself with
snow and the strongest soap, God would have to plunge him into
a muddy pit and make him filthy again, so that his very clothes
would shudder as he put them on; for otherwise his sin would not
match the punishment he was receiving. (For comparable
metaphors see Ps. 51:7; Isa. 1:18, 25; Lam. 4:14.)

Do these bitter verses tell us that Job has tried the easy
optimism of traditional advice and admitted to God that he was a
sinner and waited expectantly to be restored? I think that they do,
and that they are therefore crucial verses. We who have been put
off by Job's thunderous protestations of innocence have now a
context in which to place them. This man knew well what a
terrible thing sin is and how it angers God and brings his
retributory rules into operation. And in the early days of his

illness Job had told God often how sorry he was that he had offended him. But joy and happiness had not come to him. How long then could he go on meekly entreating and dredging up ever more morbid confessions of depravity before he had purged his contempt and was released from his prison? From the scale of his agonies, it seemed for ever.

But why does Job introduce this line of reasoning at this stage, *after*, not before, he has accused God of flouting justice and pursuing him without cause? Was his experience of contrition ignored and prayer unanswered not exactly the kind of experience that had led him to make his scathing inference that God and justice had nothing in common? Why then does Job renew the emphasis on the link between sin and suffering as though such a God equated them in making his judgments? And why the powerfully stressed "I know" of verse 28 ("I know that thou wilt not hold me innocent") when it was obvious that God did not care whether he or anyone else was innocent or guilty? (Sentences of Job beginning with "I know" occur not only here, but in 10:13; 13:18; 19:25; 30:23; 42:2. Nearly all are addressed directly to God, and all, without exception, introduce an assertion about God's behaviour, past or future, which takes us into Job's very heart.)

There can only be one explanation. Job does not find it quite so easy to dispense with the idea of a God of justice as he thought. We see him here in effect resiling from his own desolate logic and in a roundabout way admitting to himself that he must go on looking for justice even from a God who stood convicted of setting justice at naught. We may even see him, in a still more roundabout way, beginning to recoil from the selfish logic that had, in the face of the friends' accusation of high wickedness, led him to claim ever more perfection for himself.

(vi)

That Job has passed the half-way mark in his struggle through his Slough of Despond is also, I believe, hinted at in the final paragraph of this chapter (vv. 32–35).

On a surface reading we seem in this passage to be confronted with a man slipping even deeper into despair. Past experience has taught him that prayer is fruitless and he is spurred on by the thought of this to wish that somehow someone would turn up to arbitrate, *ie* be an umpire (AV, "daysman") between God and himself, someone who would persuade God not to take advantage of his vastly superior might and knowledge but be willing to speak with Job on equal terms; then he, Job, would not be tongue-tied for fear, but would at last be able to present his case and be certain it had been heard. It is, of course, at the literal level, a ludicrous wish for anyone in Old Testament times to make, and Job is fully aware of this, which is why he rejects the idea in advance with his brusque statement that God is not a man as he is that they can enter court together and sit on opposite sides of the same table. The passage is thus, on the surface, saying much the same as has already been said in verse 3 ("one could not answer him once in a thousand times") or verse 16 ("I would not believe that he was listening to my voice") or verse 20 ("Though I am innocent, my own mouth would condemn me").

But might there not be a hidden and sincerer plea behind the ludicrous one? What if Job is subconsciously piercing suddenly to the core of his distress? What if in reality he is appealing not for an intervention from outside which he knows is impossible, but to the God of goodness and justice to keep in check the God of irresponsibility and power? Or, to put it as we ourselves might, if we dared to think the thought, what if he is appealing to God's own better self? What if Job is coming round to the view that God *has* a better self? The passage then becomes a most significant one for the message of the Book of Job as a whole, and deserves to be classified along with two others of its kind which we have still to come to. These are the ones which begin at 16:19 ("Even now behold, my witness is in heaven") and, familiar to everyone, 19:25 ("For I know that my Redeemer lives"). Both of these passages attract a lot of attention from commentators and properly so, because in them Job does seem to appeal to God against God, or to hope that God will vindicate him against God. And both of them follow hard, as this one does, upon passages of the blackest desolation.

Taken together, these three passages supply the necessary counterpoint of faith and trust without which Job's contribution to the human quest for God would be almost entirely negative and onesided. They may (with a very few other passages like 10:10ff. where Job speaks warmly of God) be regarded as the equivalent in Job's laments to those cries of trust and confidence which are so prominent in the *lamentation* psalms, and which make us question sometimes whether that title may not be a misleading one. That there are only a tiny number of such passages scattered throughout the long tirades of Job, may at one level sadden us. But at another level, it is surprising—and therefore doubly welcome—that there are any.

This interpretation of mine is made not more obvious but at any rate more feasible by the rendering of the New International Version, which involves one small change of a vowel in verse 33 (instead of *lo*, "not", it reads *lu*, "would that"):

He is not a man like me that I might answer him,
    that we might confront each other in court.
If only there were someone to arbitrate between us,
    to lay his hand upon us both,
someone to remove his rod from me,
    so that his terror would frighten me no more,
Then I would speak up without fear of him,
    but as it now stands with me, I cannot.

The New English Bible adopts the same small emendation and has a very similar thrust to its rendering.

(vii)

Can we go further and see in these closing verses of chapter 9, if not a prophecy, at least a distant intimation of the Incarnation? As long as we are careful how we phrase it, and do not put into Job's mouth anything that would be meaningless to him or to those listening to his story, I am sure we can. There is probably, beneath the surface of Job's despairing wish for an arbiter or umpire, an intense longing that the Lord of hosts, whom the Old Testament knew all about, should be kind—and kind not only in the sense that an Oriental potentate could be kind, dispensing occasional beneficence from his high throne, but humane in the true meaning of that word, accessible to his creatures as a human father is to his children (the great New Testament name of God—Father—is remarkably rare in the Old Testament). In short Job wished that God could be a real Immanuel, "God with us". It is a longing which the writers of the Old Testament, never guilty of bringing Creator and creature too near to each other, do not often allow to come to expression. And in this book Job will not be encouraged to become familiar with the God who in the end condescends to answer him; for he will speak to him out of a whirlwind. But the longing is there, in the present passage and in the two other passages in chapters 16 and 19 which I have mentioned. And we who are Christians can understand it well; for we believe that God has indeed come to earth in human form to share our infirmities and griefs and agonies, and to comfort us with the nearer presence of a friend—and, as God in human form, to bring us and God together. Let us then sympathize as we can with Job in his anguished hope, and honour him for his profound, if tentative and momentary, glimpse into the heart of eternity.

THY HANDS FASHIONED AND MADE ME

Job 10:1–22

> [1]"I loathe my life;
>   I will give free utterance to my complaint;
>   I will speak in the bitterness of my soul.
> [2]I will say to God, Do not condemn me;
>   let me know why thou dost contend against me.
> [3]Does it seem good to thee to oppress,
>   to despise the work of thy hands
>   and favour the designs of the wicked?
> [4]Hast thou eyes of flesh?
>   Dost thou see as man sees?
> [5]Are thy days as the days of man,
>   or thy years as man's years,
> [6]that thou dost seek out my iniquity

and search for my sin,
⁷although thou knowest that I am not guilty,
and there is none to deliver out of thy hand?
⁸Thy hands fashioned and made me;
and now thou dost turn about and destroy me.
⁹Remember that thou hast made me of clay;
and wilt thou turn me to dust again?
¹⁰Didst thou not pour me out like milk
and curdle me like cheese?
¹¹Thou didst clothe me with skin and flesh,
and knit me together with bones and sinews.
¹²Thou hast granted me life and steadfast love;
and thy care has preserved my spirit.
¹³Yet these things thou didst hide in thy heart;
I know that this was thy purpose.
¹⁴If I sin, thou dost mark me,
and dost not acquit me of my iniquity.
¹⁵If I am wicked, woe to me!
If I am righteous, I cannot lift up my head,
for I am filled with disgrace
and look upon my affliction.
¹⁶And if I lift myself up, thou dost hunt me like a lion,
and again work wonders against me;
¹⁷thou dost renew thy witnesses against me,
and increase thy vexation toward me;
thou dost bring fresh hosts against me.

¹⁸"Why didst thou bring me forth from the womb?
Would that I had died before any eye had seen me,
¹⁹and were as though I had not been,
carried from the womb to the grave.
²⁰Are not the days of my life few?
Let me alone, that I may find a little comfort
²¹before I go whence I shall not return,
to the land of gloom and deep darkness,
²²the land of gloom and chaos,
where light is as darkness."

(viii)

The change we have noticed in Job's demeanour is hardly evident
as perplexity closes around him once more. But it is there, and it

is vital that, from now on, we look for signs of it. Sick of life and with, it seems, nothing more to lose, he takes his courage in his two hands and questions his Maker again. He flings his questions into the empty void where he knows there is a God of might who is not interested in replying; but the difference is that he now also hopes that out there, there may be a God of justice who will give a rational explanation of what is happening to him. In keeping with the faith he ought in logic to have abandoned but could not bring himself to, the questions are an impassioned cry for light in darkness, and, pointed and indeed impertinent though they are, they lack the insolent irony which overlay the questions he had addressed to God in chapter 7.

Job begins with a plain unvarnished request to God not to condemn him out of hand. His afflictions are a clear proof to everyone that God was proceeding against him, and he must know why. Could it be (v. 3) that God got pleasure out of maltreating and despising the creatures he had made, and out of advancing the policies of wicked men? Or (v. 4) was he affected by a human inability to see things as they really were (contrast 1 Sam. 16:7)? Or (vv. 5–7) were his days, like man's, so few in number that God had no time to catch Job out, but had to invent sins for him, knowing he was innocent, so that he could then punish him before he escaped his clutches? The questions show Job still mesmerised by the notion of a "human" God, although the centre of comparison has shifted from man's more desirable to his less desirable qualities. They are thus sarcastic questions, and increasingly so. But they are also increasingly absurd, and it is obvious that Job does not mean them to be taken seriously.

Nevertheless, he is in deadly earnest. In his bewilderment he is casting about desperately for any motive that might explain God's treatment of him. And finding none, he is left with the same old paralysing contrast between God *then* and God *now*. He describes it this time round (v. 8) in terms of the incompatibility between God's actions in once giving him life, and his actions now in destroying him. And this way of putting it starts him off on another tack.

(ix)

In verse 9 he compares God to a potter lavishing the utmost care on his vessel and then, dissatisfied, reducing it to dust again. It is not certain whether he is simply using a well known image to describe his own fate at God's hands or whether there is, as in Eliphaz's vision (see 4:18–19), an added pessimistic allusion to the story of man's creation in Genesis, chapters 2–3, and its outcome. It is quite likely that there is, but we should not make too much of it; for his new line of thought leads him into the first really warm and positive words which he has so far addressed to God.

Without seeing any ultimate contradiction with the idea of man being made from dust, Job goes on to picture his conception and growth in the womb in more naturalistic terms. In verse 10, the craft of cheese making and, in verse 11, the art of knitting or weaving, supply the metaphors. The seminal fluid clots inside the womb and forms a framework to which his bones and sinews are added. These verses are important for the insight they give us into how the ancient world understood the process of fecundation and the development of the foetus. But what is much more important is that for Job, the whole complicated process is supervised by God. It is God, and not a human father, who implants the liquid seed; and God, not a human mother, who nourishes it and brings it to maturity. Like every human being, he, Job, is a marvellously wrought work of art, and God is the sole artist, planning, neglecting no detail, displaying all his powers of concentration and creativity.

Job does not say so out loud, but there can be little doubt that his feelings at this point are those of the author of Psalm 139 who, thinking similar thoughts, exclaims (v. 14, AV):

I will praise thee;
    for I am fearfully and wonderfully made:
marvellous are thy works;
    and that my soul knoweth right well.

Rather than reminding us of Genesis 2–3, the verses remind us of Genesis 1 with its insistent refrain, "And God saw that it was good." And (RSV v. 12) God's "care" (literally "visitation";

see 7:18) continues beyond Job's birth, as he who has granted him life brings him to manhood through his steadfast love.

(x)

But then, having tended him so well and for so long, God appears suddenly to have changed. Or has he? It seems to me that Job, having moved out of the logic in which he was trapped before, is now wondering if that is in fact so. He has rejected the idea, to which he was forced in chapter 9, that God was only a God of power and might. And earlier in this chapter he has rejected the ideas that God enjoyed hurting his creatures, or that he so resembled his creatures that he was swayed by motives like theirs. The idea he is now pursuing is God's infinite capacity for taking pains. And the devastating thought strikes him—note the strong "I know" of verse 13, and compare 9:28 and the other passages listed there—that, far from having modified his ways, God's present devotion to his misery is of a piece with his former devotion to his creation and preservation.

Verses 13–17 do not, therefore, as most commentators suppose, accuse God of dissembling or cheating. There is no malicious predestinarianism here. Job was misled, but that was because he did not think that God would be every bit as punctilious in punishing as in preserving. Just as he had spared no effort in looking after Job all these years, so he had also, all that time, been marking the balance sheet of his behaviour. He had not let a single sin of Job's, however minor, go unnoticed, but had registered every last one of them—and he was now exacting the fullest penalty possible. In his extravagant musings, Job has, he thinks, stumbled on a reason to explain his own afflictions without charging God with inconsistency or malignity. He was suffering, not because God cared nothing for justice, but because he cared too much. Under such an obsessively stern regime even the best of men were doomed to be swept into perdition as they paid to the last farthing for ordinary human failings and omissions that a more considerate judge would have overlooked.

I suggest the following free translation of these very difficult verses (13–17):

Yet all the while you were laying up torments for me in your heart;
    I realize that it was your intention,
whenever I should sin, to take careful note,
    and not allow me to escape my guilt.
If I should join the wicked, woe betide me!
But even if I should remain a righteous man,
    I would not be able to raise my head
    for the shame filling me and the affliction overwhelming me.
Proud as a lion, you keep hunting me down;
    again and again you work your wonders upon me.
You keep sending fresh plagues to witness against me,
    and get angrier and angrier with me.
    Incessant warfare is my lot.

(xi)

Job's new insight into what he thinks is the divine mind is free of the vitriolic satire of chapter 7 and the blasphemous rage of chapter 9; and it involves him in the admission of at least some faults and weakness on his own part, although it is not an admission that is made with very much grace. But the new insight still does not brighten his spirits very much. He has discovered a God who may be consistent but who is too just by half, and the end result for him is the same. He can hope in this God no more than he could in the evil God of these earlier chapters. So once again he finds himself (vv. 18ff.) wishing he had never been born to endure the attentions of such a solicitous presence which, as surely as if God had been wholly evil, will hound him to his doom. And he pleads for a moment's easing of his pain that he may have the chance to smile once more before he goes to the land where all is darkness and gloom for ever.

There is a stunning passage in Robert Louis Stevenson's great unfinished novel *Weir of Hermiston* where, in Edinburgh's Justiciary Court, a wretch of a man called Duncan Jopp is on trial for his life before the renowned "hanging" judge. If it is possible by a human analogy to catch the atmosphere of Job's imagined confrontation with God towards the end of chapter 10, Stevenson's passage catches it. Having described the abject terror of the guilty man, it goes on to picture the harsh representative of Scottish law, upright to a fault, quite incorruptible, but completely lacking in the milk of human kindness:

> Over against him, my Lord Hermiston occupied the bench in the red robes of criminal jurisdiction, his face framed in the white wig. Honest all through, he did not affect the virtue of impartiality; this was no case for refinement; there was a man to be hanged, he would have said, and he was hanging him. Nor was it possible to see his lordship, and acquit him of gusto in the task. It was plain he gloried in the exercise of his trained faculties, in the clear sight which pierced at once into the joint of fact, in the rude, unvarnished gibes with which he demolished every figment of defence . . . The rag of man with the flannel round his neck was hunted gallowsward with jeers.

Yet, as we think back on this scarifying, yet magnificent, speech of Job—surely one of the wonders of world literature—is it not rather the beautifully positive lines on Job's evolution from foetus through birth to manhood, under the minute and providential care of a good and loving God, that linger longest in our memory? The abandoned soul on the ash heap is gradually, in spite of the frenzied thoughts that seem to carry him in every direction but the right one, rediscovering the God he had once known and loved. There is, as we would say, light to be seen at the end of a very long tunnel.

CAN YOU FIND OUT THE LIMIT OF THE ALMIGHTY?

Job 11:1–20

¹Then Zophar the Naamathite answered:
²"Should a multitude of words go unanswered,
and a man full of talk be vindicated?
³Should your babble silence men,
and when you mock, shall no one shame you?
⁴For you say, 'My doctrine is pure,
and I am clean in God's eyes.'
⁵But oh, that God would speak,
and open his lips to you,

⁶and that he would tell you the secrets of wisdom!
  For he is manifold in understanding.
 Know then that God exacts of you
  less than your guilt deserves.

⁷"Can you find out the deep things of God?
  Can you find out the limit of the Almighty?
⁸It is higher than heaven—what can you do?
  Deeper than Sheol—what can you know?
⁹Its measure is longer than the earth,
  and broader than the sea.
¹⁰If he passes through, and imprisons,
  and calls to judgment, who can hinder him?
¹¹For he knows worthless men;
  when he sees iniquity, will he not consider it?
¹²But a stupid man will get understanding,
  when a wild ass's colt is born a man.

¹³"If you set your heart aright,
  you will stretch out your hands toward him.
¹⁴If iniquity is in your hand, put it far away,
  and let not wickedness dwell in your tents.
¹⁵Surely then you will lift up your face without blemish;
  you will be secure, and will not fear.
¹⁶You will forget your misery;
  you will remember it as waters that have passed away.
¹⁷And your life will be brighter than the noonday;
  its darkness will be like the morning.
¹⁸And you will have confidence, because there is hope;
  you will be protected and take your rest in safety.
¹⁹You will lie down, and none will make you afraid;
  many will entreat your favour.
²⁰But the eyes of the wicked will fail;
  all way of escape will be lost to them,
  and their hope is to breathe their last."

Zophar possibly speaks last because he is the youngest of the
three friends. It is clear from his graceless tirade that he has been
impatient to get at a man whom he had once respected, but whose
whining inability to recognize the danger he was in had cancelled
out any sympathy he may have had for him. But it is also clear that

he has used his time of waiting to good effect; for when he does speak, it is with a cool, controlled anger, and quite a few of his rapier thrusts strike home.

(i)

In upbraiding Job for speaking long and speaking intemperately, Zophar has the classical teaching of the Book of Proverbs behind him. Unlike the lamentation psalms, it did not approve of "letting off steam". To Israel's sages it was the man who weighed his words and thought before he spoke who was wise.

He who guards his mouth preserves his life;
    he who opens wide his lips comes to ruin. (Prov. 13:3)

Do you see a man who is hasty in his words?
    There is more hope for a fool than for him. (Prov. 29:20)

Job, a man formerly famous for his wisdom, should therefore have known better than to suppose (v. 3) that he could win an argument by shouting down his opponents, or by sneering at the things they held dear. It was preposterous of him (v. 4) to advance his sarcastic attacks on God's providence as a theology worthy of their consideration, and even more preposterous to claim that the God whom he so attacked must know he was innocent. If only (v. 5) God would do what Job was always asking him to do, and deign to answer him, he would soon find out what a blasphemous fool he was.

Verse 6 is very obscure, as a look at the different translations in the various English versions will confirm. The RSV changes the text a little, but the New International Version (11:5-6) keeps closer to the Hebrew, and is for that reason to be preferred;

Oh, how I wish that God
    would speak . . . . . .
and disclose to you the secrets
    of wisdom,
for true wisdom has two
    sides.

Know this: God has even
    forgotten some of your sin.

Zophar's point seems to be that if God were to open Job's eyes
to the hidden principles by which he governed the world, he
would see how far superior divine wisdom was to human. Job had
refused to accept the verdict of human wisdom that his afflictions
proved him to be a sinner but, confronted with divine wisdom, he
would realize that God was in fact letting him off lightly.

(ii)

This is deadly invective. Zophar is every whit as orthodox as
Bildad and no more inclined than he to regard Job's sufferings as
exceptional. Indeed, on the basis of that orthodoxy, he goes
further than Bildad dared to, and quite unambiguously lets Job
know that he considers him to be a wicked man paying for his
wickedness. But whereas Bildad had simply mouthed the old
platitudes and backed them up with the sanction of human
tradition, Zophar uses Job's own style of reasoning to ridicule
him. He senses Job's confusion as he pries into matters that are
beyond him and cunningly suggests to him that the unknown
might relate to the known in a way that he has not envisaged.
Instead of winning through to a God who would admit to him that
he was a good man, he might find one who told him he was lucky
that he was not being punished more.

Warming to his theme, Zophar then asks Job whether he
seriously imagines that with all his wild questioning he could
penetrate the unfathomable mysteries of God or remotely
approach the limits of his knowledge. Such things are higher than
heaven, so how could he find the strength to climb up to them?
They are deeper than the underworld, so how could he know the
way to them? Even if he were to compass both land and sea in his
search for them, he could never catch up with them. As the AV
puts it, memorably but rather inaccurately, in verse 7: "Canst
thou by searching find out God?"

One is again reminded of Psalm 139. In Job's last speech, his
words (in 10:9–12) on God's care for him, from the moment of his

conception, closely parallel its second half, and now Zophar's
words on God's omniscience parallel just as closely its first half,
especially the well-known lines (Ps. 139:7–10) beginning,
"Whither shall I go from thy Spirit?" But whereas the psalmist is
amazed and grateful that God knows all about him, and that,
even should he want to, he cannot escape his unseen presence, it
is the negative aspect of the "all-seeing eye" on which Zophar
concentrates. He even takes up (in v. 10) Job's reproachful
statement in 9:11–12 and turns it back on him. There God's
hidden power was felt by Job as something not only irresistible,
but menacing and irrational. Zophar agrees that it is irresistible;
but to him it is thus not because God is vindictive, but because his
knowledge is infinite. Worthless men may deceive themselves or
others about their true moral state, but (v. 11) he knows who they
are and he sees their wickedness without having to look for it.
God's power is in fact nothing other than his wisdom in action
against evil.

But (v. 12) one may as soon expect a "stupid" (literally, a
hollow) man to understand this as a "wild ass" to be born (tame
as) a man.

(iii)

In making his venomous comparison in verse 12 (see also Gen.
16:12) Zophar obviously has Job in mind. But he does not quite
spell it out. This is because, like the other counsellors, he feels
duty bound to leave Job a route back to God. So he issues
Wisdom's usual exhortation to the foolish man to mend his ways.
But on his lips it is a much colder and more barbed exhortation
than Eliphaz's in 5:8ff., or even Bildad's in 8:20ff. Job will not
only have to beg for forgiveness but will have to get his thinking
straightened out and consciously put away his personal sins
before the promised blessing can be his. Only then will his misery
vanish and light dawn for him in darkness. Only then will
tranquillity and hope return to him and he will become as popular
and sought after as before.

And Zophar concludes on a distinctly sour note. Bildad had
contrasted Job's restored happiness with the fate of Job's enemies

(8:22). Zophar, in 11:20, speaks only of the hopelessness and death of the wicked in general, and pointedly does not exclude Job.

Far more than the speeches of his older colleagues, in which condemnation is either kept in the background (Eliphaz) or concealed behind soft words (Bildad), this speech of Zophar's, so openly hostile, must have cut Job to the quick. Did he feel a twinge of conscience as he remembered how savagely he had berated the friends for their lack of sympathy when only the most sympathetic of the three had spoken (6:14ff.)? His words then had been too cruel and we found it difficult to justify them. But now they would have been more than merited. Zophar's evangelistic appeal is a sham, for in his heart he has quite given Job up for lost and his animosity shines through everything he says. Even more than Bildad, Zophar shows up, for the detestable thing it is, that nauseating absence of humanity which seems so often to characterize the most zealous practitioners of divinity. Is there a more scandalous thing on God's earth than to issue the Gospel call of God's love with hatred in one's heart?

Beside Zophar's vicious and rancorous onslaught on a good man going through physical and mental torture, Job's harsh dismissal of an earnest Eliphaz's attempts to be kind to him pales into insignificance. In his selfish agony Job is thoroughly nasty to his friends, but Zophar is out to destroy a fellow human being and, in God's name, to damn him eternally—and under his prompting the other two will soon follow. That he is an able theologian who argues forcefully for his own position only makes it the more inexcusable. There must be a special place reserved in Hell for those who are clever enough with words to use God to humiliate men.

I make two final observations, both of them ironic: the *first* is that of all the friends' speeches it is this one of Zophar's that is nearest in its content (if not in its intention) to the great speeches of the Lord out of the whirlwind which finally bring an over-righteous Job to his knees. The *second* is that, whereas God will have every right to talk about his own omniscience, Zophar has no more right to do so than Job. But we will leave Job to make that point for himself when he takes up Zophar's taunts in his next speech and shows himself to be an even abler theologian than he.

I AM A LAUGHINGSTOCK TO MY FRIENDS

Job 12:1–6

> [1]Then Job answered:
> [2]"No doubt you are the people,
>   and wisdom will die with you.
> [3]But I have understanding as well as you;
>   I am not inferior to you.
>   Who does not know such things as these?
> [4]I am a laughingstock to my friends;
>   I, who called upon God and he answered me,
>   a just and blameless man, am a laughingstock.
> [5]In the thought of one who is at ease
>   there is contempt for misfortune;
>   it is ready for those whose feet slip.
> [6]The tents of robbers are at peace,
>   and those who provoke God are secure,
>   who bring their god in their hand."

Jolted out of his emotional turmoil by Zopher's icy spite, Job displays, in his final speech in the first cycle (chapters 12–14), a measure of calm control and lucidity of thought that is as welcome as it is unexpected. By the disarmingly simple expedient of taking his and the other two friends' arguments more seriously than they did themselves, he shows that he has a far worthier conception of divinity than they have. He is therefore entitled to accuse them, as he does with considerable relish in chapter 13, of thinking that they could argue God's case better than God could. And what more baleful charge can one convict a theologian of than that? With the confidence gained from this rout of his earthly opponents, Job then tries with similar aplomb to take on God, challenging him again to appear and explain himself. The challenge is delivered with a mixture of frank effrontery and touching faith that must almost have moved God to intervene there and then, if not on his behalf, at least to put him in his place. But God is clearly not yet ready to answer, and Job is left lamenting his sorry lot once more, a lament which broadens out, as the speech finishes, into a magnificently morose protest at the helplessness of the human race confronted by an unknown and contrary providence.

(i)

Job begins sarcastically by berating all three friends for preaching platitudes at him, for rehearsing in his ear as though they were the first to have discovered them, those attributes of divinity—holiness, might, wisdom and the rest—which are the common stuff of religion. Did they suppose such amazing insight gave them the right to look down their noses at him? Then, with more hurt than scorn in his voice, he remarks on the peculiar irony which had turned him, a good and righteous man who had once enjoyed God's blessing, into a figure of ridicule to them and others around him. It showed the contempt that the healthy and well-heeled, secure as they thought themselves to be in God's favour, had for those who were ill or had fallen on bad times. Did they get enjoyment out of the thought that misfortune was lying in wait for those who stumbled on life's pebbles (v. 5)? They would be far better advised to direct their attention to the real wicked, to those who prospered while setting the true God at naught, and making a god out of their crime and greed (this is probably what the cryptic third line of v. 6 is getting at).

It is surprising that Job does not make more of this cutting riposte. It will soon become apparent that the friends have been offended by that element in it which condemned their rigid orthodox Wisdom for not taking into account the plain facts of life. For in their next speeches all of them will try with all their might to convince Job that the wicked do indeed get their deserts. But although Job will, in chapter 19, call again despairingly on the friends to have pity on him, he will not develop further his accusation that they seem almost to glory in his suffering as a sign of his guilt.

I cannot but be reminded of the evil done in my own land of

Scotland by the harsher interpreters of a quite different, but equally rigid, theological system. The logic of high Calvinism also demanded that mankind be divided into two groups; those (the many) damned because of original sin no matter how earnest and kind, and those (the few) saved by divine grace in spite of any sins they might commit. And there were never lacking those who, like Russell (the Reverend John Russell, minister of the High Kirk of Kilmarnock) in Robert Burns' poem *The Twa Herds*, were keen to apply God's eternal decree on his behalf:

> He kenn'd the Lord's sheep, ilka tail,
>   Owre a' the height;
> An' saw gin they were sick or hale,
>   At the first sight.

But perhaps the most noisome feature of this high Calvinism in practice (apart, that is, from the misery it brought to those who were made to feel that they belonged to the reprobate majority) was the gratification that the more hypocritical among the "elect" drew from contemplating their own superiority, and anticipating the torments awaiting those who were not of their number. Could they—and their counterparts in other communities of the faithful—be more fiercely and effectively lampooned than by Burns in his notorious *Holy Willie's Prayer*?

> O Thou, that in the heavens does dwell,
> Wha, as it pleases best Thysel',
> Sends ane to heaven an' ten to hell,
>   A' for Thy glory,
> And no for onie guid or ill
>   They've done afore Thee!

> I bless and praise Thy matchless might,
> When thousands Thou hast left in night,
> That I am here afore Thy sight,
>   For gifts an' grace
> A burning and a shining light
>   To a' this place.

When we think harder about what Burns is saying in this poem, and of its relevance to what Job is saying here, we will not laugh too loudly at its acid humour.

WILL YOU PLEAD THE CASE FOR GOD?

Job 12:7–13:12

<blockquote>

[7]"But ask the beasts, and they will teach you;
    the birds of the air, and they will tell you;
[8]or the plants of the earth, and they will teach you;
    and the fish of the sea will declare to you.
[9]Who among all these does not know
    that the hand of the Lord has done this?
[10]In his hand is the life of every living thing
    and the breath of all mankind.
[11]Does not the ear try words
    as the palate tastes food?
[12]Wisdom is with the aged,
    and understanding in length of days.

[13]"With God are wisdom and might;
    he has counsel and understanding.
[14]If he tears down, none can rebuild;
    if he shuts a man in, none can open.
[15]If he withholds the waters, they dry up;
    if he sends them out, they overwhelm the land.
[16]With him are strength and wisdom,
    the deceived and the deceiver are his.
[17]He leads counsellors away stripped,
    and judges he makes fools.
[18]He looses the bonds of kings,
    and binds a waistcloth on their loins.
[19]He leads priests away stripped,
    and overthrows the mighty.
[20]He deprives of speech those who are trusted,
    and takes away the discernment of the elders.
[21]He pours contempt on princes,
    and looses the belt of the strong.
[22]He uncovers the deeps out of darkness,
    and brings deep darkness to light.

</blockquote>

²³He makes nations great, and he destroys them:
  he enlarges nations, and leads them away.
²⁴He takes away understanding from
    the chiefs of the people of the earth,
    and makes them wander in a pathless waste.
²⁵They grope in the dark without light;
    and he makes them stagger like a drunken man.

¹"Lo, my eye has seen all this,
    my ear has heard and understood it.
²What you know, I also know;
    I am not inferior to you.
³But I would speak to the Almighty,
    and I desire to argue my case with God.
⁴As for you, you whitewash with lies;
    worthless physicians are you all.
⁵Oh that you would keep silent,
    and it would be your wisdom!
⁶Hear now my reasoning,
    and listen to the pleadings of my lips.
⁷Will you speak falsely for God,
    and speak deceitfully for him?
⁸Will you show partiality toward him,
    will you plead the case for God?
⁹Will it be well with you when he searches you out?
    Or can you deceive him, as one deceives a man?
¹⁰He will surely rebuke you
    if in secret you show partiality.
¹¹Will not his majesty terrify you,
    and the dread of him fall upon you?
¹²Your maxims are proverbs of ashes,
    your defences are defences of clay."

(ii)

But it is the friends' view of God, rather than their view of man, that Job is at this juncture most concerned to counter. It is noteworthy that the "you" of verse 7 is singular. Presumably it is Zophar that he now chiefly addresses. He is intent on giving over against the friends' his own appraisal of God's "wisdom and might" (v. 13) and he concentrates naturally on what Zophar had to say on this subject in chapter 11. But as Job gives that appraisal, he also manages to get in some telling digs at Eliphaz's speech in chapter 5 and at Bildad's in chapter 8.

Resuming his sarcasm, Job upbraids Zophar for gratuitously teaching him lessons which could easily be learned from the beasts and birds and plants and fish. All nature knew instinctively who was in charge of its destiny, and who gave life and breath to all living things. (Verse 9 speaks of the "hand of the Lord", using the special name of the God of Israel which Job, as a foreigner, is not supposed to use; but, as a glance at a concordance will show, the phrase is so common in Scripture that the author is probably employing it idiomatically, almost like our legal phrase "act of God".) What then was so remarkable in Zophar's claim (11:11) that God was aware of who the wicked were? As Job might have said, with the same friend's jibe in 11:12 in mind, even a "donkey" could understand that. But of course what Zophar had really meant was that he—Job—was wicked. Did Zophar really think that Job could not see what his game was in the same way that he could distinguish a good meal from a bad one (12:11)? If that was all that Zophar's praise of the divine wisdom led to, then he, Job, would have none of it. And if that was all that the vaunted "wisdom" of the "aged", which Bildad had spoken so warmly of, had to teach, Job was glad he had rejected it.

(iii)

Verses 13–25 form, with their frequent echoes of the language of the Psalms, another of Job's lyrical stretches. But, as in 9:4ff, his intention is not to inculcate a feeling of admiration and awe. Rather, it is to spell out how, to anyone who looked at the world through unclouded spectacles, God's power and wisdom worked out in reality. Men were helpless to oppose God (v. 14). Fierce nature had to obey his whim (v. 15). God held in his hand the fate both of those who, like the friends, were confident they had access to his counsel, and of those whom, like Job, the friends had tried to dupe (v. 16). And in particular (v. 17ff.), God controlled, for his own hidden purposes, the course of history. Ministers of state, judges, kings, priests and all the other great men who thought that their decisions were crucial to progress were but puppets dancing to his tune. Either they met a bad end or their plans came to nothing.

Verse 22 in such a context can hardly mean that God makes everything plain, to Job or to anyone else. So either Job is being ironical and we should add an exclamation mark at the end of the sentence, or the dark things, which are being brought to light, are the schemes and ambitions of rulers and statesmen. (cf. Isa. 29:15). It is God who exalts nations and brings nations low, while their leaders wander like lost souls, or grope in the darkness as though blind, or stagger helplessly like drunk men.

It is a morbid critique of the human scene and of the inscrutable providence of the God who oversees it, but it is given with a cool detachment that contrasts vividly with the passionate anger of chapter 9. There Job in his despair described a world delivered by God into the hands of evil men. Here it is the hard evidence of the posturing of nations and the pretensions of the great ones of the earth on which Job draws. There he was railing against God's injustice. Here he is setting forth his particular proof of God's wisdom and claiming it to be much nearer the truth, as it presents itself to the seeing eye, than Zophar's.

And, we might add, if the world's strong and clever are so overruled by God, what is to be said of the world's poor and humble, towards whom, according to Eliphaz (see 5:9ff.), God was supposed to have a bias? The only ones in fact whom Job does not mention in his "psalm" are the wicked. The implication is obvious. He can detect in the way that God in his wisdom governs the world, nothing to make him change his opinion, expressed in verse 6, that "the tents of robbers are at peace".

(iv)

Having given his own analysis of the "facts of the case", Job repeats in 13:1–2 his claims to know as much about God's attributes as the friends. He needed no lessons from them in this regard. But of course his real desire was not to argue *about* God, but to get through to him and argue *with* him. In that quest, which, even as they spoke their platitudes, was eating his heart away, they were no help to him at all. So in his anger he accuses them, directly to their faces, of telling lies about God and of covering the hard truth about God's actions with the whitewash of piety. The medicine they prescribed for his tortured soul was useless. If only they, as physicians of Wisdom, had enough wisdom to observe the silence they were constantly urging on him!

It is not entirely fair of Job to suggest that his friends are talking too much when he is accorded three times as much space for his own arguments (see 11:3). But there is no doubt that he is entirely justified in the vitriolic onslaught he now mounts upon them. There they were, standing beside his sick-bed, intoning truisms, marvelling at God's greatness and majesty and inscrutability, whereas all the time they had God summed up! How dare they speak falsehood and deceit on his behalf! What presumption to show partiality to God, to "accept his person" (AV, v. 8: the Hebrew is literally, "Shall you lift up his face?"), to twist verdicts in his favour, when he himself had no respect of persons (Deut. 10:17)! Was God a suppliant in their court that he craved a kind word from them? Would they be "special pleaders" for God (Moffatt)? By so restricting him to their own limited vision, they were demeaning him and recreating him in their own small image. And by shamelessly assuming that he must side with them, they were placing themselves in mortal danger.

In verse 9 Job bitingly flings back at the friends the threats they had uttered against him. God would not be mocked by the so-called faithful any more than he would be mocked by his open enemies (cf. Gal. 6:7), and he would see to it that they were suitably pursued and punished. "In secret", in 13:10, probably meant that their sentiments sounded fine on a first hearing but were, when examined, no more than base sycophancy. At least he, Job, was afraid of God. It would be better for them if they showed a like dread and did not treat him as though he were in their pocket. Their *apologetic*, to use the technical term for that branch of theology which defends the faith against attack, was a sham, and the aphorisms which tripped so smoothly from their lips crumbled to nothing when tested against the evidence of life as men had to live it.

Thus does Job put in the dock the professional theologians of every age who write their pathetic treatises justifying the ways of God to men, and with them all preachers and clergy who, in their sermons or their pastoral visits, laud the mysteriousness of God, yet have a pat answer for every religious problem. His words contain an awesome warning for those of us who have answered the call to preach God's word, and to bring his comfort and admonition to a weary and suffering and sinful humanity. It is an honourable profession to aspire to—none more so—but surely only if wc keep it in perspective, and practice it literally in the fear of God, knowing that we are playing with fire. Only then will we be able to prevent ourselves from falling into that most Stygian of all hells—the hell of those who patronise God and arrogate to themselves the task of defending his honour, because in their heart of hearts they are not sure that he is capable of doing it for himself.

THOUGH HE SLAY ME, YET WILL I TRUST IN HIM (AV)

Job 13:13–19

¹³"Let me have silence, and I will speak,
  and let come on me what may.
¹⁴I will take my flesh in my teeth.
  and put my life in my hand.
¹⁵Behold, he will slay me; I have no hope;
  yet I will defend my ways to his face.
¹⁶This will be my salvation,
  that a godless man shall not come before him.
¹⁷Listen carefully to my words,
  and let my declaration be in your ears.
¹⁸Behold, I have prepared my case;
  I know that I shall be vindicated.
¹⁹Who is there that will contend with me?
  For then I would be silent and die."

(v)

It is difficult not to feel a little sorry for the friends as they reel
under as severe a mauling as the well-meaning must ever have
received. It was a mauling they richly deserved; for they had,
albeit with the best of intentions, been playing God with a good
man's life and reputation. But how Job turns the knife once he
has plunged it in! And how contemptuously, whenever he recalls
his resolve in verse 3 to do his arguing not with the monkey but
with the organ-grinder, he leaves them vanquished on the field
and turns to his battle with the major foe!

The oration which begins at this point and carries through to
the end of chapter 14 is the noblest of all Job's addresses. It lacks
the insolent passion of chapter 9 or the unutterable pathos of
chapter 19 or the frantic assurance of chapter 31. Or rather it
sounds such notes, when it sounds them, in a quieter key. But
there is also about it, as there is about no other of his speeches, a
defiant greatness of spirit. The most miserable imaginable of
human beings draws near to death's door, yet he is still able,
through a gloom pierced with only a ray or two of hope, to present
(as it had never been presented before and hardly has since) what
I can only term, man's case against God. Ultimately it is a case
that will not stand; but *ultimately* is the operative word. The
friends are scandalized by it, and perhaps any religious person
ought to be. But for God's sake (and I mean this overused
expletive quite literally) let us not rush, at this of all moments, to
put the man who argues it in his place. Let us rather leave God to
do that for himself when the proper time comes, and ask why he is
at the present time willing to let this man have his say. And let us
conclude, as surely the author of the book means us to conclude,
that Job is here saying something that God wanted him to say,
something indeed that he *had* to say before the voice out of the
whirlwind could become audible.

As he opens the oration in 13:13, Job is still addressing his
colleagues and demanding from them a silence which I would
guess that they, in their dazed condition, were only too ready to
concede until they were able to redeploy their scattered forces.
Well aware of what he is attempting in citing God to appear in

court, Job is filled with terror. But it is not the terror that afflicted him in chapter 9—that he would be so flustered and tongue-tied in the presence of God's erratic, but overwhelming power, that he would end up by condemning himself. This Job of chapter 13 is sufficiently confident of God's interest in justice to declare that no "godless" man would be allowed to stand before him (v. 16). This adjective in the Old Testament usually describes a person given to profanity, and it was used in this sense by Bildad in 8:13, where it is paralleled by the phrase "all who forget God": see also 17:8; 20:5; 27:8. A related word in Arabic denotes an "apostate" from the Muslim religion. But in Aramaic and Rabbinic Hebrew it may mean "hypocrite" (AV) or "flatterer". These last meanings are exactly what are required in the present context. Job is asserting that God had no time for sycophants like the friends, but (if he listened to anyone) God would respect an honest suppliant like himself who spoke to him from the heart. Dr. Gordis quotes an apposite example from the Talmud: "The prophets know that their God is a God of truth who cannot be flattered."

Job then is prepared, having glimpsed through his terror a God of justice, to take his life in his hands (v. 14) and defend his integrity before God (v. 15), confident (v. 16) that his consciousness of innocence will secure him God's verdict.

(vi)

It is in the middle of this bold declaration of intent that there come the oft-quoted words (v. 15) rendered in the AV, "Though he slay me, yet will I trust in him", but usually translated in modern versions in such a way as to give almost the opposite sense. It is not easy to decide which one is right—the AV or the modern versions. For both can draw on earlier Jewish tradition.

The received Hebrew text contains the word *lō*, spelt in this way to mean "not"; but the margin (what the scholars call the Massoretic notes; the Massoretes being mediaeval Jewish scribes and textual experts) has the same word spelt slightly differently, so as to give the meaning "to, for, in him". We may compare this with English homonyms like *son* and *sun*, or *bare* and *bear*. The modern versions follow the text, arguing that, in this passage, Job is conjuring up courage out of the depths of despair, and that to have him suddenly changing gear in mid-stream and confessing trust or hope in God, would be to diminish its defiant force. He is appealing to a God who is treating him as though he was his enemy (v. 24), and appealing magnificently, but in his innermost being he knows that he will not be given a hearing. Thus;

(RSV) Behold, he will slay me; I have no hope.
(Moffatt) He may kill me—what else can I expect?
(JB) Let him kill me if he will; I have no other hope.
(GNB) I've lost all hope, so what if God kills me?

I do not disagree that, when this great oration is over, Job's final conclusion will be a pessimistic one. But I feel that there is a stronger case to be made out for the Authorized Version's rendering, than its rejection by almost all the more recent translations might lead us to suppose. (Only the NIV supports it, although it also gives the negative alternative in a footnote.) The reading "to, for, in him" has a very long pedigree. It is the reading presupposed by the *Septuagint* and most of the other ancient versions. There is also a passage in the *Mishnah* (completed about 200 A.D.), where two rabbis argue, much as we are doing now, about whether the reading "to, for, in him," or the reading "not" should be preferred. But most significantly there is the important verse (14:14) to which we will come soon, and in which Job wonders briefly whether there might not indeed be an afterlife and declares that, if there should be, he would be ready to "wait" for as long as it took for God to answer him. The verb translated as "wait" at that point, is the same verb as the AV interprets as "trust", and the RSV and other modern versions translate as "hope". In the Old Testament as a whole this verb rarely has as forceful a meaning as "trust", although it often means "hope", but in the Book of Job it mostly has its basic meaning of "wait"; see (in addition to 14:14) 6:11; 29:21; 30:26; 32:11, 16.

Let us admit, then, that the AV overdoes it with its glorious "yet will I trust in him" (13:15). Nevertheless, we ought to see in this verse something more than despair. This nuance of

"something more" can be imparted even to *lo*, *ie* "not", by adding
the adjective "other", as the Jerusalem Bible does ("I have no
other hope"). But it can be even more effectively achieved
through a combination of the reading *lo*, "for him", and the
translation "wait". Although Job does not at this point look
beyond his own death, the seed of the thought is planted in his
mind which will be expressed out loud in 14:14, although it will
then, before the speech ends, be swallowed up once again in
melancholy. I suggest the following free translation for verses
15–16:

> Though he slay me, yet will I wait for him.
> Only I must be able to defend my conduct before him.
> That is the only way I shall be saved,
> since no hypocrite would dare to approach him.

Job knows the risk he is taking in pleading innocence before a
God who seems to have pronounced him guilty. Probably God
will peremptorily finish him off, but in spite of that he can do
nothing other than wait for him to appear. Perhaps God will
answer him before he has to quit this life. But whether or not he
does, Job must keep on trying to get through to him. There may
not be a God of justice behind the God of wrath who is presently
laying him low, but he must assume that there is, and that he will
respond to Job's straight talking.

(vii)

By this time Job has patently left the friends behind and is in
effect addressing God. But he makes (v. 17) one last plea to them
to listen carefully to what he is saying. He will not crawl to God.
The case he has prepared is an unanswerable one and he knows
(v. 18; this is one of the "I know" passages to which attention was
drawn at the end of ch. 9) that he will be vindicated. There cannot
surely be any human adversary who will dare to oppose him
further.

In a similar passage, in Isaiah chapter 50, the prophet, speaking
for a martyr Israel which had suffered for God's sake in exile, sees
Israel's vindication drawing near and (vv. 8–9) challenges the

world to contradict; far from Israel having been cursed by God, God *himself* was about to bring her agonies to an end and enable her to hold her head up once more among the nations which had despised her. It is that passage from Isaiah, which is in turn taken up by St Paul in Romans 8:31ff., where he celebrates the unshakeable confidence of the Christian who knows that God is "for us". "Who shall bring any charge against God's elect?" We have not long since seen how such confidence could be nauseatingly overstretched by people like Job's friends, or like Burns' Holy Willie, who too easily concluded that they were God's favourites and could do or say no wrong. But the prophet and the apostle were not addressing people basking in the sunshine of self-satisfaction, but people who had gone through, and were still going through, the dark valley of persecution. It was because they had nothing to be confident about in themselves, that preacher and letter-writer raised their followers' eyes towards One in whom they could be confident, and One who would deliver them from pagan sneers.

Job is, of course, not in the position of the Babylonian exiles or the Roman Christians either. He has still too much confidence in himself. But he is a lot nearer their position than the comfortable friends. The man on the ash heap is gradually struggling through a period of trial to a proper view both of God and of himself. He has a long fight still ahead of him, but instead of receiving support and understanding in his quest from those around him, he has been subjected to a constant nagging. His faith is yet fitful, but it is infinitely stronger than the friends', because he can wrestle with God while they have him wrapped in cotton-wool for his own protection. He cannot believe that he will not be given a verdict of *not guilty*, and the thought of them returning to the field from which he had driven them, and, again in their false God's name, pronouncing the verdict of *guilty*, suddenly appals him. If, while he is desperately trying to reach the true God and has just got him in his sights, they were to start preaching at him again, he could not bear it and would rather die on the spot. They must allow him this chance to protest his innocence to heaven, for it may be his last.

WILT THOU FRIGHTEN A DRIVEN LEAF?

Job 13:20–14:6

20"Only grant two things to me,
    then I will not hide myself from thy face:
21withdraw thy hand far from me,
    and let not dread of thee terrify me.
22Then call, and I will answer;
    or let me speak, and do thou reply to me.
23How many are my iniquities and my sins?
    Make me know my transgression and my sin.
24Why dost thou hide thy face,
    and count me as thy enemy?
25Wilt thou frighten a driven leaf and
    pursue dry chaff?
26For thou writest bitter things against me,
    and makest me inherit the iniquities of my youth.
27Thou puttest my feet in the stocks, and watchest all my paths;
    thou settest a bound to the soles of my feet.
28Man wastes away like a rotten thing,
    like a garment that is moth-eaten.

1"Man that is born of a woman
    is of few days, and full of trouble.
2He comes forth like a flower, and withers;
    he flees like a shadow, and continues not.
3And dost thou open thy eyes upon such a one
    and bring him into judgment with thee?
4Who can bring a clean thing out of an unclean?
    There is not one.
5Since his days are determined,
    and the number of his months is with thee,
    and thou hast appointed his
    bounds that he cannot pass,
6look away from him, and desist,
    that he may enjoy, like a hireling, his day."

(viii)

Job has informed his friends what he means to do, and now he does it. We can almost see him turning away from them and raising his eyes defiantly towards heaven. He admits to God that he has felt resentful towards him; but he is willing to swallow his resentment if God will only give him some sign that he is not out to humiliate him but has good reason for maltreating him. It is the same request as he had made at the end of chapter 9, but this time there is more sharpness in it. In chapter 9, verses 32–35, he had wondered plaintively whether an umpire might be found to ensure that God would not take advantage over Job, using his vastly superior power. Here, in chapter 13, verses 20–22, Job asks God outright to break his silence and appear before him divested of the trappings of divinity. If the dispute between them is to be resolved, either God must accuse Job openly and let him defend himself, or he must be prepared without equivocation to answer the charges that Job brings against him.

But God is not having any of this, and the loud silence on his side continues. For yet another time Job is forced to address his plea to empty space and although, as he begins, his new found courage still buoys him up, he is, before he finishes, to be weighed down again by the pessimism which has been enveloping him since his tragedies struck. And again he can only conclude that this God, whose attentions he could not escape, did not consider himself bound by the same rules of decency and fair play which he demanded of his creatures. It is this conclusion—which I described earlier as man's case against God—that he develops in the last few verses of chapter 13 and throughout chapter 14.

He begins with a series of questions that remind us of those he asked of God in chapters 7 and 10; but there is a difference. There is impertinence and irony still in Job's words, but there is none of the insolent sarcasm that characterized the former of these chapters, nor any of the frantic logic which led him astray in the latter. Indeed his very first question (13:23) conceals an admission that he has sinned. It is by no means a contrite confession, but neither is it, as I read it, a pseudo-confession like the ones in 7:20–21 and 10:14–15. Job sincerely wants to know how often and how far he has fallen. This may be because he is convinced that the answer will convict God of punishing him more than he deserved, that it will show God's treatment of him to be quite out of step with anything he could have done to offend him. But at least he is, if belatedly and indeed temporarily, abandoning his pretence of perfection, and looking askance at his former way of life of which so far he has been so inordinately proud. The balance sheet is, for the present, no longer all black on God's side and all white on Job's.

Why, then, when Job is ready to make a movement towards God, does God so insistently refuse to move in his direction? Why does God, instead of answering him plainly, keep avoiding him and treating him as his enemy (v. 24)? Why does God harass and pursue one who is already as frail as a leaf before the wind, and as helpless as stubble lying on the ground (v. 25)? Why does God keep so assiduous a record of his misdemeanours and bring into the reckoning after so long the indiscretions of Job's youth, which were no worse than those of others (v. 26; cf. Ps. 25:7)? And why, finally, does God now put him in the stocks and stick to him like a gaoler accompanying a prisoner on his circumscribed round of exercise (v. 27)? All this makes no sense to Job. It is as though he were no better than a rotting piece of wood or a moth-eaten garment, fit only to be kicked aside or flung out.

(ix)

These are not, when they are examined with any care, proper questions for anyone to put to God. Indeed, it could be said that Job is not yet willing to give God his freedom any more than the friends were. He is afraid of God, which is more than the friends were, but his picture of God also is too restricted; too limited by his own troubles. And this is true even when he widens his complaints to take in others as well as himself. For it is suffering humanity Job has chiefly in mind as he launches out in chapter 14 upon a magnificent lament over man's weakness and finitude. Forgotten is his brief, but glorious, eulogy in chapter 10 (vv. 8ff.) of the God who had so carefully made and so lovingly cared for him, as, in his gloom, Job expatiates on the shortness of man's life and the distress that is his invariable lot.

There is little for our comfort in the poignantly beautiful verses with which chapter 14 opens. Nor, in their sentiment, are they alone in the Old Testament. We think immediately of Isaiah chapter 40, where in verses 6–8, "all flesh is grass" which withers, whereas "the word of our God shall stand for ever"; or of Psalm 103, where, in verses 14ff., man, whose "days are like grass" and "like a flower of the field" is contrasted with his Maker whose mercy is from "everlasting to everlasting". Yet compared with our passage, these are supremely positive lines, turning our thoughts away from our own temporality towards God's eternity, in which alone is our hope. We have to listen, for an apter parallel, to the sombre tones of Psalm 90. There again (vv. 5–6) mankind is compared to the grass which is soon cut down and withers, but (vv. 9–10) the leading thoughts are of the wrath of God in which they have to pass their few allotted days, and the sorrow and trouble which he sends on them.

But even Psalm 90 is more optimistic than Job. While the psalmist prays for God to "return" (v. 13) and have mercy on his people, Job can only plead with God to "look away" from his poor weak creatures that they may enjoy a little rest before their time of toil is ended. And while the psalmist is able to muster some feelings of gladness and expectancy as he waits for a stern God to show his kinder face, Job can only marvel that the God with whom he has to deal should be so persistently severe with a pathetic creature like man. Job has ceased for the moment to remember the good and just God whose face he had so recently glimpsed through his terror, and he now sees only absurdity before him. Of God's greatness he has no doubts, but he is simply unable to comprehend why the providence of such a God should issue in a life that is so short, nasty and brutish for his creatures.

Not even man's moral uncleanness is left out—and this is new for Job. In his present cooler frame of mind, he can allow himself to admit that not only he, but all men, are corrupt. But he does not advance this as a reason for the unceasing torment of human existence. Man's imperfection is, like his frailty, part of his finitude, and is to that extent his Creator's fault rather than his own; or, at any rate, it never remotely explains the suffering and servitude to which, under God's regime, he is subjected.

(x)

It is easy enough to pick holes in Job's doleful analysis of the human condition. Where is there in it (as there was in chapter 10) a mention of the good things of life showered on men by a bountiful Creator? Where is there a hint of the happiness which human beings are able to conjure up for themselves out of the most depressing circumstances, and which is one of the glories of their species? Or where, on the other side of the coin, is there a recognition (as there is, for instance, in Gen. chapters 1–11) of the awfulness of man's pride and his rebellion against his Maker which have so much to do with his present parlous situation? Job has, to our relief, said a little about human imperfection and his own sin, but it is not nearly enough. The analysis is too lopsided and, even for the Old Testament, places too much emphasis on God's responsibility for everything and man's utter helplessness to do anything to extricate himself.

But we ought not, for all that, to criticize too much in case, unwittingly, we land ourselves alongside the friends and begin to exonerate God at Job's expense. If God could put up for so long with this complaining servant of his, can we do less? And if God found it possible in the end to pronounce in Job's favour, surely we must steel ourselves to do likewise, hard though it may be for us. There is a charge against God in this speech of Job's which conventional piety, like the friend's, too quickly suppresses. For the vast majority of the human race, even in these enlightened days of technical achievement, life *is* as Job here describes it: weakness and corruption and decay; unremitting toil to win a crust of bread; disease and misery; no chance to effect an improvement in their lot; no freedom to act before death brings a quick end to their transient existence—are these not the things that mark for far too many all that they can look forward to?

Yet God allows these things to be! We seek for our little explanations, but do they really satisfy us? Must we not sometimes protest with all our being at the enormity of it all? Can we lay hand on heart and say that Job here, the insolence burned out of him and only a cold and uncomprehending anger left, does not speak for all of us at least some of the time? And one last thought: will God himself have any respect for us if we do not follow this despairing servant of his into his God-forsaken darkness, where the divine voice has ceased to speak, and only man's bitter and forlorn tears are found? Is it not one of the lessons of this book that, unless we do so as we are able, assuredly we will not feel the warmth of God's light when it eventually dawns?

IF A MAN DIE, SHALL HE LIVE AGAIN?

Job 14:7–22

> ⁷"For there is hope for a tree,
>   if it be cut down, that it will sprout again,
>   and that its shoots will not cease.
> ⁸Though its root grow old in the earth,
>   and its stump die in the ground,
> ⁹yet at the scent of water it will bud
>   and put forth branches like a young plant.
> ¹⁰But man dies, and is laid low;
>   man breathes his last, and where is he?
> ¹¹As waters fail from a lake,
>   and a river wastes away and dries up,
> ¹²so man lies down and rises not again;
>   till the heavens are no more he will not awake,
>   or be roused out of his sleep.
> ¹³Oh that thou wouldest hide me in Sheol,
>   that thou wouldest conceal me until thy wrath be past,
>   that thou wouldest appoint me a set time, and remember me!
> ¹⁴If a man die, shall he live again?
>   All the days of my service I would wait,
>   till my release should come.
> ¹⁵Thou wouldest call, and I would answer thee;
>   thou wouldest long for the work of thy hands.
> ¹⁶For then thou wouldest number my steps,
>   thou wouldest not keep watch over my sin;

¹⁷my transgression would be sealed up in a bag,
and thou wouldest cover over my iniquity.

¹⁸"But the mountain falls and crumbles away,
and the rock is removed from its place;
¹⁹the waters wear away the stones;
the torrents wash away the soil of the earth;
so thou destroyest the hope of man.
²⁰Thou prevailest for ever against him, and he passes;
thou changest his countenance, and sendest him away.
²¹His sons come to honour, and he does not know it;
they are brought low, and he perceives it not.
²²He feels only the pain of his own body,
and he mourns only for himself."

(xi)

In the last part of his final speech in the first cycle, Job wins through briefly to another vision of hope, but no sooner is it caught sight of, than it vanishes, and a black and morbid pessimism descends on him again. The vision has to do with the thought of his survival after death, and the blackness returns, if anything more densely than before, when he realizes that in so musing he is chasing a mirage.

A tree that is cut down does not die. It can never regain its former height and splendour; yet out of its rotting stump, if there is sufficient moisture in the soil, new shoots will suddenly, when all seems lost, sprout. But man does not even have that half-hope. Death for him means complete extinction. Like a shrinking lake, or a disappearing stream in time of drought, he fades away to nothing. Job had previously—and most unusually for someone in Old Testament times—yearned for death because it would bring him relief from the pains and alarms that gnawed incessantly at him, and from the God who caused them (see 3:21ff.; 7:15–16; 10:18ff.). But with thoughts like these pressing in upon him, it has clearly come home to Job what the "nevermore" of death means. Till the heavens ceased to be—and they were in Hebrew metaphor scarcely less enduring than the eternal God himself (see Pss. 72:7; 89:36–37; 102:25–27)—he would not awake from his last sleep.

I recall the fine lines of the Scottish mediaeval poet, William Dunbar, with their insistent Latin refrain ("the fear of death perplexes me"):

> I that in heill wes and gladnes
> Am trublit now with gret seiknes
> And feblit with infermite:
> > *Timor Mortis conturbat me.*
>
> Our plesance heir is all vane glory,
> This fals warld is bot transitory,
> The fleshe is brukle [frail], the Fend is sle:
> > *Timor Mortis conturbat me.*
>
> No stait in erd heir standis sickir [sure];
> As with the wynd wavis the wickir [willow],
> wavis this warldis vanite:
> > *Timor Mortis conturbat me.*

It is that kind of fear that now grips Job, not simply the selfish dread of what is going to happen to "me" when the call comes, but a sinking feeling in the gut that life—my life, your life, any man's life—has no meaning; that *life* is, in fact, as Macbeth in his final moments of disintegration saw it;

> . . . but a walking shadow; a poor player,
> That struts and frets his hour upon the stage,
> And then is heard no more: it is a tale
> Told by an idiot, full of sound and fury,
> Signifying nothing.

The consolations of a Resurrection faith did not prevent Dunbar and Shakespeare from penning these dark lines. Neither, I would argue, is this the place for us to bury our heads in Christian piety. Job, living when he did, had no hope of life beyond the grave like the one unleashed on the world when Jesus rose on the third day. But, like the two great poets I have quoted, we must be aware that such a hope is difficult to sustain. Indeed, if we wish to put ourselves in Job's position in this black chapter, we need only look around us and see how our contemporaries view death. The fear of death has not been banished from our society and we deceive ourselves if we think that quoting an Easter hymn or two will banish it from our own hearts. So let us honestly admit that we know very well what Job is getting at here.

(xii)

That should prepare us to see what he is getting at when he allows himself, in verses 13ff., the luxury of speculating about his own survival. In the precisest terms, Job is not wishing for eternal life in the Christian sense, but is asking for God to intervene in the process of dying as the Hebrews understood it. Like other ancient peoples, they held the belief that when people died, something of them lasted on for a temporary period in a shadowy world beneath the earth, presumably until their bodies had mouldered to dust in the ground. Only then did the whole personality finally cease to exist.

Job is therefore not contemplating immortality when he asks God to come to him in *Sheol*. Nevertheless—and again most daringly for a man of his time—Job is piercing beyond the *no* of death and demanding from God a *yes* which will give more than a passing meaning to the short and troubled life of his which is so soon to come to an end. We will not grasp the poignancy of that demand if we shake our heads and pity Job for not having won through, as we have, to a full belief in life after death. He is in fact making, for the age to which he belonged, a truly remarkable leap into the darkness.

There are several passages in the Psalms where sick and troubled people plead with God to rescue them from *Sheol* (*eg* Ps. 49:15). Christian readers of the Old Testament almost invariably get these wrong when they interpret them in the light of the Easter message. In their original setting, they are in fact no more than heartfelt prayers to be spared an early death. This is made clear by a Psalm like 116, for example, where in verses 8–9, an ertswhile sufferer thanks God for delivering him from the approaching power of death so that, now recovered, he is able to appear before God in the Temple among his living worshippers. Job's plea goes some way beyond that. He knows that he is near to death and that nothing can stop it, yet he can ask the God, who is presently deaf to his cries, to name a day when he will at last listen to them. So carried along is he by this vision of the future, that he quite forgets about getting his innocence acknowledged, and seems to accept that he is guilty. It is God's ultimate intervention that he desires, and for which he is willing to wait (see 13:15) for as long as he has to. God is about to bring about his death and hide him out of his sight in *Sheol*, but he foresees a time when the same God will remember him (cf. Gen. 8:1) and call to him there, cancel the accusation against him, tie up his transgressions in a bag, and show kindness once more to the creature he had once so lovingly formed.

The nearest parallel to this amazing flight of the imagination is Ps. 139:8, where the psalmist states his faith that even although he is in *Sheol*, his God will find him there. This faith also breaks through the common understanding of the age (see, for example, Ps. 88:10–12) that God did not interfere in what happened in *Sheol*. But neither Job, nor the author of Ps. 139, speculate further. Nor in Job's case in particular is there any thought of a return to life on earth. He is in effect expressing his longing that the dispute between him and God may one day be peaceably settled, and so intense is the longing that he is not prepared to let even his physical death stand in the way of that day's dawning.

(xiii)

But the longing, intense as it is, cannot be sustained. Job's famous words, "If a man die, shall he live again?" (v. 14) are, in the last analysis, words of deepest melancholy. The words demand, and are given by Job, the answer *no*; and his startling vision of a day in *Sheol*, when God will finally drop all charges against him, quickly evaporates in the very strong "but" of verse 18. Even the seemingly permanent features of the natural world fall victim to decay. Mountains can crumble away and rocks can be moved from their place; and the waters of a river slowly but surely wear away the stones and carry off the soil on its bed. In the same way

God erodes the hopes of all mankind. He is far too strong for it and must always have his own way.

Job, in his mounting despair, even ridicules the persistent hope of Old Testament man that, although he will not himself survive, his name will live on among his sons, and that, through their achievements, he will be remembered and honoured. Probably they too will be brought low and only repeat his failure. That failure, and the pain and sorrow it brings in its wake, is all that any man knows for sure. Such despair would, in our modern age, have long ago dispensed with the idea of God. But that option is not there for Job, and so he has to put God in the dock. He does not hear the groans of his creatures, and he does not care. Indeed, if Job's experience is anything to judge by, God enters the ring against them. Human life is nothing but a grim farce, and who but God can be held responsible, since all power to act effectively is on his side, not man's?

It is a relief to know that the author of the book does not leave Job in this desolate mood. And indeed, here and there, he has already dropped the markers which hint at the way by which Job will, in the end, make his peace with God. Nevertheless, we owe it to him to face up seriously to the deadly thought which he makes Job, at this point in the debate, plant in our minds. We do not need to be reminded of all the evil and tragedy that exists in our world as it existed in Job's. But can we blame all of this on human disobedience and sin, or for that matter on the Devil? Ought we not to blame some of it on God? Where in heaven's name is his promised kingdom? When is he who is all-powerful going to listen to the prayers of his oppressed children and do something about it? Think of these questions and you may conclude, with the help of his despondent, yet realistic, servant of old, that there is indeed a case for God to answer.

YOU ARE DOING AWAY WITH THE FEAR OF GOD

Job 15:1–16

[1]Then Eliphaz the Temanite answered:
[2]"Should a wise man answer with windy knowledge,

and fill himself with the east wind?
³Should he argue in unprofitable talk,
   or in words with which he can do no good?
⁴But you are doing away with the fear of God,
   and hindering meditation before God.
⁵For your iniquity teaches your mouth,
   and you choose the tongue of the crafty.
⁶Your own mouth condemns you, and not I;
   your own lips testify against you.

⁷"Are you the first man that was born?
   Or were you brought forth before the hills?
⁸Have you listened in the council of God?
   And do you limit wisdom to yourself?
⁹What do you know that we do not know?
   What do you understand that is not clear to us?
¹⁰Both the gray-haired and the aged are among us,
   older than your father.
¹¹Are the consolations of God too small for you,
   or the word that deals gently with you?
¹²Why does your heart carry you away,
   and why do your eyes flash,
¹³that you turn your spirit against God,
   and let such words go out of your mouth?
¹⁴What is man, that he can be clean?
   Or he that is born of a woman, that he can be righteous?
¹⁵Behold, God puts no trust in his holy ones,
   and the heavens are not clean in his sight;
¹⁶how much less one who is abominable and corrupt,
   a man who drinks iniquity like water!"

Of the three friends Eliphaz is the most entitled to feel aggrieved
at Job. In his first speech, in chapters 4 and 5, he had honestly
tried to sympathize with Job, and had encouraged him to look for
an explanation of his suffering not directly in his own
wrongdoing, but in the common imperfection of a human race
which had to live with trouble as its birthright. He had received a
dusty and ungracious response. Instead of taking the well trodden
route of turning humbly to God in prayer, Job had insisted on
blaming God—and blaming him vehemently—for what was

happening to him, and had gone on at unseemly length about his own innocence. The man whom he had once been pleased to count as his colleague, and who did seem to him to be getting more than his fair share of mankind's misery had, to his chagrin, turned out to be a rebel at heart. Indeed, it was now clear to him that if ever there was a case to which the traditional doctrine of retribution applied, it was Job's. So in his second speech, we find the old philosopher, who had at first been brave enough to express his disquiet at the rigidity of orthodox Wisdom, espousing it as enthusiastically as Bildad and Zophar, and joining them in blanket condemnation of Job. After Job had, in chapter 13, so ungratefully and cruelly despised their well-meaning advice, it was the only weapon they had left.

(i)

Eliphaz's speech falls into two parts, in the first part of which (vv. 1–16) he attacks Job personally. Gone is his praise of Job's virtuous former life, and in its place is his new conviction that Job's wild language betokened a deep-seated evil within him that was only now coming to the surface. Not only was Job a windbag, but a dangerous one who was undermining all that religion stood for. He was clever, but not wise, and his claim to be so was self-deception. Did Job think that, like Adam in the Garden, he had a "hot line" to the Creator and was privy to the knowledge that only God possessed? (Eliphaz may have in mind in v. 7 the familiar story of Genesis, but it is more likely that he is alluding to the rather different version, perhaps pagan, preserved in Ezekiel's sardonic lament over the king of Tyre: see especially Ezek. 28:12–15.) Eliphaz himself, and many other teachers of Wisdom, were older and wiser than Job. Why had Job refused to be contrite before God as he advised, or refused to taste the rich consolations which he urged upon him? What did he hope to gain from venting his rage and spite in the only quarter from which help could possibly come?

At this point Eliphaz reverts to the visionary experience of which he had apprized Job in chapter 4. Through it, with a force that had caused his hair to stand on end, he had been led to the conclusion that the God who had little cause to trust his heavenly servants, had even less cause to trust his earthly creatures whose life, compared to his eternity, was as short as a moth's. As he reported it at that early stage in their confrontation, it was his intention to comfort Job with the thought that he was not alone in his pain and misery, and he ought, therefore, like many an ill-used believer before him, to be flinging himself on God's mercy. But as he reports it here, it has become merely an additional reason for execrating Job. Indeed, Job was now a living proof of its truth, and a particularly loathsome example of a corrupt humanity which imbibed evil as readily as a drink of water

(ii)

Some of the points made by Eliphaz are valid points and echo our own sense of shock at Job's intemporate language. On many occasions we have used the word *blasphemy* to describe it, and have had a hard struggle to remember that Job was in fact an innocent sufferer. Perhaps, therefore, we should not rush too sanctimoniously to criticize Eliphaz. We should note in addition that Eliphaz's sarcastic questions in verses 7ff. (like Zophar's in 11:7ff.) are not all that obviously different from the questions God will himself address to Job in chapter 38. There is an irony to be savoured here.

Nevertheless, it has to be admitted that Eliphaz's harshness and intolerance are frightening. It is hard to conceive how the gentle counsellor of chapters 4 and 5, pompous and tactless though he may sometimes have been, could turn his coat quite so thoroughly, or how the quizzical sceptic of those chapters could emerge quite so wholeheartedly on the side of the Bildad of chapter 8, *that* dogmatic upholder of the "good old-time" religion, who saw only good men and bad men and no one in between. So severely has his *amour-propre* been dented that personal vindictiveness has all but shut out memory and affection. For someone who belonged to antiquity's equivalent of one of the caring professions, to allow that to happen was unforgivable.

There is another irony in this particular confrontation, and it rebounds to Job's discredit no less than it does to Eliphaz's. We felt it right to castigate Job for earlier misconstruing Eliphaz's intentions, and savagely attacking him and his colleagues in chapter 6 for being no true friends of his. Yet, in his most recent speech, Job seemed to be coming round, partially at any rate, to Eliphaz's way of thinking (see 13:23; 14:1; 14:4). How sad that he did not do so sooner! And how sad that Eliphaz should fail to notice when he did, and that he has ears only for Job's more outrageous utterances! But how typical all this is of a lot of human controversy, in the religious, as in any other, sphere! Why did Job and Eliphaz so perversely refuse to acknowledge the common ground between them, and why do we today, in our various allegiances, so often repeat their mistake?

THE WICKED MAN WRITHES IN PAIN ALL HIS DAYS

Job 15:17–35

17"I will show you, hear me;
  and what I have seen I will declare
18(what wise men have told,
  and their fathers have not hidden,
19to whom alone the land was given,
  and no stranger passed among them).
20The wicked man writhes in pain all his days,
  through all the years that are laid up for the ruthless.
21Terrifying sounds are in his ears;
  in prosperity the destroyer will come upon him.
22He does not believe that he will return out of darkness,
  and he is destined for the sword.
23He wanders abroad for bread, saying, 'Where is it?'
  He knows that a day of darkness is ready at his hand;
24distress and anguish terrify him;
  they prevail against him, like a king prepared for battle.
25Because he has stretched forth his hand against God,
  and bids defiance to the Almighty,
26running stubbornly against him
  with a thick-bossed shield;

²⁷because he has covered his face with his fat,
    and gathered fat upon his loins,
²⁸and has lived in desolate cities,
    in houses which no man should inhabit,
    which were destined to become heaps of ruins;
²⁹he will not be rich, and his wealth will not endure,
    nor will he strike root in the earth;
³⁰he will not escape from darkness;
    the flame will dry up his shoots,
    and his blossom will be swept away by the wind.
³¹Let him not trust in emptiness, deceiving himself;
    for emptiness will be his recompense.
³²It will be paid in full before his time,
    and his branch will not be green.
³³He will shake off his unripe grape, like the vine,
    and cast off his blossom, like the olive tree.
³⁴For the company of the godless is barren,
    and fire consumes the tents of bribery.
³⁵They conceive mischief and bring forth evil
    and their heart prepares deceit."

(iii)

In the second part of his speech (vv. 17ff.) Eliphaz, having
assigned Job to the category of the wicked, describes for him at
length their agonies and their fate. The wicked man is defined as
one who would "play the hero" (v. 25; RSV has "bids defiance")
before the Almighty and dare to take him on in battle. Such
brazen impertinence is bound to bring him inner turmoil and
anxiety. Marked down for the sword, destined to be hunted and
plundered, he will become the victim of unceasing alarm and fear.
And his dread will not be misplaced. Declared an outcast from
decent society, he will make no enduring wealth and sink no
permanent roots. Like a tree burned by fire or blasted by the
wind, he will be destroyed and thus fully requited for the vanity of
his ways, and the godless and mischievous company he keeps.

The terrible images of retribution are not always consistent,
but their drift is clear. Job should know that, by virtue of his
assaults on providence, he was already experiencing the agony of
body and mind that was his due, and that unless he abandoned

tout de suite his defiance of heaven, it would work itself out in bitter and final disaster. But it is noteworthy that the "unless" is scarcely audible. Only verse 31 ("Let [such a man] not trust in emptiness") sounds a warning note. To all intents and purposes, Job's doom is already written, and it is others who, if they are wise, will take to heart the lesson of his fate.

(iv)

In his characteristic way (cf. 4:8) Eliphaz wants us to believe that he had seen the principle he enunciates operate consistently in human experience. He does not convince us. We are much more likely to agree with Job's assessment in 12:6 that "the tents of robbers are at peace". This is not rejecting what Eliphaz thinks of as the pure teaching of the fathers (vv. 18–19) before it became affected by alien modern ideas. It is simply being realistic. There are areas of life in which it is apparent that a man will reap what he sows; and there are many harmful and damaging actions and habits which inevitably draw down dire consequences on the heads of those who adopt them. Israel's Wisdom teachers knew all about these, as any chapter of the Book of Proverbs testifies. But it is by no means an observable fact that the wicked in this world always, or even generally, get their just deserts. On the contrary, they are, as often as not, sleek and contented in their wickedness, "flourishing like a green bay-tree", as the Prayer Book version of Psalm 37:35 has it. The confidence of the Book of Proverbs did not prevent the Hebrews worrying a lot about this. Indeed, it worried them every bit as much as the suffering of the righteous did. The Old Testament is full of rather desperate advice to believers not to "fret" because of the wicked (Ps. 37:1); see also Psalms 49 and 73. And, far too frequently for our taste, it calls down curses upon them, revealing how their prosperity needled its writers, as in imprecation psalms like 109; see also Psalm 139:19ff.

It would be unfair to put all these passages down to envy and vindictiveness. Most of them are, in reality, fervent prayers that justice may not only be done but may be seen to be done among men. And if we are feeling generous, we may be disposed to grant that Eliphaz shares that prayerful concern. But we cannot leave it at that. His tirade is worse than that even of Psalm 109; for it is directed against one man, not merely a class of men. And it is directed against that man not for his overt actions, but for his words. It is a vicious performance on behalf of which we dare not enter any mitigating plea. Moreover, considering his major shift of theological ground since his previous speech, there is the rank smell of hypocrisy about it as well. In the interests of the survival of established religion a bumbling but likeable old Wisdom teacher, who in his first speech was almost as sceptical as the Job of chapter 14, has turned himself into a malicious and rancorous "Holy Willie". Our blood cannot but run cold as we see him doing what he regards as his God-appointed duty. It will run even colder when we see his two younger colleagues follow him with undisguised relish.

HE HAS TORN ME IN HIS WRATH

Job 16:1–17

¹Then Job answered:
²"I have heard many such things;
 miserable comforters are you all.
³Shall windy words have an end?
 Or what provokes you that you answer?
⁴I also could speak as you do,
 if you were in my place;
I could join words together against you,
 and shake my head at you.
⁵I could strengthen you with my mouth,
 and the solace of my lips would assuage your pain.

⁶"If I speak, my pain is not assuaged,
 and if I forbear, how much of it leaves me?
⁷Surely now God has worn me out;
 he has made desolate all my company.
⁸And he has shrivelled me up,
 which is a witness against me;
and my leanness has risen up against me,

   it testifies to my face.
⁹He has torn me in his wrath, and hated me;
   he has gnashed his teeth at me;
   my adversary sharpens his eyes against me.
¹⁰Men have gaped at me with their mouth,
   they have struck me insolently upon the cheek,
   they mass themselves together against me.
¹¹God gives me up to the ungodly,
   and casts me into the hands of the wicked.
¹²I was at ease, and he broke me asunder;
   he seized me by the neck and dashed me to pieces;
   he set me up as his target,
¹³   his archers surround me.
   He slashes open my kidneys, and does not spare;
   he pours out my gall on the ground.
¹⁴He breaks me with breach upon breach;
   he runs upon me like a warrior.
¹⁵I have sewed sackcloth upon my skin,
   and have laid my strength in the dust.
¹⁶My face is red with weeping,
   and on my eyelids is deep darkness;
¹⁷although there is no violence in my hands,
   and my prayer is pure."

Job is overwhelmed by the new turn in the friends' arguments. No
longer is there even a pretence of guiding him back to the right
path. As a result he now feels completely isolated and alone.
Both man and God have failed him and turned against him. But
although his friends' enmity hurts, it is God's hostility that
mortifies him most. His desperate appeal to God to explain why
he has been so treated by him has gone unanswered. So just as he
had followed his lament of chapter 3 with a fierce attack on God
in chapters 7 and 9, here too Job follows the gloom and pessimism
of chapters 13 and 14 with a renewed offensive against a cruel and
uncaring heaven, an offensive that fills much of this speech and
spills over into the one after it.

But there is a crucial difference between the new offensive and
the one he had mounted in the first cycle. With the rising dismay
there comes a rising faith. Job has not forgotten the passing

glimpses he has been given of a juster and more merciful divine
face behind the tyrannical face which confronts him. And even in
his alienation these glimpses of a good God return to plague him
with hope. There is now a balance between protest and trust
which is reminiscent of the marvellous balance achieved in the
great psalms of lamentation (see, for example, Pss. 22 or 42–43 or
102). Job is, despite his friends and, as yet, despite God,
continuing his slow climb out of spiritual madness into spiritual
sanity.

(i)

As in chapter 6, Job replies to Eliphaz's speech with a sarcastic
attack on all three friends. It is as though he sensed that they
would take their cue from him. He was wrong about this in
chapter 6 but here he is spot on; for Bildad and Zophar will do
little more in their next speeches than mimic Eliphaz's ill-natured
description of the downfall of the wicked. So his suffering is the
result of his sin? How easy it was for them to say that! They did
not even have to enquire about his real character. Their dogmas
made it plain that he was evil.

Job goes on to imagine their positions being reversed. He could
equally well have played the rôle of "miserable comforter". He
could, like Eliphaz, have strung together any number of
conventional phrases drawn from the Wisdom textbooks. Or he
could, like all of them (we can almost see them grimacing in the
background), have shaken his head in disapproving silence at
what he saw. But he hopes rather (v. 5) that he would have tried
the way of genuine encouragement, whether in words or by
keeping silent (the second half of the verse should be translated
". . . or sympathy would restrain my lips").

(ii)

For the moment, however, Job says no more to the friends, but
abruptly recalls the enmity of a greater One than they. In verse 6
he still talks of speaking out and of remaining silent, but he is no
longer thinking of how he would have approached the friends had
they been in his shoes and he in theirs, but of how he has been

approaching God. Neither his words of complaint or appeal, nor
his reproachful silences (ought we to have made room for more of
these in our interpretation of his speeches?) have budged God an
inch. In the reality of his anguish he can find no relief. For God
has seen to it that he is beyond help. No human comfort remains
for him, and his emaciated form makes it obvious that he has
offended heaven and forfeited its comfort. Or so it seems.

An incoherence invades Job's words at this juncture. Where in
verse 7 the RSV has "God", the Hebrew simply has "he"; and
where in the second line the RSV has "he", the Hebrew has
"thou". The "he" of verse 8 is also "thou" in the Hebrew. Then
after the "he" of verse 9 and the "they" of verse 10 (not "men" as
in the RSV) God's name is mentioned for the first time in verse
11. Job sees only violence and hatred all around him—God's first
and foremost, but also, under his prompting, the violence and
hatred of men; and his language becomes shrill to the point of
paranoia.

In verse 9, Job's "adversary" is a wild animal tearing him to
pieces. In verse 10, false witnesses press upon him, striking him
and maligning him. In verse 11, God surrenders him to the
wicked and the ungodly. In verse 12, God is a wrestler of
superhuman strength who suddenly picks him up and dashes him
down again. Then Job is God's target, and (in v. 13) God calls on
his archers to let fly at him and slash his body open. Finally in
verse 14, God is laying him under siege, breaching his defences
and rushing through Job like a warrior in the heat of battle.
Under these incessant accusations and assaults, Job dons the
sackcloth of mourning and his eyes are swollen and red with
weeping as the shadow of death settles upon him.

Yet he is innocent of any wrong, and time and time again in his
prayers he has told God so. It is this simple fact, his conviction
that he is guiltless of anything that might conceivably justify such
murderous suspicion and maltreatment, that empties Job's world
of all reason and sense. The similarity of Job's words in verse 17 to
those used about the suffering Servant of the Lord in Isaiah 53:9
must be coincidental (no notion that suffering can have a
vicarious purpose ever surfaces in the Book of Job), but it adds a

poignancy to this unbearable scene that we, if not the book's first readers, can readily appreciate. We must not, however, carry the similarity over into our interpretation. To Job, his suffering is meaningless. He has seen his friends start off by acknowledging his goodness and end up by accusing him of all manner of depravity. God also—no, God above all—must know he is innocent; yet he has been orchestrating this ordeal as though he were punishing one who was the guiltiest of all sinners. Job feels it in his bones that, if only he could get through to God, the misunderstanding between them (for that is what it had to be) would be cleared up and his vindication achieved. But—the unkindest cut of all—the judge is nowhere to be found. The only one who could give him the verdict he craved for was too busy hounding him to spare the time to take his place on the bench, where he would have to abandon his bias and look at Job's case with the dispassionate eyes of justice.

All these thoughts and more are involved in Job's simple cry of *not guilty*, as he prepares to make one of the sudden changes of gear which are so characteristic of this middle section of the book.

(iii)

Nightmarish is perhaps the best word to describe Job's language as, in this and the succeeding speech, he veers between the emotional extremes of *hopelessness* and *hope*. It is almost impossible to decide which emotion is the stronger. Is it *hopelessness*, because these speeches both end on a note of depression? Or is it *hope*, because they contain brighter visions, and the flame of these is so intense that it can never quite be put out by the surrounding gloom? I am inclined towards the second view; but it is a very close call. Thus Dermot Cox can argue that these speeches "show a disorientated mind fluctuate from despair to hope to despair, but despair is dominant. Hope serves merely as a dramatic device to heighten it." He may be right. It is the glory of this book that it has drawn, down the centuries, so many marvellously contrary interpretations from so many wise and thoughtful commentators, and of no section is this truer than of the superb and climactic section of the Book of Job which we have just entered. It behoves us therefore to tread humbly. No man has penetrated further into the mystery of the Godhead than the wretch on his ash heap whom we see before us, and whose words of unutterable sadness and expectation we are privileged to overhear.

EVEN NOW, BEHOLD, MY WITNESS IS IN HEAVEN

Job 16:18–17:16

[18]"O earth, cover not my blood,
    and let my cry find no resting place.
[19]Even now, behold, my witness is in heaven,
    and he that vouches for me is on high.
[20]My friends scorn me;
    my eye pours out tears to God,
[21]that he would maintain the right of a man with God,
    like that of a man with his neighbour.
[22]For when a few years have come
    I shall go the way whence I shall not return.
[1]My spirit is broken, my days are extinct,
    the grave is ready for me.
[2]Surely there are mockers about me,
    and my eye dwells on their provocation.

[3]"Lay down a pledge for me with thyself;
    who is there that will give surety for me?
[4]Since thou hast closed their minds to understanding,
    therefore thou wilt not let them triumph.
[5]He who informs against his friends
    to get a share of their property,
    the eyes of his children will fail.

[6]"He has made me a byword of the peoples,
    and I am one before whom men spit.
[7]My eye has grown dim from grief,
    and all my members are like a shadow.
[8]Upright men are appalled at this,
    and the innocent stirs himself up against the godless.
[9]Yet the righteous holds to his way,

and he that has clean hands grows stronger and stronger.
[10]But you, come on again, all of you,
    and I shall not find a wise man among you.
[11]My days are past, my plans are broken off,
    the desires of my heart.
[12]They make night into day;
    'The light,' they say, 'is near to the darkness.'
[13]If I look for Sheol as my house,
    if I spread my couch in darkness,
[14]if I say to the pit, 'You are my father,'
    and to the worm, 'My mother,' or 'My sister,'
[15]where then is my hope?
    Who will see my hope?
[16]Will it go down to the bars of Sheol?
    Shall we descend together into the dust?"

(iv)

The series of pictures of a persecuting and implacable deity, hell-bent on the humiliation and annihilation of a human being, which is given to us in the first part of this oration, is hardly matched even by the abandoned onslaught of chapter 9 on a malign divinity who causes, and then mocks at, earth's calamities. But as he did then, Job, without a break and with no rhyme or reason that we can detect, suddenly sees the contorted and malevolent features of his God crumble, and a friendly face appear. The Job who had been plunged into near blasphemous despair is raised in an instant to desperate assurance.

As in Genesis 4:10, innocent Abel's blood cries out for redress, or, as in Ezekiel 24:7–8, the blood of Babylon's victims spurs God on to wreak vengeance upon her, so here Job imagines his blood, after his death, carrying his silent plea for vindication up to heaven. In Genesis, Abel's blood finds a "voice" and calls from beneath the ground, but in Ezekiel, the blood shed by Babylon lies uncovered on the bare rock that it may be a more visible reminder of her crimes. It is the second idea that Job makes use of, as he foresees an untimely, violent death for himself, and summons the earth not to cover his blood, thus removing the evidence of his unjust murder. His "cry" must be heard. (Incidentally, "cry" is a word worth studying for the depth of passion invested in it in so many Biblical passages; see Gen. 27:34; Exod. 2:23; 3:7; Esth. 4:1; Pss. 107:6; 142:5–6; and cf. Luke 18:7.)

Job is not so optimistic as to demand instant vindication. Only when he is dead—and at God's bloodthirsty hands!—will the strange figure (whom he called in 9:33 an "umpire" and will in 19:25 call his "redeemer", but to whom here he gives the name of his "witness") arrive on the scene to plead his case for him. The noun translated "he that vouches for me" (16:19) is better known in Aramaic, and means exactly the same as "my witness"; see Genesis 31:47 (*Jegar-sahadutha* and *Galeed*) where the two words are part of alternative names for the same area. But "vouches for" carries the right nuance. In Hebrew legal procedure there is neither a prosecutor nor a defending counsel in our sense of these terms. An offended party did his own prosecuting and the accused defended his own case, each calling witnesses as required. And the witnesses on both sides did more than give evidence under oath. They took an active part in condemning or exonerating.

A defending witness stood to the right of the accused, a fact which explains several allusions in the Psalms to God appearing at the worshipper's right hand (*eg* 16:8; 109:31). The metaphor of God as a "witness" is therefore not a new one. See also Psalm 142, where the psalmist looks in vain to his right but, finding no man to take notice of him, has to "cry" (v. 5) to the Lord to be his refuge.

Job, therefore, as he looks around him, sees the open derision of his friends, and he knows that his days (oddly the text has "years") are numbered, and that he has very little time before he has to take the journey from which there can be no way back. There shall be no recovery for him in this life. His "spirit is broken" (17:1; or perhaps the NEB is better, since Job is at this moment being borne up on wings of faith, with the translation "my mind is distraught"). The grave is ready for him (Coverdale: "I am harde at deathes dore"); and as he goes to his doom, he hears only the mocking curses of his erstwhile colleagues (17:2).

Yet in his mind's eye, he also sees a future assize in heaven at which he himself will not—alas!—be present. But as God sits on the bench, another God will be there to speak for him and to say better than Job ever could, the things that had to be said. To that God he now pours forth his anxious and tearful prayer that he will win for him, from the other God, the verdict that is his due. The second part of 16:21 should be more precisely translated "as a man will plead for his fellows" (Jerusalem Bible, NIV). Job's point is that if a mere human can get justice for his friend in an earthly court, how can God do less for him in his own heavenly court?

(v)

The paradox of Old Testament theology could not be more starkly set forth than in that verse which has just been mentioned and which I will render as following:

> . . that he [God] might remonstrate for a man with God,
> as a man remonstrates for his friend.

Add, at the end of the second line, "with whoever is wronging him" and the meaning becomes crystal clear. God has wronged Job, and only God can right the wrong. Job therefore has to appeal to God against God in a way that makes us feel distinctly uncomfortable. But we have encountered before in this book, the contradiction within the Godhead that arises from a view of reality that is not afraid to place both good and evil under the direct will of God. And I have suggested before (see the commentary on 1:6–12) that we ourselves may, in moments of crisis, have more in common with that view than we suspect. Whenever we let the guard of our careful theological language slip, and in frustration blame God for what is happening to us, we are to that extent at one with Job and the many loudly protesting souls in the Old Testament who know who is in charge of their lives, and are therefore as likely to reproach him as praise him, and to be resentful at his absence as thankful for his presence. Perhaps, guided by them, we should not be as ashamed of these moments of frustration as we tend to be. Perhaps a God who is always nice and consistent and never at fault, is too small a God, a God who is not doing his job properly.

But if that strikes the reader as too risky a theological line to take, let me try another line, a line which I have already tried with the "umpire" passage at the end of chapter 9. Is not the deepest meaning of Job's flight here, from a stone-deaf God to a God who will answer his despairing prayers, to be found in the belief of 1 John 2:1 that "we have an advocate with the Father, Jesus Christ the righteous"; or of Hebrews 9:24 that Christ has entered heaven "now to appear in the presence of God on our behalf"; or of Romans 8:34 that no one can now condemn us because of Christ Jesus "who died, yes, who was raised from the dead, who is at the right hand of God, who indeed intercedes for us"? There may be no room in these Christian passages for a confidence in one's own righteousness as strong as Job's, but do they not in their own way encourage troubled souls to call on God to argue their case for them before God, and to win "justice" for them? Is there not a tension within the Christian Godhead too? Are we not, whenever we pray—and in a sense more real than we may ever imagine—, fleeing from God to God, as Job does so resolutely in this glorious passage?

(vi)

By 17:3 Job's hope is beginning to fade and his faith to falter. But before he is enveloped in grief and melancholy again, he demands a sign, a token before he dies that would give him some assurance that he would be declared innocent at that future assize. Moffatt catches the sense of the verse well, if somewhat freely:

> Give me a pledge that thou thyself will act;
> who else would undertake my cause against thee?

It is, of course, a vain request; for were it granted, his struggles would there and then have been over. His good God would have shown himself, and he would have been free. (There is a partial parallel to Job's request in Isa. 38:14–15, where King Hezekiah, near to death, asks the God who has caused his illness to be his "security", *ie* to give him a pledge that he will recover; in the AV, "undertake for me". In his case the prayer is answered.)

At this point Job thinks of the friends again. Blinded by the same God who had it in for him, they were far from giving him any guarantee of help; and he hopes they will be punished for it. Again Moffatt's translation of verse 5 is better than the RSV's: his colleagues were;

> like one who bids friends to a feast,
>   and lets his children starve!

But his bewilderment only increases and yet more tears well up in his eyes as he dwells on the contempt in which he is held by them and, it would seem, by everyone else around. Surely there must still be some men of honour left in the world who would be appalled at what was happening to him and who would try, wherever they were, to see to it that goodness was not trampled underfoot! Surely there must be some people somewhere who, like himself, held to their integrity, and who, unlike himself, received their due recompense!

Then (vv. 10ff.) in a last act of defiance, Job calls on the friends and all like them to return to the attack and do their worst. His course was run and they had succeeded in turning light into darkness. He had already booked his bed in Sheol and was about to make the acquaintance of his new relatives, the "pit" and the "worm". All that remained was for his cancelled hope and himself, together, to descend into the dust.

The final verses of Job's fourth speech are in the same vein as the lugubrious passage in chapter 14, where the *no* that death writes on human hopes and aspirations first came home to him with all the force of a door being slammed in his face. Quite gone now is the plaintive, and indeed peevish, welcoming of death which marked his utterances in the first cycle (see 3:20–22; 7:15–16; 10:18–22), where he was more concerned to be free of God's attentions than to seek his intervention. In that all-consuming quest, which is fast becoming the only thing that matters to him, death is a barrier not an escape.

SHALL THE EARTH BE FORSAKEN FOR YOU?

Job 18:1–21

[1]Then Bildad the Shuhite answered:
[2]"How long will you hunt for words?
Consider, and then we will speak.
[3]Why are we counted as cattle?
Why are we stupid in your sight?
[4]You who tear yourself in your anger,
shall the earth be forsaken for you,
or the rock be removed out of its place?

[5]"Yea, the light of the wicked is put out,
and the flame of his fire does not shine.
[6]The light is dark in his tent,
and his lamp above him is put out.
[7]His strong steps are shortened
and his own schemes throw him down.
[8]For he is cast into a net by his own feet,
and he walks on a pitfall.
[9]A trap seizes him by the heel,
a snare lays hold of him.
[10]A rope is hid for him in the ground,
a trap for him in the path.
[11]Terrors frighten him on every side,
and chase him at his heels.
[12]His strength is hunger-bitten,
and calamity is ready for his stumbling.
[13]By disease his skin is consumed,
the first-born of death consumes his limbs.
[14]He is torn from the tent in which he trusted,
and is brought to the king of terrors.
[15]In his tent dwells that which is none of his;
brimstone is scattered upon his habitation.
[16]His roots dry up beneath,
and his branches wither above.
[17]His memory perishes from the earth,
and he has no name in the street.

¹⁸He is thrust from light into darkness,
    and driven out of the world.
¹⁹He has no offspring or descendant among his people,
    and no survivor where he used to live.
²⁰They of the west are appalled at his day,
    and horror seizes them of the east.
²¹Surely such are the dwellings of the ungodly,
    such is the place of him who knows not God."

As Job strikes out on new paths of theology and experience, now
raised to glorious hope, now plunged in deepest gloom, the
friends retreat with ever hastening steps into the safe haven of
their conventional beliefs. Bildad is enraged by Job's hard words
against them. In 16:2 Job had called them "miserable
comforters"; in 17:4 he had suggested that God was withholding
understanding from them; and in 17:8ff., Job had as good as said
that they did not belong to the truly righteous since these, if they
existed, would have been shocked at what God was doing to him.
This to Bildad was turning truth on its head. God was not tearing
Job apart; Job was tearing himself apart. He was asking the world
to stop for him, and the whole moral order to be overturned,
simply because he felt hard done by.

This last point is a good one, but it is the only good point he
makes. For, after his short remonstrance is over, Bildad proceeds
to read Job the same cruel lesson as Eliphaz had on the fate of the
wicked. If there is a difference between them, it is that, whereas
Eliphaz concentrated on the effects of a wicked man's
wrongdoing on his conscience, Bildad dwells on the external
results of the retribution he has brought upon himself. Job's light
is put out; his schemes come to nothing; he falls into traps; fears
surround him; his strength fails; disease stalks him; the
"first-born" of death (an angel of the underworld? or simply a
metaphor for mortal illness?) is about to summon him before the
"king of terrors" himself; no name will survive him, and only the
infamy he has earned will outlast him to remind people far and
wide that he ever existed. "Such", he concludes, "is the place of
him who knows not God". He does not say in so many words,

"You are the man" (2 Sam. 12:7), but he hardly needs to.

Bildad's comments form a well-structured poem, made up of beautifully regular verses and full of powerful images. Bildad is the least effective thinker of the three friends, but he is the best poet, perhaps because, as an admirer of tradition, he had immersed himself in the language of his "scriptures". As in chapter 8 we recognize his gifts but, as there, we lament his essential inhumanity. It is not surprising that he should think that Job considered him "stupid" (v. 3). Job probably did. But, as Job's words in his very next speech will show, he is far more anguished by Bildad and his colleagues' pitiless hatred.

HAVE PITY ON ME, O YOU MY FRIENDS

Job 19:1–22

¹Then Job answered:
²"How long will you torment me,
    and break me in pieces with words?
³These ten times you have cast reproach upon me;
    are you not ashamed to wrong me?
⁴And even if it be true that I have erred,
    my error remains with myself.
⁵If indeed you magnify yourselves against me,
    and make my humiliation an argument against me,
⁶know then that God has put me in the wrong,
    and closed his net about me.
⁷Behold, I cry out, 'Violence!' but I am not answered;
    I call aloud, but there is no justice.
⁸He has walled up my way, so that I cannot pass,
    and he has set darkness upon my paths.
⁹He has stripped from me my glory,
    and taken the crown from my head.
¹⁰He breaks me down on every side, and I am gone,
    and my hope has he pulled up like a tree.
¹¹He has kindled his wrath against me,
    and counts me as his adversary.
¹²His troops come on together;
    they have cast up siegeworks against me,
    and encamp round about my tent.

¹³"He has put my brethren far from me,
and my acquaintances are wholly estranged from me.
¹⁴My kinsfolk and my close friends have failed me;
¹⁵ the guests in my house have forgotten me;
my maidservants count me as a stranger;
I have become an alien in their eyes.
¹⁶I call to my servant, but he gives me no answer;
I must beseech him with my mouth.
¹⁷I am repulsive to my wife,
loathsome to the sons of my own mother.
¹⁸Even young children despise me;
when I rise they talk against me.
¹⁹All my intimate friends abhor me,
and those whom I loved have turned against me.
²⁰My bones cleave to my skin and to my flesh,
and I have escaped by the skin of my teeth.
²¹Have pity on me, have pity on me, O you my friends,
for the hand of God has touched me!
²²Why do you, like God, pursue me?
Why are you not satisfied with my flesh?"

In the first cycle Job almost ignores Bildad's contribution, showing his contempt for a man so tied to tradition that he had no real views of his own. But this time round the traditional platitudes have more bite. Even Eliphaz has taken them on board, and every sentence of Bildad's speech has made it obvious that he, Job, was being got at personally. Job senses more acutely than ever before that everyone around him is against him, and this naturally leads on to the thought once again that God too is against him. Abjectly he laments his double estrangement in words that, for all their self-centredness, would draw blood from a stone. But then with the same abruptness as in chapter 16, his mood changes. And as in that chapter, it is Job's unalterable consciousness of his own innocence that induces the change; that, and the answer of his heart that his redeemer, his vindicator, lives.

(i)

Job begins, as usual, by expressing his irritation with the friends, using the plural and thus including the other two with Bildad. Their constant insinuations were weighing him down and crushing his spirit. Were they not ashamed to be casting endless aspersions on his integrity? Even if he had done wrong—it is not a gracious admission, but we have to remember whom he was addressing—he had not hurt *them*, only himself, and they had no call to add to his suffering. Their talk of Job deserving his punishment was motivated by pure malice. He was suffering not because of anything he had done but simply because God had willed it so. If they wanted to make a great fuss of his degradation, that ought to be a good enough argument for them. It was one with which he could himself readily agree. Although he was not in the wrong, God had put him there (v. 6).

(ii)

But even as Job draws the friends' attention to the sole cause of his misery, he is aware that he is not just making a clever debating point. His agonies were only too real to him. They came from a God who had committed "violence" against him (a very strong word which often has connotations of ruthlessness and hatred, and which is not elsewhere brought into such close relation with God's activity; see Gen. 6:11 and contrast Hab. 1:2, although the prophet's language is very similar to Job's). And the same God had given Job no answer when he had "cried" to him (for this verb see 16:18). It was the same when he had prayed for justice; he got none. This was what being put in the wrong by God meant for him.

First (vv. 8–10), God had deprived Job of hope. He had hemmed him in, cutting off all escape and obscuring his path ahead. He had stripped him of the dignity that his righteousness ought to have won for him (cf. 29:14). God had engineered the collapse of Job's fortunes like a house falling down, and uprooted his hope for the future as though it were a mere tree.

Second (vv. 11–12), God had openly and visibly assailed him as though he were his enemy. He had assembled his troops to lay siege to him as to a hostile city, and they were casting up their earth mounds against him and closing in for the kill. Job is here, as in 6:4 and 10:17, probably referring to his physical ailments and pains.

Third (vv. 13ff.), God had isolated Job from all human contact and affection. At this point the metaphors cease and in the directest language Job describes his abandonment by kinsfolk and acquaintances alike. Those to whom he had extended hospitality did not want to know him. The serving girls in his house treated him like a foreigner. His manservant refused to obey him, however much Job entreated him. His wife found him repulsive, his brothers turned from him in disgust, even little children reviled and mocked him. Those whom he had befriended avoided him, and those whom he loved showed no love in return.

Job is not thinking here so much of Eliphaz, Bildad and Zophar, as of his immediate family and neighbours, or, at any rate, of those who were left (it may be significant for his state of mind that his dead sons and daughters are not mentioned). Perhaps some of them were there looking on, part of that wider audience in the background whose presence we sometimes detect in Job's words elsewhere. But whether or not they were present, he is sure that they too, arguing from his emaciated condition, have concluded that he is a sinner.

But then as he sums up his feeling of utter dereliction he does turn to the three men whom he has for so long been engaging in frantic debate. He is as good as dead. (The quaint phrase "escaped by the skin of my teeth" makes us ask "What skin?", and must have been a common Hebrew idiom, although it occurs only here in the Old Testament.) Had they not an ounce of pity to spare for him? What pathos is packed into the two short lines of verse 21, with its repetition of the imperative verb "pity me" and its unambiguous reminder that God alone had to be held responsible for the whole meaningless tragedy of his life!

In explicitly saying that the divine *animus* against him is the sole reason for his anguish, Job is of course implicitly denying that his own behaviour has anything to do with it. He does not shout his innocence abroad in this chapter, but he has not in the slightest retreated from his burning attachment to it. And he hints at it again in a final riposte in the friends' direction. Why did they join so enthusiastically with God in relentless pursuit of an innocent man? Why had they not given up their spite and settled for the success that they—or rather God—had already achieved?

(iii)

The haunted cry of verse 21 shows beyond question that what Job is really after in this first part of chapter 19 is a modicum of human sympathy and understanding. He does not ask with Juliet;

> Is there no pity sitting in the clouds,
> That sees into the bottom of my grief?

It is *justice*, not *pity*—not, even by this time, *relief*—that Job seeks from God. But surely the human spectators of his shame need not be as driven by lust for his blood as is the One who is shaming him! And surely Job is right to reproach them for their brutality!

Yet we cannot avoid the impression that Job is overdoing it. There is a whining as well as a piteous quality to his complaints. Without denying for one moment that God is in some sense behind Job's suffering—there would be no problem in the book if that were not so—we cannot help asking when Job is finally going to give up the very personalized terms in which he has so far, with the exception of his cooler speech in chapters 12–14, insisted on conducting the confrontation between them. Had God, as he keeps on implying, been mustering all his majesty and might with the sole intent of squashing him? And, in particular, could God fairly be accused of turning Job's nearest and dearest against him?

And what of these people, including the poor wife whom he had so harshly dismissed when his troubles were beginning? If we are not disposed by this stage to say a lot in favour of the "official" friends of Job, can we in justice assume that he has good reason for so maliciously upbraiding them? They were not professional theologians out to defend God's honour and, although they must have asked themselves what he could have done to deserve his troubles, they must also have asked themselves why God should be so hard on him. It is a common delusion of people who are sick that the whole world—doctors, nurses, relatives, visitors, God—is conspiring against them. That does not mean that it is. We may even have experienced these feelings ourselves, and we will know that it is simply not true.

We should therefore be prepared to acknowledge that, heart-rending though they are, Job's words at this point in chapter 19, even more so than his words in chapters 16 and 17, have about them the whiff of paranoia. Like Milton's Satan in Pandaemonium after his defeat;

> ... he hears
> On all sides, from innumerable tongues,
> A dismal universal hiss, the sound
> of public scorn.

But there is too much in him of Shakespeare's Richard:

> There is no creature loves me!

The paranoia will—alas!—return (although never as strongly as here), but just for now it is—mercifully!—about to be swamped in another return, the return of a vision, as the "umpire" of chapter 9 and the "witness" of chapter 16, become the "redeemer" of the second half of this tempestuous speech.

I KNOW THAT MY REDEEMER LIVES

Job 19:23–29

> [23]"Oh that my words were written!
>   Oh that they were inscribed in a book!
> [24]Oh that with an iron pen and lead
>   they were graven in the rock for ever!
> [25]For I know that my Redeemer lives,
>   and at last he will stand upon the eartn;

²⁶and after my skin has been thus destroyed,
    then from my flesh I shall see God,
²⁷whom I shall see on my side,
    and my eyes shall behold, and not another.
    My heart faints within me!
²⁸If you say, 'How we will pursue him!'
    and, 'The root of the matter is found in him';
²⁹be afraid of the sword,
    for wrath brings the punishment of the sword,
    that you may know there is a judgment."

(iv)

From the verdict of an unpitying God and, imitating him, an unpitying generation of his own human kind, Job turns first to the verdict of posterity. If only his words could be written down in a scroll—no, better, if only they could be carved with an iron tool on solid rock that they may last the longer, and each letter of them filled with lead that they may stand out the clearer—then future generations would learn about him, and they, in a less charged and biased atmosphere, would be bound to recognize the truth, to acknowledge his integrity, and to be angry on his behalf that God had treated him so.

But even as he utters the wish, he realizes that this could never be. Why should they, worshippers of the same God as he, take his side against God any more than his own contemporaries?

So next, desperately, Job finds himself once again gripped by the strange logic of faith, and is impelled to turn away from the God of the present and place his trust in the God of the future. He remembers that, in a similar moment of inspiration in his last speech, he had seen beyond his death to a time when his future God would be his witness and defend him before his present God. Although he himself, dead and buried, would not be there, he was able to trace, in the foresight of his imagination, the shape of two divine figures, and one was interceding for him with the other and wresting from him the verdict which he longed to hear (16:19–21). Now, building on that earlier vision, he is able to raise himself once more to assurance, and to such a pitch of assurance that his two Gods coalesce into one.

(v)

Verse 25 should begin with "but", as in the Revised Version of 1885, rather than the "for" of the Authorized Version and the RSV. Job has given up the vain wish for a memorial in human words; even his own human words, and even a memorial which would survive as long as an inscription on rock. He is moving on to a more radiant certainty which is based on what he now regards as the most enduring aspect of his God's character; that of the "redeemer" of his people.

The Hebrew noun meaning "redeemer", is *go-el* from the verb *ga-al* (both pronounced with two syllables). In their primary usage both noun and verb belong to the sphere of family law and denote the duty of a relative to protect and defend the rights of a member of his family who was in trouble. Thus, if an Israelite had to sell himself into slavery in order to pay his debts, he was to be "redeemed" by one of his relatives, his brother first, or, if he had none, his uncle or his cousin or whoever thereafter had the closest ties of blood with him (Lev. 25:47–49). Or if for similar reasons he had to sell his property, such a relative must be given first refusal so that the property might, if possible, be kept within the family (Lev. 25:25; Ruth 4:1–6). Or, most seriously of all, there was the old tribal obligation of blood-revenge. The blood of a kinsman must be avenged by the nearest relative killing the one who had shed it or, failing him, a member of his clan. This law could still be invoked in David's time, to judge by Joab's killing of Abner for slaying his brother, Asahel (2 Sam. 3:22–32). But in the legislation of Numbers 35:9–34 and Deuteronomy 19:1–13, although still sanctioned, its force has been mitigated by the institution of "cities of refuge" to which the offender could flee, and by the requirement of legal proof of his guilt. There is nothing, however, in Israel's legislation allowing in such cases, as there was in Arab Bedouin practice, the payment of a ransom or compensation in money. The slaying of the slayer comprised the "redemption".

The idea of a redemption price is connected chiefly with another Hebrew verb "to redeem", *padah*. This sometimes overlaps in its usage with *ga-al*, but it has no necessary implications of family duty. Thus a betrothed woman may be "redeemed" (*padah*) if her prospective husband finds her unsatisfactory (Exod. 21:8). And it is this verb which is used to denote the "redemption" by a fixed payment of the first-born, who "ideally" should have been sacrificed to God; see Numbers 18:15–16.

Both *ga-al* and *padah* are frequently applied to God, whether as deliverer of his people from bondage in Egypt (Exod. 6:6; 15:13; Deut. 7:8; 9:26; Pss. 77:15; 103:4; 106:10), or as the one who is about to deliver them from slavery in exile (Isa. 43:1; 44:22–23; 51:10–11; 52:9), or indeed as their deliverer from any kind of trouble (Gen. 48:16; Ps. 25:22), including sickness and death (Pss. 34:22; 49:15; Hos. 13:14) but not, with one exception (Ps. 130:8), sin. In few of these passages is it possible to say with any certainty that the writer has a reason for preferring one verb to the other, because both equally emphasize the weakness and need of those who are "redeemed".

But this is not the case with God as *go-el*. This title (there is no equivalent noun from *padah*) is used a few times in the Psalms (*eg* 19:14) and elsewhere (*eg* Prov. 23:11; Jer. 50:34), but it is a particular favourite of the "Second Isaiah", chapter 40 onwards (*eg* 41:14; 43:14; 49:7, 26; 54:5). And in many of these passages there are patent hints of the original legal usage. Note especially the ideas of God taking vegeance in Isaiah 49:26, and of God as his people's close relative in Isaiah 54:5, and of God pleading their case in Proverbs 23:11 and Jeremiah 50:34 (see also for the latter meaning, the verbal form in Ps. 119:154). But missing yet again are the ideas of God as *go-el*, delivering his people from sin or guilt, or of him paying a redemption price on behalf of his people. Indeed, the latter idea is specifically excluded by Isaiah 52:3, where a verbal form of *ga-al* is used: "You were sold for nothing, and you shall be redeemed without money".

I have intentionally drawn attention to the absence from the Old Testament concept, of "redemption", of the ideas of being saved from sin, or of God meeting the penalty which the sinner himself ought to have met. This is because these two ideas are (in addition to good Old Testament ideas of deliverance from evil or death) fundamental to the New Testament conception. The following passages all use parts of the Greek words which are the equivalents of Hebrew *ga-al* and *padah*: Mark 10:45; Romans 3:24–25; Ephesians 1:7; Colossians 1:13–14; 1 Timothy 2:5–6; Titus 2:14; 1 Peter 1:18–19. There is a temptation for Christian piety, mesmerised by such passages, always to connect redemption with sin and guilt and, without thinking, to read this connection into any Old Testament passage where "redeemer" or "redeems" or "redemption" are mentioned. It is a temptation that we must assiduously resist, and nowhere more so than in the case of the present passage, which is so well known to us from its very Christian context in Handel's *Messiah*; but in which, in its original Hebrew context, it is not at all the forgiveness of his sins, but rather the vindication of his innocence, that Job expects from his "Redeemer".

(vi)

What Job confidently looks forward to in verse 25 is a pronouncement in his favour by God. He is himself about to die, but God is the living God. God will live on, and will be not only Job's "Redeemer" but *the one who comes after* him. This phrase, translated "at the latter *day*" in the AV or, less specifically, "at last" in the RSV, is not adverbial, but adjectival describing God and meaning simply "the last one" or, as I have rendered it, "the one coming after". And this *coming one* will, as the Hebrew says literally, "stand upon the dust". This may mean "upon the dust [of my grave]" (cf. Job 17:16; Ps. 22:15, 29) or, more generally, somewhere "on the earth" (cf. Job 41:33, where the Hebrew also has "dust"). It is on either rendering a peculiar phrase; but on either rendering there is a perceptible advance on the previous vision.

There (16:19) Job's vindication was to take place in heaven, after he had died; but, here in verse 25, God is to come down to declare it in person, after Job is dead, on earth. The verb, "stand", is probably used in its legal sense of rising up as a witness or as a judge in court (see Pss. 3:7; 12:5; 76:9). But it is not necessary to envisage a formal assize as in chapter 16. In that future heavenly assize, Job had watched, in his imagination, as a God who believed in justice defended him against a God who did not, and won for him an acquittal. Now, acutely aware that his friends and relatives have failed him, and seeing no prospect of his own words surviving to plead his case for him, he looks in frenzied anticipation to a newly united God, his true Next-of-kin, his only Avenger, his Redeemer, to do his duty by him and, when he is in his grave, to gain for him, among men on earth, the recognition of his innocence and the cancelling of the charges against him that he had already gained for him in heaven.

That Job should have struggled through to a position where he can lavish upon the God who has been his implacable foe not simply the cool titles of "umpire" and "witness", but the warm and vibrant title of *go-el* or "Redeemer", with all its associations of family affection and solidarity, is a remarkable testimony to the limpet-like quality of his faith. Once he had "known" that God would not hold him innocent (9:28); then he had suddenly "known" that, if he could only find him, he would be vindicated (13:18); now he "knows" that the eternal and living God is, whatever may seem to the contrary, in reality his *go-el*, his redeemer, and that he is ready to stand by his poor, oppressed kinsman. For the first time the reality of Job's faith is proving stronger than the reality of his suffering.

But even the "knowledge" that his faith brings him, miraculous as it is when measured against his present torment, is not enough for Job in this moment of exaltation. He wants not only to "know" what God will do, but to "see" him.

I SHALL SEE GOD

Job 19:23–29 (*cont'd*)

(vii)

It is very frustrating for a commentator that the famous passage we are studying should not only be so difficult in the Hebrew, but also seared into the consciousness of the English speaking peoples through the magnificent, but quite tendentious, translation of it in the King James Version. We have already seen what it makes of verse 25. The same version, verses 26 and 27 reads;

> And *though* after my skin *worms* destroy this *body*,
>   yet in my flesh shall I see God:
> Whom I shall see for myself,
>   and mine eyes shall behold, and not another . . .

When Handel in his *Messiah* juxtaposed these three verses of the Authorized Version in the same ravishing *soprano aria* with the words of St. Paul from 1 Corinthians 15:20 (namely "For now is Christ risen from the dead, the first-fruits of them that sleep") he was doing no more than responding to the invitation built into them by the translators. The "at the latter day" (AV) of verse 25 takes us forward to the Last Judgment and the resurrection of the dead at the end of the age, when Christ will return to earth to inaugurate God's final kingdom; and we, escaping, through the merits of our "Redeemer", the threat of an adverse verdict, shall rise from our graves, leaving behind us the earthly bodies which the "worms" have destroyed, and shall live for ever in God's nearer presence, enjoying "in [our] flesh", *ie* in our new resurrection bodies, the beatific vision. These are the kind of thoughts that the Authorized Version's translators intend Job's soaring vision to raise in the Christian reader's mind as they, in essence, detach it from its context and make it a veiled, yet unambiguous, prophecy; one placed in the patriarch's mouth by the Holy Spirit which tells of the redeeming work of Jesus of Nazareth and of his Second Coming. What, faced with such a powerful tradition of interpretation, can a poor commentator do?

He can say first, as I now do, that he has no wish to deny that, in its deepest meaning, the passage lifts the Christian believer up into the hope and comfort of the Gospel. There may not be in it, as there is in the passage on the "umpire" in chapter 9, and on the "witness" in chapter 16, the thought of God mediating for us with God, but like these two passages it expresses a yearning in Job's heart for a saviour who will not only be divine, but human; and it goes beyond these two passages in visualizing him as a kinsman no less, one who will defend his own through thick and thin, even through the boundary of death. But that is as far as Job's imagination carries him, and it is in fact almost too far for him. It is here surely that we should find a reason for the difficulty of the Hebrew. It must reflect a searching for words on Job's part as he tries to describe what the religious language of his day had no words to describe.

An honest commentator must, therefore, further ask his readers to recognize this and not to fill out what Job "knows" with what we *know*. In short, we may know what the deepest meaning is, but Job does not. He can only glimpse it from afar. Job catches sight of his redeemer coming to his aid after he is dead, but his redeemer is God, not yet God's Son, and he is clearing Job's name, not clearing him from guilt. The time when this will happen is undetermined, but it is certainly not when the last trump shall sound; and, if we are to keep this passage in line with chapter 14 ("If a man die, shall he live again?") and chapter 16 ("my witness is in heaven . . ." but "I shall go the way whence I shall not return") it is quite impossible that Job, even in visionary ecstasy, should be thinking of resurrection, far less immortality, for himself.

(viii)

How then does Job put into words his conviction that he will "see" God? If on his lips it cannot mean what Revelation 22:4 means, what *does* it mean?

It is important to notice that in the Hebrew of verse 26 not one of the three words in the Authorized Version, "though", "worms", and "body", actually appears, as the italics in our printed Bibles indicate. It is the same with "day" in the previous verse, as we have already discovered. But remove these words and we remove the overt "Christian" interpretation from our range of options. (Is the RSV, rather mischievously, hanging onto that interpretation by printing *Redeemer* with a capital, something which not even the AV did, although Handel's librettist did?) I believe in fact that we are left with only two viable interpretations.

Either (with the NEB and the GNB) Job is expecting to have his vision before he dies, in which case we may translate verses 25–26 thus:

> But I know that my *go-el* is now living
> and that he will stand up last upon the earth;
> and after my skin has [all but] peeled away—[I know] this,
> that while still in my flesh I shall see God.

Or (as with most other versions, and in keeping with my own view in this commentary so far) Job does not expect to have his vision until after he dies, in which case we may render the verses as follows:

> But I know that my *go-el* does not die
> and that as the one who will come after me
> he will take his stand over my grave;
> and after my skin has [wholly] peeled away—[I know] this,
> that even without my flesh I shall see God.

(The Hebrew preposition in the final line is literally "from", as in the RSV, but depending on the context it can sometimes mean "away from" and sometimes "in".)

The only point in favour of the first of these interpretations is the fact that, at the end of the book, God does appear to Job while he is still alive, and restores him. But how was Job at this moment to know that? On the contrary, in nearly everything he has said up until now, Job has assumed, whether wishfully or resentfully, that he was going to die soon and that any hope of acquittal for him lay on the other side of the grave. Thus in chapter 16, he had in his mind's eye seen his vindication taking place in a future court in heaven. But in this speech he has been more concerned about his innocence being recognized on earth. No mere written record left behind him would achieve this. Only God could bring it about. That is the stage Job has reached as he begins to speak these verses. In my view the whole context of the passage points indubitably towards the second of the above interpretations.

I hesitate to go further than to translate it. But, if I have to, it seems to me that what, in his halting words, Job is saying is this: I know that I have a *champion* (Moffatt) in heaven and that, when I am dead, he will see to it that my integrity is no longer impugned among those who knew me; and I, a bodiless shade in Sheol, will be aware of this, for he will appear to me there.

In the Old Testament only Psalm 139's equally breathtaking leap into the unknown (v. 8) can be compared: "If I make my bed in Sheol, thou art there!" Elsewhere God does not interfere in the underworld (see also the commentary on 14:7–22).

Verse 27 is also ambiguous. Either Job is speaking of seeing God "for myself" (AV), or "for me" in the sense of being "on my side" (RSV). In a context which has God as *go-el* taking the part of a dead *kinsman*, the latter rendering is the more apposite. The RSV could, however, have improved on its rendering by translating the last word of the second line as "stranger" instead of "another". I suggest for the two lines;

I shall see him to be on my side;
    my very own eyes shall look [on him] and [he will] no [longer
        be a] stranger.

(ix)

There remain the third line of verse 27 and Job's final words to his friends, with whom he had been pleading for sympathy just before his great cry of assurance and hope.

Verse 27 is literally, "My kidneys fail [or, are consumed] in my inside". We would be more likely to say, "My heart fails within me". But in Hebrew psychology, the kidneys are the seat of the strong emotions of longing and affection, whereas the heart is more often associated with the will or even the intellect (see, *eg*, 1 Sam. 7:3; Pss. 19:14; 90:12; 139:23). But what is the thrust of this short phrase? Does it betoken, like the extended final verses of Job's previous speech (see especially 17:11ff.), a flooding back of realism and dejection? As the vision fades, is Job in effect saying "[Alas! this cannot be, therefore] my heart sinks within me", as the Jerusalem Bible translates it? With the verb "fails" in this pessimistic sense, compare Psalms 69:3; 143:7. Or, as the level of exaltation inevitably drops, does some optimism remain? Should we translate the line from verse 27 thus: "[But can this possibly be?] My heart yearns within me" (NIV)? There are parallels to this meaning in Psalms 84:2 (where the RSV has "faints") or 119:81 (where it has "languishes").

I am strongly inclined towards the second interpretation. The very curtness of the line is itself evidence that Job is not on this occasion collapsing into black despondency, as he had so often done before, but is determined to hold on to his new found assurance that God is not his enemy but his redeemer. There are to be moments of anger and frustration, even paranoia, for him yet, but I believe that a second watershed in his spiritual pilgrimage has been reached. The first was reached at the end of chapter 9 when he caught behind the God, who until then he was convinced was out to humiliate him without reason or cause, a brief glimpse of another God who could be moved to act justly. Now the two Gods, who in chapter 16 he had watched struggling with each other for his soul, have become one again, and the one name above all that he has found to call him is *go-el*, kinsman, defender, avenger and redeemer.

Two verses of a psalm, which has quite a few points of contact with the Book of Job, come to mind as a fitting summary of Job's state of mind as he speaks this marvellous passage which in so many ways marks the zenith or apogee of the whole book:

Whom have I in heaven but thee?
    And there is nothing upon earth that I desire besides thee.
My flesh and my heart may fail,
    but God is the strength of my heart and my portion for ever.
(Ps. 73:25–26)

The second of these verses uses the verb "fail" in a pessimistic sense, but that hardly matters. Job's love for God has been rekindled and not even when he eventually "sees" God in the whirlwind in the book's last (or rather, last but one) scene and is driven to his knees, will we encounter a better Job. He has hard lessons still to learn and contrition still to show, but here a proud man adores God, unaided by God, just as in chapter 14, a sad and angry man had found the courage to reproach God for his mismanagement of the universe. Prometheus may have to be bound if God is to be God, but Prometheus can love and adore as well as accuse and defy. Let us honour this Prometheus for that.

(x)

The last two verses of the chapter contain a rebuke and a warning to the three friends. If they continue to persecute him they will suffer for it. The phrase which Job puts into their mouths, "the root of the matter is found in him", is the second idiom that has passed into the English language via Job chapter 19 (the other is "I have escaped by the skin of my teeth" in v. 20). By using these words the friends clearly mean that the real cause of his afflictions is to be traced to his own behaviour, not God's. We are reminded, therefore, at the end of the chapter, of Job's still unquenched and very Old Testament reliance upon his own righteousness. We will undoubtedly be grieved by this, as we will by Job's vindictive tone so soon after he himself has discovered One whom he hopes will be kind to him. Job is patently not yet ready to forgive them (as he will eventually do in the dénouement of 42:7–9), and indeed he seems almost to be inviting his *go-el* to avenge him (Job) on them. This too is a very Old Testament trait; see how such beautiful psalms as 137 and 139 are marred by their quite vicious concluding paragraphs. We may try to understand these and other passages like them, but we cannot possibly condone them. For all the clouds of glory which it trails in its wake, the passage we have been studying comes to us, as do Psalm 137 with its "Happy shall he be . . . who dashes . . ." and Psalm 139 with its "I hate them with perfect hatred", from God's old dispensation and not his new. It is salutary to remember this as we turn to Zophar's horrifying second speech.

THE EXULTING OF THE WICKED IS SHORT

Job 20:1–29

[1]Then Zophar the Naamathite answered:
[2]"Therefore my thoughts answer me,
  because of my haste within me.
[3]I hear censure which insults me,
  and out of my understanding a spirit answers me.
[4]Do you not know this from of old,
  since man was placed upon earth,
[5]that the exulting of the wicked is short,
  and the joy of the godless but for a moment?
[6]Though his height mount up to the heavens,
  and his head reach to the clouds,
[7]he will perish for ever like his own dung;
  those who have seen him will say, 'Where is he?'
[8]He will fly away like a dream, and not be found;
  he will be chased away like a vision of the night.
[9]The eye which saw him will see him no more,
  nor will his place any more behold him.
[10]His children will seek the favour of the poor,
  and his hands will give back his wealth.
[11]His bones are full of youthful vigour,
  but it will lie down with him in the dust.
[12]Though wickedness is sweet in his mouth,
  though he hides it under his tongue,
[13]though he is loath to let it go,
  and holds it in his mouth,
[14]yet his food is turned in his stomach;
  it is the gall of asps within him.
[15]He swallows down riches and vomits them up again;
  God casts them out of his belly.
[16]He will suck the poison of asps;
  the tongue of a viper will kill him.
[17]He will not look upon the rivers,
  the streams flowing with honey and curds.
[18]He will give back the fruit of his toil,
  and will not swallow it down;
 from the profit of his trading

he will get no enjoyment.
¹⁹For he has crushed and abandoned the poor,
he has seized a house which he did not build.

²⁰"Because his greed knew no rest,
he will not save anything in which he delights.
²¹There was nothing left after he had eaten;
therefore his prosperity will not endure.
²²In the fulness of his sufficiency he will be in straits;
all the force of misery will come upon him.
²³To fill his belly to the full
God will send his fierce anger into him,
and rain it upon him as his food.
²⁴He will flee from an iron weapon;
a bronze arrow will strike him through:
²⁵It is drawn forth and comes out of his body,
the glittering point comes out of his gall;
terrors come upon him.
²⁶Utter darkness is laid up for his treasures;
a fire not blown upon will devour him;
what is left in his tent will be consumed.
²⁷The heavens will reveal his iniquity,
and the earth will rise up against him.
²⁸The possessions of his house will be carried away,
dragged off in the day of God's wrath.
²⁹This is the wicked man's portion from God,
the heritage decreed for him by God."

Zophar, like Eliphaz and Bildad before him, is oblivious to Job's anguished cries for human understanding and sympathy. Job had put himself beyond the pale by his continuous whining at God and his refusal to listen to the warnings his two colleagues had given about the fate of the wicked. And now he was making mad claims that the God whom he had vilified was about to come to his aid and tell the world how innocent he was! This was insufferable. There was no way this man could be saved from the retribution he was bringing on himself; but perhaps he could yet be made to recognize his arrant folly in challenging the constitution of the universe. For was it not a fact beyond dispute from the earth's beginnings not only that the downfall of the sinner was inevitable but that it was never delayed for long? Any prosperity he enjoyed was but to give him somewhere to fall from, and it could not last.

(i)

To illustrate this variation on the only tune the friends have played throughout the second cycle, Zophar draws the picture of an arrogant and greedy man hurtling in the midst of well-being to a well merited doom. He may reach for the sky, but he will disappear quicker than his own dung, leaving his children to beg from the poor. He may savour his crimes like gourmet's food, but they will turn to serpent's gall in his belly. He may gulp down his wealth in his rapacity, not caring whom he hurts, but he will hold none of it; God will make him vomit it all up again. He will suddenly be assailed by God's wrath, run through by arrows which will glisten with his blood when they are withdrawn, and perish as a pauper and in torment, unmissed and unmourned.

It is a quite appalling diatribe, replete with the most nauseating metaphors. Zophar's finger was, of course, pointing straight at Job. Not every scene which he sketches fitted his case, but Job cannot have been in any doubt that the parable was about him. He was being told in effect that he was fortunate to have enjoyed his possessions and his happy family life for as long as he had. The sickening impact it must have had on him so soon after his plaintive appeal to the friends to "have pity, have pity", and after his heartening vision of a God who would yet be his redeemer and vindicator, is almost impossible to imagine. Nor can we easily conceive the kind of mind which, in order to prove a dogma true that is so patently not true, could dredge up from God knows where such venom and filth.

And yet . . . if we only pause to think, how often, how very often has religious rivalry down the ages produced its Zophars, and how they have outdone benighted pagans in the invective of scurrility and hate! It is a sobering lesson for all religious enthusiasts to ponder. Is it not Zophar—and all who in our various Churches are like him—who is beyond the pale? Must dividing mankind into "us" and "them" lead to this?

(ii)

A few statistics from our book should help to drive this point home. List (A) gathers together sections of the friends' speeches in which the topic is the happiness that comes to the righteous; list (B) has those in which it is the fate awaiting the wicked.

			Verses
(A)	(Eliphaz)	4:7; 5:17–26; 22:19–30	23
	(Bildad)	8:5–7, 20–22	6
	(Zophar)	11:13–19	7
(B)	(Eliphaz)	4:8–11; 5:2–7; 15:17–35	29
	(Bildad)	8:4, 11–19; 18:5–21	27
	(Zophar)	11:6, 11–12, 20; 20:4–25	26

Threat in these speeches outweighs the promises, and punishment the curses, in a proportion of no less than 82 verses to 36; and even that revealing statistic may misrepresent the true balance if we take into account the strident "ifs" in the (A) passages of Bildad in 8:5–6, of Zophar in 11:13–14, and of Eliphaz in 22:23–25. Only Eliphaz in his first speech and Bildad at the end of chapter 8 exude any genuine warmth in the prospects they hold out before Job. On the other hand, the passages in list (B) form a rising crescendo of menace and hate that would be hard to match in the worst outpourings of the gutter press. These represent the real message the friends have for Job, and it is that message alone which is graced by them with the accolade of tradition or orthodoxy (see 8:8–10; 15:18; 20:4). Need anything more be said?

IS MY COMPLAINT AGAINST MAN?

Job 21:1–34

[1]Then Job answered:
[2]"Listen carefully to my words,
   and let this be your consolation.
[3]Bear with me, and I will speak,
   and after I have spoken, mock on.

⁴As for me, is my complaint against man?
   Why should I not be impatient?
⁵Look at me, and be appalled,
   and lay your hand upon your mouth.
⁶When I think of it I am dismayed,
   and shuddering seizes my flesh.
⁷Why do the wicked live,   .
   reach old age, and grow mighty in power?
⁸Their children are established in their presence,
   and their offspring before their eyes.
⁹Their houses are safe from fear,
   and no rod of God is upon them.
¹⁰Their bull breeds without fail;
   their cow calves, and does not cast her calf.
¹¹They send forth their little ones like a flock,
   and their children dance.
¹²They sing to the tambourine and the lyre,
   and rejoice to the sound of the pipe.
¹³They spend their days in prosperity,
   and in peace they go down to Sheol.
¹⁴They say to God, 'Depart from us!
   We do not desire the knowledge of thy ways.
¹⁵What is the Almighty, that we should serve him?
   And what profit do we get if we pray to him?'
¹⁶Behold, is not their prosperity in their hand?
   The counsel of the wicked is far from me.

¹⁷"How often is it that the lamp of the wicked is put out?
   that their calamity comes upon them?
   that God distributes pains in his anger?
¹⁸that they are like straw before the wind,
   and like chaff that the storm carries away?
¹⁹You say, 'God stores up their iniquity for their sons.'
   Let him recompense it to themselves, that they may know it.
²⁰Let their own eyes see their destruction,
   and let them drink of the wrath of the Almighty.
²¹For what do they care for their houses after them,
   when the number of their months is cut off?
²²Will any teach God knowledge,
   seeing that he judges those that are on high?
²³One dies in full prosperity,

being wholly at ease and secure,
²⁴his body full of fat
and the marrow of his bones moist.
²⁵Another dies in bitterness of soul,
never having tasted of good.
²⁶They lie down alike in the dust,
and the worms cover them.

²⁷"Behold, I know your thoughts,
and your schemes to wrong me.
²⁸For you say, 'Where is the house of the prince?
Where is the tent in which the wicked dwelt?'
²⁹Have you not asked those who travel the roads,
and do you not accept their testimony
³⁰that the wicked man is spared in the day of calamity,
that he is rescued in the day of wrath?
³¹Who declares his way to his face,
and who requites him for what he has done?
³²When he is borne to the grave,
watch is kept over his tomb.
³³The clods of the valley are sweet to him;
all men follow after him,
and those who go before him are innumerable.
³⁴How then will you comfort me with empty nothings?
There is nothing left of your answers but falsehood."

It is in his final speech in each of the first two cycles that Job chooses to meet head on the arguments of his three friends. Throughout the first cycle the friends had defended the consistency of the divine providence and Job had attacked it; but it was only in chapters 12–14 that he felt able to marshall his theological forces, as it were, and drive the friends in disarray from the field. In the process some of his own wilder ideas of God's nature and purposes were abandoned; but it was his sober and sombre analysis of the divine power holding sway over a world whose human inhabitants could see no hope or meaning in their lives, that won the first battle in their war of words. In the second cycle the friends do not again dare to take up the weapons of debate on behalf of their doctrine of God. Instead, fastening

onto Job's brief reference to the "tents of robbers" being at peace
and those who provoke God being secure (12:6), they attempt in
their second speeches to prove to Job that the opposite is the case.
Why they should shift to ground where their fighting position is to
our eyes patently weaker than it was in the first cycle, is not easy
to credit. But we should remember that the friends are
representatives of a supremely confident ethic, that of the Book
of Proverbs, whose writers had few qualms about dividing
mankind into two, the wise or good and the foolish or bad, or
about predicting the rewards and punishments which each group
would inevitably earn for itself. The friends do not think that they
are on weaker ground, but they are about to find out, as Job,
compelled by Zophar's pitiless tirade to abandon briefly his
turbulent search for an absent God, decides to be quit of them
once and for all.

(i)

Sarcastically Job contrasts the "consolations of God" which they
had offered him (15:11) with the only consolation he has to offer
them, that of hearing the truth. After he has finished they may
mock, a reference no doubt to their three harangues on the fate
of evil men with their scarcely veiled condemnations of himself.
They had been out to get him (their savagery had hurt), but *he*
was not out to get *them*. His basic complaint was not against men
but against God (who had hurt him far more).

It was what God had done to him that had led Job, as the first
cycle was ending, to paint a dolorous picture of a providence that
destroyed the hopes of ordinary faithful people and consigned
them to lives of misery and frustration. And it was what God had
done to him that was leading him now to the equally distressing
conclusion that, in the divine dispensation, the rewards that
ought to have gone to ordinary faithful people went to those who
lived in open sin and flouted the laws of common decency. Why
did his friends so kick against the pricks of reality? Let them
forget their textbooks and look out on the great big world and see
what was actually happening there, and be struck dumb. Let

them share his dismay and tremble with him at what he had
discovered.

HOW OFTEN IS IT THAT THE LAMP OF THE WICKED
IS PUT OUT?

Job 21:1–34 (*cont'd*)

(ii)

Cooly and devastatingly Job develops his thesis along three lines.

First, in verses 7–16 he simply describes the outward prosperity
of the godless in general. But how uncannily his description
echoes so many Old Testament passages where the blessings that
attend the righteous are seductively set forth (*eg* Pss. 1 and 128;
Prov. 3:13–18; or even Eliphaz's words in 5:24ff.)! The wicked do
not fall under God's rod, but survive to old age with their families
around them, their homes safe, their herds prolific, the sound of
music and rejoicing everywhere, and they come to the grave in
peace. Yet they do not acknowledge God or attend his Temple,
but boast openly of having ignored him and got away with it.
"What profit is there in prayer?" (v. 15) could be their motto. In
verse 16 Job expresses his abhorrence that they should find
success so easy; but that they do, and that God lets them, he does
not doubt.

Second, in verses 17–26 Job counters some of the arguments
advanced by the friends to support their case. His series of
questions in verses 17 and 18 gives the lie to Bildad's claim, in
18:5ff., that the light of the wicked is put out and that all manner
of disasters overtake them. Then in 21:19 Job brings up an
argument which is implicit rather than explicit in the friends'
speeches (see Zophar's words in 20:10 and cf. also 27:13–15,
given to Job as the text stands, but more likely to have been
originally intended for one of the friends). Nevertheless it is an
argument that forms an integral part of the Old Testament
doctrine of retribution elsewhere, even appearing in the Second

Commandment (Exod. 20:5) although perhaps best known from the old proverb cited by both Jeremiah (31:29) and Ezekiel (18:2): "The fathers have eaten sour grapes, and the children's teeth are set on edge." In Job's view (as in that of the two prophets) it would make better sense if the fathers' own teeth were set on edge and they suffered the Almighty's wrath themselves! (For the survival even in New Testament times of the belief that the fathers' sins are visited by God on their children, see John 9:2–3.)

Verse 22 should, like verse 19, be prefaced for clarity with "You say" (this phrase is not in the Hebrew of verse 19 but has been added by the RSV). Job is not here being pious but is alluding to a constant theme of the friends (see 11:7ff.; 15:8; and, in Eliphaz's next speech, 22:12ff.), namely that God's wisdom is not to be questioned. In the context of a debate on retribution they mean, of course, his actual distribution of rewards and punishments. In other words, there were the wicked they knew about by their actions and there were a lot of others whom God knew about, but who only became known to the friends when God brought those others low and they saw the visible marks of his judgment. This was, of course, one of the ways, if not the chief way, by which the friends had come to place Job in the ranks of the wicked; and Job himself had felt the sinister force of the argument. To both the friends and himself, his tragedies and illness were proof of God's displeasure; it was only in the conclusions they drew from it that they differed. Job's refutation of this argument is oblique. But in its clear-headed pessimism it is worthy of Ecclesiastes (see 2:14–16; 9:2, 11–12). One man dies in full security and blooming health, another in misery, never having tasted the good things of life. Job does not say that one is a sinner and the other a righteous man, nor even whether death comes to them soon or late. And he does not say so precisely because it makes no difference. Death levels all men and renders comparisons, based either on their known circumstances or on their public characters at the time, not only odious but vain.

Third, in verses 27–33 Job anticipates a possible question the friends might fling back at him: "Give us proof that we are wrong.

Show us the house, still standing, of a great and arrogant man (for "prince" in this opprobrious sense see Job 12:21 and the very similar words in Ps. 107:40) or the house (tent) still occupied of a truly wicked man". In replying to this imagined taunt Job does not ask them to use the evidence of their own eyes, suspecting that, confronted with the most flagrant wickedness, they would be quite capable, the way their minds operated, of calling it goodness. Rather, he appeals to the judgment of the generality of mankind and invites them to ask their question of any who have travelled the world's roads. Their unbiased testimony would be that the wicked and powerful always escape the calamities that come to lesser men. None presumes to accuse them and none is strong enough to oppose them. They die, yes, but they are borne to the grave in high honour, accompanied by innumerable respectful mourners, and even their shadowy existence in Sheol (amid "the clods of the valley") is sweet to them.

(iii)

Job is at this point clearly finished with the friends. Nothing that they have said since Eliphaz's first speech has brought him a grain of insight or comfort; and all that remains of their counsel is falsity and untruth (v. 34). Eliphaz will in the next chapter make one last confused and thoroughly spiteful attempt to reason with him, but Job will not dignify it with a reply. Indeed the plural "you", if we discount 27:5 as part of a section which may not belong to the original work (see below), will not pass his lips again. The "thou" of God is what alone will concern him hereafter.

(iv)

It is only when Job's replies to the friends are considered in their full scope that it strikes us what a revolutionary thing it is that Job has done in this chapter—or rather, that the author of this book has done through him. We are witnessing the collapse of the whole edifice of Hebrew Wisdom or, at any rate, of the theological and ethical reasoning that underpinned it. No sensitive Jew or Christian (I say nothing of the mirror-images of

Eliphaz, Bildad and Zophar, who have appeared in every generation and are—alas!—still with us) will, after this, read the Book of Proverbs, or the first or the thirty-seventh or even the forty-ninth or the seventy-third Psalms with complete approval or ease. He will find much in these writings to edify and warn and comfort and sustain him, but he will be unable to share, without grave reservations, the unclouded confidence of their authors, that there are only two types of men; the good whom God always or eventually blesses, and the wicked whom he always or eventually assigns to perdition. The Book of Job has for ever destroyed the neat equations between virtue and reward, and between sin and punishment, on which the Wisdom movement was founded—or, to be more precise, it has destroyed these equations as rules by which it can be claimed that God governs his creation. Retribution will no longer be seen as the way by which God normally proceeds in his dealings with the children of men.

Whether Job himself at this stage grasps all the corollaries of what he has been saying is another matter. It will soon become apparent that he does not, any more than he fully takes to himself what it means that he should now be able to call God his redeemer. To put it bluntly, Job may have dealt with the friends (and God will in the end acknowledge that he did it very well), but God has still to deal with him.

THERE IS NO END TO YOUR INIQUITIES

Job 22:1–30

[1]Then Eliphaz the Temanite answered:
[2]"Can a man be profitable to God?
  Surely he who is wise is profitable to himself.
[3]Is it any pleasure to the Almighty if you are righteous,
  or is it gain to him if you make your ways blameless?
[4]Is it for your fear of him that he reproves you,
  and enters into judgment with you?
[5]Is not your wickedness great?
  There is no end to your iniquities.

⁶For you have exacted pledges of your brothers for nothing,
  and stripped the naked of their clothing.
⁷You have given no water to the weary to drink,
  and you have withheld bread from the hungry.
⁸The man with power possessed the land,
  and the favoured man dwelt in it.
⁹You have sent widows away empty,
  and the arms of the fatherless were crushed.
¹⁰Therefore snares are round about you,
  and sudden terror overwhelms you;
¹¹your light is darkened, so that you cannot see,
  and a flood of water covers you.

¹²"Is not God high in the heavens?
  See the highest stars, how lofty they are!
¹³Therefore you say, 'What does God know?
  Can he judge through the deep darkness?
¹⁴Thick clouds enwrap him, so that he does not see,
  and he walks on the vault of heaven.'
¹⁵Will you keep to the old way
  which wicked men have trod?
¹⁶They were snatched away before their time;
  their foundation was washed away.
¹⁷They said to God, 'Depart from us,'
  and 'What can the Almighty do to us?'
¹⁸Yet he filled their houses with good things—
  but the counsel of the wicked is far from me.
¹⁹The righteous see it and are glad;
  the innocent laugh them to scorn,
²⁰saying, 'Surely our adversaries are cut off,
  and what they left the fire has consumed.'

²¹"Agree with God, and be at peace;
  thereby good will come to you.
²²Receive instruction from his mouth,
  and lay up his words in your heart.
²³If you return to the Almighty and humble yourself,
  if you remove unrighteousness far from your tents,
²⁴if you lay gold in the dust,
  and gold of Ophir among the stones of the torrent bed,
²⁵and if the Almighty is your gold,
  and your precious silver;

²⁶then you will delight yourself in the Almighty,
and lift up your face to God.
²⁷You will make your prayer to him, and he will hear you;
and you will pay your vows.
²⁸You will decide on a matter, and it will be established for you,
and light will shine on your ways.
²⁹For God abases the proud,
but he saves the lowly.
³⁰He delivers the innocent man;
you will be delivered through the cleanness of your hands."

The debate between Job and his friends has ground to a sad, but
long inevitable, halt. The well tried and tested precepts and
procedures of Israel's "wise men" have failed in the face of a man
in Job's extreme position. It remains for Eliphaz in effect to admit
this before the three of them depart from the scene, or—since
they are still present at the end of the book, let us say more
truthfully—leave the centre of the stage. Eliphaz tries to salvage
some dignity as he retires and, as always, he speaks beautifully;
but his speech is the speech of a devout man turned hunter of
heretics, and the sparks of malice and hypocrisy fly from it in all
directions.

(i)

Eliphaz begins shamelessly by pronouncing the sentence which
he feels he and his two fellow judges have been guided by an even
higher Judge to pronounce. We can almost see him looking at
each of them in turn and getting their nods of assent.
Peremptorily he tells Job that God does not gain anything when a
man lives a good life and cannot therefore be punishing him for
his piety. He must be putting him under judgment because he is a
sinner and, since the judgment is so severe, he must be a mighty
sinner. His strident attempts to excuse himself are only added
proof of his guilt; for no one could go on claiming such perfection
as Job, unless he had something very suspicious to hide. It is a
pernicious line of reasoning, worthy of the most sycophantic
judge in any totalitarian regime one cares to name. Only, the
higher authority this minor judge seeks to please is God!

And there is worse to come as Eliphaz takes it upon himself to specify the crimes of which Job must have been guilty to merit so black a sentence. The kindest thing one can say is that the old scholar has simply consulted his textbooks again and devised a short catalogue of the most heinous sins to which a man of Job's former rank and wealth might be tempted. There is truth in this observation; for in chapter 31 Job will construct a similar list of crimes with the contrary purpose of denying that he ever committed them; and it will include all four here laid at his door by Eliphaz, *viz.*

> verse 6, exploitation of the destitute; compare 31:19–20
>   and Deuteronomy 24:12–13
> verse 7, inhumanity towards the needy; compare 31:16–17
>   and Isaiah 58:7
> verse 8, misappropriation of another's land; compare 31:38–40
>   and 1 Kings 21
> verse 9, disregard of the defenceless; compare 31:16–17, 21
>   and Deuteronomy 14:29.

But, however conventional his words, we must surely also register our horror at the lengths to which this once gentle soul is willing to go to maintain the orthodoxy of which he is now a hooked and landed victim. Human righteousness is trampled in the mud to magnify divine righteousness, and the facts are the last thing to be allowed to stand in the way. The atmosphere is redolent of the Inquisition on the prowl. It is fortunate for Job that the only power his friends have over him is the power of words.

(ii)

In 22:12ff. Eliphaz for once argues well, or should we rather say cunningly? He gives a sinister twist to a belief that Job has actually held, namely that God did not care what went on on earth. He suggests that what Job really believes is that God is too far above men, too up in the clouds, as it were, to notice what they do. This is not at all the same thing; but it is very similar to the attitude Job ascribed to the ungodly in his previous speech, and

Eliphaz turns the screw by quoting some of the words Job used there; compare verses 17–18 with 21:14–16. He thus saddles Job with a view he had expressly said he abhorred. It is clever, but what end does it serve?

The real nastiness in this part of his speech is reserved for verse 18 and verses 19–20. In verse 18 the wicked are said to show no gratitude to God for the blessings they receive from him—and, we are meant to conclude, Job had been ungrateful when he was prosperous. And in verses 19–20 the righteous are said to be glad when they see the wicked bite the dust. Eliphaz is able here to use the language of the Psalms and could almost be quoting from Pss. 52:6 or 107:42—which does not say a lot for these two psalms. (See also the commentary to 12:1–6.)

(iii)

Then after all that, Eliphaz reverts to the traditional evangelical appeal, an appeal none of the friends has seen fit to employ since the first cycle. If Job, even at this eleventh hour, is willing to change his ways, to receive instruction from God rather than give it to him, to humble himself before God and abandon his reliance on wordly things (riches above all), making the Almighty his treasure, then the God, who abases the proud and lifts up the truly innocent, will yet deliver him; he will delight himself in God's favour, all his prayers will be answered and all his enterprises succeed. The honeyed words trip easily from Eliphaz's tongue; but when we recall that Job is being invited to repent of sins he had never committed and to stop trusting in possessions that had been taken away from him, we dare not allow ourselves to be impressed. There are times when the Gospel call is irrelevant to man's needs, and one of these is when he is being dangled over hell-fire and shouted at to recant or else.

There are touches in this speech of the Eliphaz whom Job had once known, but they are lost to sight in an amalgam of half-truths and downright lies, of sweet enticements and bloody threats that the most ranting demagogue could not better. Job is fully justified in responding to it with the contempt of silence and in thereafter hazarding his life with the real God, not the caricature of him which his spokesmen in this book present. Of course the friends are not wrong all of the time, but they are wrong so often and so hypocritically and so maliciously and so unashamedly, that it is a relief to see the back of them.

OH, THAT I KNEW WHERE I MIGHT FIND HIM!

Job 23:1–17

[1] Then Job answered:
[2]"Today also my complaint is bitter,
　　his hand is heavy in spite of my groaning.
[3]Oh, that I knew where I might find him,
　　that I might come even to his seat!
[4]I would lay my case before him
　　and fill my mouth with arguments.
[5]I would learn what he would answer me,
　　and understand what he would say to me.
[6]Would he contend with me in the greatness of his power?
　　No; he would give heed to me.
[7]There an upright man could reason with him,
　　and I should be acquitted for ever by my judge.

[8]"Behold, I go forward, but he is not there;
　　and backward, but I cannot perceive him;
[9]on the left hand I seek him, but I cannot behold him;
　　I turn to the right hand, but I cannot see him.
[10]But he knows the way that I take;
　　when he has tried me, I shall come forth as gold.
[11]My foot has held fast to his steps;
　　I have kept his way and have not turned aside.
[12]I have not departed from the commandment of his lips;
　　I have treasured in my bosom the words of his mouth.

[13]"But he is unchangeable and who can turn him?
　　What he desires, that he does.
[14]For he will complete what he appoints for me;
　　and many such things are in his mind.
[15]Therefore I am terrified at his presence;
　　when I consider, I am in dread of him.

¹⁶God has made my heart faint;
   the Almighty has terrified me;
¹⁷for I am hemmed in by darkness,
   and thick darkness covers my face."

On the view taken in this commentary, chapter 23 gives us more or less the whole of Job's next speech, and chapter 24 does not belong with it. I shall argue shortly that chapters 24–27 consist of a number of fragments of speeches which the author preserved along with the main body of his work because he thought they might be useful, either as additions or as alternatives to existing passages, in a future revision. These were then subsequently gathered together and inserted in their present position by a disciple or scribe who was not quite sure what else to do with them. A third cycle with only two speeches in it seemed to him the most likely place to put them. He thus, in my opinion, unwittingly but seriously compromised the author's original intention, which was to conclude the disputation between the friends and Job at this point with a short and sharp final confrontation between him and their chief spokesman.

We have just listened in chapter 22 to Eliphaz's last effort to persuade Job of his folly. And it may not be without significance that, after a long period in which he and his colleagues did nothing but condemn Job, Eliphaz closes with an appeal to him to repent and turn to God. It is sincerely enough meant (a good evangelist never gives up hope!); but it is nevertheless tantamount to a confession that the three of them have nothing more to say to him and are leaving his future fate in God's hands. In chapter 23 Job does not deign to reply to him, but he accepts the force of his logic. Only God can help him now. But the same thought then strikes him as had struck him before whenever the friends had counselled him to seek God in prayer. What an absurd thing to advise when God refuses to listen to him! So, in a soliloquy which is not obviously addressed either to the friends or to God, Job releases all his pent up frustration and despair in a shrieking protest against the unfathomable mystery of a God who is inaccessible to the creatures he has made, and who leaves them

unaided to make what they can of life's inconsistencies and
tragedies. It is not by any means the first such protest, but in its
very terseness and in its poignant admixture of bewilderment and
confidence, of stubbornness and helplessness, of frantic hope and
black despondency, it has all the marks of a dramatic climax.
After this, we feel, God must either say something for himself or
Job must try another tack.

(i)

After setting forth succinctly in verse 2 the gravamen of his
complaint (namely that, in spite of his groaning and lamenting
and protesting and appealing, God's hand still lies heavy upon
him), Job gives vent to his feelings in three crisp but forlorn
paragraphs.

In verses 3–7 Job expresses his earnest desire that he might
come to God's tribunal and that God might not only listen to him
but answer him. He is sure that if this were to happen he would be
acquitted. Contained in short compass in these verses are Job's
wish that God would lay aside his divine power and behave with
him as a human judge would, first expressed in 9:32–35; his
conviction that God would only listen to a good and sincere man
and had no time for flatterers, first seen in 13:15–16; and the
knowledge that first came to him in full measure in 16:19–21 that,
in spite of his present treatment of him, God still cared about
justice. There is—and how could it be otherwise when, in the
interval, Job has been mainly concerned with rebutting the
friends' arguments?—a falling away from his supreme insight in
19:25–27 that God was more than a judge, that he was in fact his
redeemer, his kinsman, and by virtue of that was, in spite of all
appearances, in reality, on his side. Job has retreated into the
atmosphere of the courtroom, and of proving and disproving
charges.

Nevertheless, there is one noticeable advance on chapter 19.
Job is no longer content with vindication hereafter but wants an
acquittal now. He does not talk in this speech of waiting for as
long as it should take for God to appear, nor does he look in faith
beyond his fast approaching death. God must answer him now.

And so it will be until God speaks to him out of the whirlwind in chapter 38.

(ii)

Then, in verses 8–12 Job, as so often before, awakens to the realization of what he is asking or, rather, of whom he is asking it. How can he pin God down? "God, who is everywhere present, everywhere eludes him; he feels his omnipotent power, but in vain seeks to see his face" (A B Davidson). And the reason God eludes him is that he knows Job to be innocent (v. 10)! Paranoia creeps into Job's voice here, and even blasphemy; not since chapters 7 and 9 has Job spoken in so insolent a vein. But the paranoia quickly passes and before the verse is finished, it is replaced with self-confidence. In a remarkable glimpse into the truth which the audience, remembering the Prologue, will savour with ironic pleasure, Job talks of being tried by God and emerging as pure gold. For he has faithfully held to God's instructions and fulfilled all the demands God has laid on mankind.

We are back in these verses with the boastful Job whom we cannot, with our Christian sensitivity, easily warm to; the same Job we found in 6:30 ("Is there any wrong on my tongue?"); in 9:21 ("I am blameless"); in 10:7 ("Thou knowest that I am not guilty"); in 13:15ff. ("I will defend my ways to his face . . . a godless man shall not come before him . . . I know I shall be vindicated . . . Make me know my transgression and my sin"); in 16:17 ("there is no violence in my hands"); in 19:3ff. ("Are you [the friends] not ashamed to wrong me . . . know then that God has put me in the wrong . . . He has stripped from me my glory").

These passages make up, with the one we are commenting on and, still to come, the whole of chapter 31 (and, we may add, 27:2–6, an extra fragment which may have been intended to strengthen the present passage), much more than a claim on Job's part that, although he is a weak and sinful mortal like the rest of us, he has done nothing to deserve what has been done to him. To argue that this is all Job is saying is a false assessment of his attitude which too many Christian commentators are prone to make. Job means it, and means it passionately, when he says he is innocent, even "perfect"; and he means it when he accuses God of depriving him of his right to be known and recognized as a righteous man.

It follows from this, of course, that Job is not yet able to follow out the logic of the devastating arguments he used to demolish the orthodoxy of the friends. The plain facts of his own experience, and that of many more apart from him, set it beyond dispute that innocent people like himself can suffer horribly, and guilty sinners can sleep safe in their beds knowing that they will rarely be brought to account for their crimes. But his reaction to such facts is still one of anger and perplexity—these things ought not to be! He is (as looking back later we will realize) but a hair's-breadth away from the answer—"solution" is quite the wrong word to use in such a context as this. But it will need God to spell it out for him when he at last breaks his interminable silence. At the moment Job is still attached by an invisible umbilical cord to the Wisdom tradition on which he was raised, and the hair's-breadth is a veritable chasm, with Job on one side calling desperately to God on the other side to come over and face him. That is what I meant when I said at the conclusion of the commentary on chapter 21 that the revolutionary was not able as yet to grasp the full corollaries of the revolution he was setting in motion.

(iii)

In verses 13–17, therefore, instead of further light, Job only sees more darkness ahead. God's will cannot be changed and must work itself out in his, Job's, extinction; unenlightened and unacquitted. And he adds: "And many [other] such things are in his [God's] mind" (v. 14). The prospect, not only for himself, but for the world at large, is altogether bleak. Before the mystery and absurdity and offence of it all, he is terrified and on the brink of going mad. He can see no avenue of escape and God, being God, offers none. He is hemmed in by ignorance and only an all-encompassing gloom lies in front of him.

It is on such a note of deepest depression that, as I understand the author's intention, he wishes Job's confrontation with his human adversaries to end. A voice from off stage—not God's but that of a concerned and thoughtful onlooker—will shortly give, in the famous poem on Wisdom in chapter 28, a kind of "state of the game" report. And thereafter Job and God will be on their own.

I AM HEMMED IN BY DARKNESS

Job 23:1–17 (*cont'd*)

(iv)

Before the onlooker of chapter 28 has his say, can we ourselves encapsulate Job's state of mind at this most crucial stage in the unfolding of the drama of which he is the protagonist? I believe that we can say *six* things about it and that saying them will help to clarify our minds as we approach the book's last and greatest confrontation.

First, Job is undoubtedly guilty of *hubris*. There is about him something of that arrogance of humanity in the face of a hostile universe which was, according to the Greeks, the "primal evil, the sin whose wages is destruction" (Aeschylus, *Agamemnon*). The whole ancient world, to whom divinity was real in a way that our modern world can hardly comprehend, echoed in one form or another that fundamental belief. Nemesis stalked for those who defied heaven: for Arachne, turned into a spider by Athena because she boasted of her skill in weaving; for Aqhat in the Ugaritic story, slain by the goddess Anat because he refused to give her his magic bow; for the Assyrian emperor in Isaiah 10:5ff., ignominiously defeated before Jerusalem because he did not know when to stop in his ambition to rule the world. The friends of Job sensed this insane streak in him, and were right to sense it. The fact that in sensing it they were congenitally incapable of distinguishing their own will from God's, may detract from (but does not remove entirely) their charge (spoken by Eliphaz in 15:25ff.) that Job was stretching forth his hand against the Almighty and running stubbornly against him; or their taunt (delivered by Bildad in 18:4) that Job wanted the earth to be forsaken so that he might win his case against God. This man would have to cease overstepping the mark at some point; the ancient Hebrew culture from which our book stems could be content with nothing less.

Second, it cannot be denied that Job is *obsessed with his own righteousness*. Even in the Prologue (1:1–5) there is something unhealthy about the way this is described, as though Job's self-esteem depended on his being the father of a large family and the owner of vast possessions; and there is something rather desperate in his punctilious observance of rituals as though without them his sons and daughters would be bound to fall into sin. Then, in the poetic debate, not only does Job revert incessantly to his "perfection" (as in the list of passages cited in the previous section of this commentary), but there is a morbid unwillingness to admit even small faults on his part. Consider the hypothetical nature of the confessions he makes in 7:20 ("If I sin, what do I do to thee?"), in 9:30 ("If I wash myself with snow . . ."), in 10:14 ("If I sin, thou dost mark me"), and in 19:4 ("And even if it be true that I have erred . . ."). Only at the end of chapter 13 and the beginning of chapter 14 does Job ask God with any sincerity to let him know where he has gone wrong, and admit with any sorrow the iniquities of his youth, and acknowledge with any contrition that weakness and corruption may indeed be qualities shared by all men. We can accept that, in relation to the demands by his friends for him to recant, Job is right to maintain his innocence. But as long as the obsessional notes sound through his protestations, there is more to Job's stance than a straightforward defence of his behaviour and integrity. There is a mental imbalance which requires to be corrected.

Nor, *third*, can it be denied that Job is prone to *paranoia*, the victim far too often of the delusion that everyone is against him. His feeling of being persecuted by a divine enemy, whose one concern is to get at him, begins as early as chapter 6 (v. 4), and is still there in chapter 19 (vv. 8ff.). His friends too are accused of treachery in chapter 6 (vv. 14ff.), when only Eliphaz has spoken, and he is still demanding sympathy from them in chapter 19, instead of which they keep pursuing him "like God" (vv. 21–22).

And in the same chapter (vv. 13ff.) Job's wider circle of relatives and acquaintances, who have not spoken at all, are tarred with the same brush as he implicates them along with God and the friends in mocking at and maltreating him. In the case of the friends and, indeed, in the case of God, Job has been given reason for his persecution complex, but hardly in the case of that wider circle. In their case he is completely deluded; and even in the case of God and the friends, he, as often as not, grossly overstates; his language at times becoming intemperate to the point of unreason. It is hard to condone such loss of temper and impossible to believe that he can be allowed to continue in it.

But, *fourth*, at this moment Job is chiefly in the grip of a deep-seated *depression*, a choking presentiment that he is doomed and that nothing he may say or do can change his fate for the better. He can see no way either of attaining his goal or of finding relief, and is being compelled to the conclusion that life for himself and for all men is meaningless and absurd, quite the opposite of what the text-books of his religion, with their lovely phrases, said it ought to be. He has by this stage moved beyond the cheap peevishness of Hardy's final sentence in *Tess of the d'Urbervilles*:

"Justice" was done, and the President of the Immortals, in Aeschylean phrase, had ended his sport with Tess.

He has moved too beyond the sorrowful resentment of blinded Gloucester in *King Lear*:

As flies to wanton boys are we to the gods;
They kill us for their sport.

Perhaps he has even moved beyond the sarcastic realism of Edmund Blunden's parody of Psalm 37:25:

I have been young, and now am not too old,
And I have seen the righteous forsaken,
His health, his honour and his qualities taken.
This is not what we were formally told.

Among modern authors it is Franz Kafka who best catches Job's mood as chapter 23 closes. Like Josef K in *The Trial*, Job knows that he has been falsely accused and is relentlessly trying to find the judge who will give him justice; and it is his failure to find him that engenders his despair. Just as Josef K is finally defeated by (and indeed murdered by the agents of) a "system" in which he had all along placed his trust, so Job is sure that he is being cheated and slowly ground to nothing by a God who, in his heart of hearts, he is convinced would acquit him if he could only appear before him. But God is incomprehensibly choosing to avoid him. In the face of the contrariness and irrationality of human existence in general and of his own existence in particular, Job feels crushed and utterly alienated, sunk in grief and impotence. And the continuing indifference of heaven is the last straw. He seems on the point of giving up the struggle.

But Job does not. Defiant to a fault, arrogantly self-righteous, quick to blame anyone else but himself for his troubles, given to sudden fits of helpless melancholy, there is yet about him—his *fifth* quality—a quiet and noble *dignity* which earns our grudging respect. We should not forget that God has in fact been abominably unfair to Job. That God was, according to the Prologue, testing his loyalty and faith, does not make that fact any the less true. We may wish to transmute such simplistic language into the more careful language of theology; but even then we are confronted with the reality and the frequency of unmerited suffering like Job's, in what is supposed to be a *good* God's *good* creation. Surely Job is entitled to protest about it, and surely any who, out of a false respect for God, deny his right to do so, are treating with intolerable levity the dreadful anomalies flung up by the presence of evil in this world in which God has set us. Protest and complaint against God are not things that Christian rhetoric easily takes to. But they are things which the Old Testament in places, notably in this book and in the *lamentation psalms* on which it so often draws, almost commends. It is possible to grovel too quickly before an implacable providence which, if it does not directly cause, at least permits the most horrendous tragedies to take place. And it may

not say much for us that we do not often enough get angry enough
with God for this state of affairs. We need to learn from Job that
there are times when it is right in the name of suffering humanity
to stand up to God.

(I say a little more about this penchant of the Old Testament for
protest in my remarks on Jacob's "striving" with God at Peniel in
Genesis, volume II, in this series; see pp. 204ff.. There I quoted
Margarete Susman's profound remarks about Job and the people
with whom we share the Old Testament; they deserve to be
quoted again:

> Job, who in his suffering was delivered by God to his tempter,
> prefigures in his fate the sorrowful fate of the Jewish people in exile.
> Like Job the Jews accepted [this is not yet quite true of Job] their
> suffering as something decreed by God. But they do not simply accept
> it, they want to understand [this is most certainly true of Job]. They
> want to understand God for whose sake they suffer. Like Job they
> demand that God whose bidding and law they have accepted be
> absolutely just. Here is the reason why life for the Jews in their exile is
> one long litigation, an incessant quarrel with God.

The point for us is that the Jews, far more than we Christians,
have retained a healthy Old Testament hatred for suffering as
something to be opposed or at least argued about, and not
something to be meekly acquiesced in. We ought not too readily
to let God off the hook by telling everyone who suffers to look at
Jesus and to take up his or her cross.)

Finally, and *sixth*, there is Job's wonderful *faith*. It is there,
strongly if naïvely, in the old Job of the Prologue, in the fine
sentiments of 1:21 and 2:10. Then, after going underground for a
time, it surfaces fitfully in 9:33ff. and 10:8–12, to appear more
urgently in 13:15–16, and more urgently still in 16:18ff. In spite of
everything this man holds on to God and to a God who is in his
deepest nature *just*. And he is not only *just* but on Job's and on
mankind's side, as Job at last realizes in the vision of his
"Redeemer" at the end of chapter 19. There are not many such
passages in this lugubrious book, but they are crucial. Without

them we may have a Job who is acceptable and indeed attractive to modern humanist sensibilities, whether in his passionate indignation in the face of life's anomalies, or in his querulous dignity in the midst of alienation and disaster. He shows us a weak human being asserting, against all the odds, the essential nobility of the species that is, in its own eyes and despite its many faults, the measure of all things. That the fates against which Job battles are called God is to such sensibilities merely a form of words that come with the fact that this book is an ancient book. Take these passages seriously, however, and God is restored to his rightful biblical place; and humanism, unable to cope, shies away from the Book of Job. It becomes plain that God, not Job and not any man, is in the last analysis the measure of all things. Job has still to come to terms with what this means, and acknowledge that he must give way to One who is greater and wiser than he. But these passages indicate that, in his innermost being, he already knows that this is what he will have to do, and that the justification and relief and freedom for which he longs so intensely, will not be his, except by the willing and uncoerced verdict of God. In these passages he accepts in fact that he cannot force God's hand. In the end it will be Job's faith that will cure his madnesses and make him whole.

A NOTE ON CHAPTERS 24–27: MISPLACED OR UNFINISHED FRAGMENTS

After the impasse reached in chapter 23 all seems set for Job's final challenge to God in chapters 29–31 and God's reply out of the storm in chapters 38–41.

Yet both of these climactic scenes are tantalisingly delayed: the *first*, by the five chapters 24–28 in which, except for a few verses assigned to Bildad, Job speaks all the time and for much of it repetitively, even contradictorily; and the *second*, by the six chapters 32–37 in which a newcomer called Elihu says, at considerable length and with considerable bombastic flourish, what, when analysed, amounts to very little. If we are to retain these two long sections as we now have them, it is difficult to avoid the conclusion that they have a chiefly dramatic function, namely to increase the tension by isolating and so highlighting the two sections which really matter, *ie* the ones in which Job makes his last great defence of his integrity and in which God ultimately intervenes to put him—and all of us—in our places.

However, it cannot be without relevance that it is exactly these five and these six chapters which, for quite other reasons, have attracted the suspicion of critics. We shall look later at the doubts which they raise about the Elihu speeches (doubts which I share). Here, it is the dubious features they find in chapters 24ff. which concern us. The following three are particularly noteworthy:

(a) Chapter 24 is exceedingly difficult and disjointed, and it is ill-preserved, as the unusually high number of divergencies between the Hebrew and the ancient Greek (*Septuagint*) version shows;
(b) Bildad is given only five verses (25:2–6) and Zophar is given no third speech at all, yet many passages assigned to Job (notably 24:18–20, 24 and 27:13–23; and possibly 26:5–14 and 27:8–10) contain sentiments that, on the surface at any rate, accord more closely with the friends' known positions than with Job's;
(c) Chapter 28 is a lyric poem, complete in itself, and does not fit within an argumentative speech by either Job or the friends.

Even a conservative scholar like Dr. F.I. Andersen (in the Tyndale series) admits that something has gone far wrong with chapters 24–27 and that we can only do with them "the best we can". More liberal critics like Professor Pope (in the Anchor Bible series) have taken it upon themselves to reconstruct a full third cycle by redistributing the contents so as to yield a longer speech by Bildad, an answering speech by Job and a new third speech by Zophar. His solution is as follows:

Job's reply to Eliphaz (cont'd): 24:1–17, 21 (with some
    rearrangement of the verses)
Bildad's third speech: 25:1–6; 26:5–14
Job's reply to Bildad: 26:1–4; 27:2–7
Zophar's third speech: 27:8–23; 24:18–20, 22–25

Professor Pope does not regard chapter 28 as belonging to the original book and thus makes chapters 29–31 Job's reply to Zophar, as well as his final appeal to God. (For similar arrangements in modern printed versions, see the GNB and the Jerusalem Bible.)

Professor Westermann (in his study of the structure of the book, mentioned in the list for Further Reading) is even more radical. He thinks that most of chapters 24–27 contain fragments misplaced from

earlier or later speeches in the book, or were intended by the author
for revision of these speeches. It is not always clear which of these
opinions he holds, but in his view;

> Chapter 24:1–4, 9, 12, 21–23, 25 belongs with Job's speech
>   in chapter 21,
> Chapters 25:2–6 and 26:5–14 belong with Bildad's speech
>   in chapter 8,
> Chapter 27:2–6 belongs with Job's final speech
>   in chapter 31, and
> Chapter 27:8–10, 13–23 belongs with Zophar's speech
>   in chapter 11.

I am inclined to favour Professor Westermann's approach because
of its clear recognition that the debate between Job and his friends is in
effect ended at chapter 23; but I would not wish to be so precise as he is.
It is hard to believe that these fragments could once have been located
elsewhere and then removed to their present positions; nor, if they are
drafts for a future revision, can I see that we have enough evidence to
do any more than speculate where the author intended them to go. I
am content with the hypothesis that the author composed them, and
kept them by him, for possible use in such a revision, and that a disciple
of his, or a later copier, found them with the manuscript and inserted
them where they now are because he felt (like Professor Pope) that the
author meant to give us a third cycle commensurate in size with the first
two.

In short, I believe that we have in chapters 24–27 a number of
fragments which give us valuable insights into the author's mind but
that their present arrangement is not due to him. If that is so, then it is
clearly pointless straining to find in the chapters a consistent line of
argument that will have any real bearing on the thrust of the book as a
whole. In what follows, I identify nine separate fragments according to
theme, and simply print the RSV text of each with an occasional
change and a few explanatory comments. I do not, however, press my
solution on the reader in preference to any other scholar's. It is my way
of doing "the best I can" with the chapters, no more.

(Chapter 28, on the other hand, I regard as an integral part of the
original work, although I do not believe it was spoken by Job, as its
being joined to chapter 27 in the present text without a fresh rubric
suggests. Rather it serves a similar function to the "chorus" in a Greek
drama, offering comment from outside on what is going on. I would

attribute it, as I have already indicated, to an "interested onlooker". Of the scholars I have mentioned, Dr Andersen and Professor Westermann adopt roughly similar positions).

(A) *Job on how the poor suffer and the wicked escape punishment*
  (24:1–12, 21–23, 25)

¹"Why are not times of judgment kept by the Almighty,
  and why do those who know him never see his days?
²The wicked remove landmarks;
  they seize flocks and pasture them.
³They drive away the ass of the fatherless;
  they take the widow's ox for a pledge.
⁹They snatch the fatherless child from the breast,
  and take in pledge the infant of the poor.
²¹They feed on the barren childless woman,
  and do no good to the widow.
⁴They thrust the poor off the road;
  the poor of the earth all hide themselves.
⁵Behold, like wild asses in the desert
  they go forth to their toil,
 seeking prey in the wilderness
  as food for their children.
⁶They gather their fodder in the field
  and they glean the vineyard of the wicked man.
⁷They lie all night naked, without clothing,
  and have no covering in the cold.
⁸They are wet with the rain of the mountains,
  and cling to the rock for want of shelter.
¹⁰They go about naked, without clothing;
  hungry, they carry the sheaves;
¹¹among the olive rows of the wicked they make oil;
  they tread the wine presses, but suffer thirst.
¹²From out of the city the dying groan,
  and the soul of the wounded cries for help;
  yet God pays no attention to their prayer.
²²But he prolongs the life of the mighty by his power;
  they rise up when they should despair of life.
²³He gives them security, and they are supported;
  and his eyes are upon their ways.

²⁵If it is not so, who will prove me a liar,
and show that there is nothing in what I say?"

These verses are part of a speech by Job in which he castigates God for letting the wicked get away with cruelty and oppression, and for ignoring the cries of their victims. There is evidence of dislocation in the present text; for instance verse 9 is obviously out of place and verse 25 can hardly follow verse 24. I have done some re-arrangement in order to bring out the meaning more clearly, but there is no certainty that I have got it right. There may even be two fragments; one concerned with the wicked's maltreatment of the helpless, and the other concerned with the difficulties which poor people in general have in scraping a living. For similar sentiments from earlier in the book see 9:23–24; 10:3; 12:6; and, in particular, chapter 21.

(B) *Job on the "friends of darkness"* (24:13–17)

¹³"There are those who rebel against the light,
who are not acquainted with its ways,
and do not stay in its paths.
¹⁴The murderer rises in the dark,
that he may kill the poor and needy;
and in the night he is as a thief.
¹⁵The eye of the adulterer also waits for the twilight,
saying, 'No eye will see me';
and he disguises his face.
¹⁶In the dark there are men who dig through houses;
by day they shut themselves up;
they do not know the light.
¹⁷For deep darkness is morning to all of them;
for they are friends with the terrors of deep darkness."

Although these verses may have been composed to go along with the previous passage, they seem to make up a unit on their own. Unlike the wicked in (A) who oppress the poor and needy openly, the murderer, the adulterer and the robber ply their trades in secret and do not, like the prosperous wicked in 21:14–15, boast of defying God. The secret success of the wicked is not a theme which obviously adds anything to the argument of the Book of Job and I doubt whether, had it come to it, the author would have made use of this passage.

(C) *A friend on the fate of the ungodly* (24:18–20, 24)

¹⁸"They are swiftly carried away upon the face of the waters;
    their portion is cursed in the land;
    no treader turns towards their vineyards.
¹⁹Drought and heat snatch away the snow waters;
    so does Sheol those who have sinned.
²⁰The squares of the town forget them;
    their name is no longer remembered;
    so wickedness is broken like a tree.
²⁴They are exalted a little while, and then are gone;
    they wither and fade like the mallow;
    they are cut off like the heads of grain."

These verses are out of place in a speech by Job, thus the added rubric at verse 18 in the RSV, "You say". They could have been meant to supplement Zophar's speech in chapter 11, which does not have a section on this theme, or to replace a portion of any of the friends' speeches in the second cycle.

(D) *A friend on man's imperfectibility* (25:2–6)

²"Dominion and fear are with God;
    he makes peace in his high heaven.
³Is there any number to his armies?
    Upon whom does his light not arise?
⁴How then can man be righteous before God?
    How can he who is born of woman be clean?
⁵Behold, even the moon is not bright
    and the stars are not clean in his sight;
⁶how much less man, who is a maggot,
    and the son of man, who is a worm!"

These sour and malevolent lines on human depravity reveal more about the person who utters them, than the person (Job) to whom they are addressed. In their present context they are assigned to Bildad, but there is nothing else to compare with them in any of his speeches. They are in fact much more akin to the pessimistic message of Eliphaz's vision in 4:17ff. (cf. 15:14–16) and could well have been intended to sharpen one of his speeches.

(E) *A beginning of a speech by Job* (26:2–4)

²"How you have helped him who has no power!
    How you have saved the arm that has no strength!

³How you have counselled him who has no wisdom,
  and plentifully declared sound knowledge!
⁴With whose help have you uttered words·
  and whose spirit has come forth from you?"

These bitingly sarcastic opening lines were perhaps meant for Job's
speech in chapter 23, which, as it is, has no introduction, or for his
speech in chapter 9, where the introduction consists of only half a
verse.

(F) *Job on the greatness of God* (26:5–14)

⁵"The shades below tremble,
  the waters and their inhabitants.
⁶Sheol is naked before God,
  and Abaddon has no covering.
⁷He stretches out the north over the void,
  and hangs the earth upon nothing.
⁸He binds up the waters in his thick clouds,
  and the cloud is not rent under them.
⁹He covers the face of the moon,
  and spreads over it his cloud.
¹⁰He has described a circle upon the face of the waters
  at the boundary between light and darkness.
¹¹The pillars of heaven tremble,
  and are astounded at his rebuke.
¹²By his power he stilled the sea;
  by his understanding he smote Rahab.
¹³By his wind the heavens were made fair;
  his hand pierced the fleeing serpent.
¹⁴Lo, these are but the outskirts of his ways;
  and how small a whisper do we hear of him!
  But the thunder of his power who can understand?"

These magnificent verses are often attributed by the critics to Bildad
and linked with (D) above, but in my view they must be intended for
Job. They celebrate God's creation in terms that remind us
occasionally of Genesis 1 (see Job 26:7, where the word "void" is the
same as the word translated as "without form" in Gen. 1:2, or; and
Job 26:13, where "wind" could be rendered "spirit"), but more often
of poetic passages which draw on ancient cosmology and mythology
like Psalms 74:12ff.; 104:1–9; or, from the divine speeches later in this

book, 38:4ff. In particular, they may be compared with the hymnic passage in 9:4–13, where *Rahab* (an alternative name of Leviathan the chaos monster) is also mentioned. Doubtless they are meant, like that passage, to be taken with an overlay of irony. Job is always well aware of God's power and majesty, and when necessary, can describe it much more effectively than the friends; but it is God's justice in which he is more interested, and which he really wishes to question.

With the enigmatic "north" in verse 7, compare Isaiah 14:13, and with verse 13, compare Isaiah 27:1. The last line (26:14) reminds us of God's words in 40:9.

(G) *Job on his integrity* (27:2–6)

²"As God lives, who has taken away my right,
  and the Almighty, who has made my soul bitter;
³as long as my breath is in me,
  and the spirit of God is in my nostrils;
⁴my lips will not speak of falsehood,
  and my tongue will not utter deceit.
⁵Far be it from me to say that you are right;
  till I die I will not put away my integrity from me.
⁶I hold fast my righteousness, and will not let it go;
  my heart does not reproach me for any of my days."

These defiant verses could have been intended to supplement Job's speech in chapter 23. They would excellently follow an introduction like (E) above (cf. in particular 26:4 with verse 3 here) and would themselves be well followed by that chapter as we have it. There is an earlier passage along the same provocative lines in 13:13ff., but it does not have quite the same ring of bold finality that this passage has. Professor Westermann would link it with Job's last great defence of his conduct in chapter 31 which, in its present form, begins rather abruptly. But the reference to "you", *ie* the friends, in 27:5 would not suit there; the friends are not otherwise addressed in chapters 29–31. Chapter 31 covers much the same ground at greater length, but it is for God's ears, not the friends'.

(H) *Job on the fate of the wicked* (27:7–12)

⁷"Let my enemy be as the wicked,
  and let him that rises up against me be as the unrighteous.
⁸For what is the hope of the godless when God cuts him off,
  when God takes away his life?

⁹Will God hear his cry,
　　when trouble comes upon him?
¹⁰Will he take delight in the Almighty?
　　Will he call upon God at all times?
¹¹I will teach you concerning the hand of God;
　　what is with the Almighty I will not conceal.
¹²Behold, all of you have seen it yourselves;
　　why then have you become altogether vain?"

We find similar sentiments on Job's lips in 19:28ff. and 21:16, 34, but without the obvious irony of the middle part of this passage. If it is a unity, it shows the author toying with the idea of introducing a sarcastic note into Job's arguments with the friends on this theme. But it may not be a unity. Verses 8–10 could have been intended for one of the friends, and verses 7, 11–12 could be isolated lines for possible use in filling out earlier speeches of Job.

(I) *A friend on the fate of the wicked* (27:13–23)

¹³"This is the portion of a wicked man with God,
　　and the heritage which oppressors receive from the Almighty:
¹⁴If his children are multiplied, it is for the sword;
　　and his offspring have not enough to eat.
¹⁵Those who survive him the pestilence buries,
　　and their widows make no lamentation.
¹⁶Though he heap up silver like dust,
　　and pile up clothing like clay;
¹⁷he may pile it up, but the just will wear it,
　　and the innocent will divide the silver.
¹⁸The house which he builds is like a spider's web,
　　like a booth which a watchman makes.
¹⁹He goes to bed rich, but will do so no more;
　　he opens his eyes, and his wealth is gone.
²⁰Terrors overtake him like a flood;
　　in the night a whirlwind carries him off.
²¹The east wind lifts him up and he is gone;
　　it sweeps him out of his place.
²²It hurls at him without pity;
　　he flees from its power in headlong flight.
²³It claps its hands at him,
　　and hisses at him from its place."

See the comments appended to (C) above.

BUT WHERE SHALL WISDOM BE FOUND?

Job 28:1–28

[1]"Surely there is a mine for silver,
  and a place for gold which they refine.
[2]Iron is taken out of the earth,
  and copper is smelted from the ore.
[3]Men put an end to darkness,
  and search out to the farthest bound
  the ore in gloom and deep darkness.
[4]They open shafts in a valley away from where men live;
  they are forgotten by travellers,
  they hang afar from men, they swing to and fro.
[5]As for the earth, out of it comes bread;
  but underneath it is turned up as by fire.
[6]Its stones are the place of sapphires,
  and it has dust of gold.

[7]"That path no bird of prey knows,
  and the falcon's eye has not seen it.
[8]The proud beasts have not trodden it;
  the lion has not passed over it.

[9]"Man puts his hand to the flinty rock,
  and overturns mountains by the roots.
[10]He cuts out channels in the rocks,
  and his eye sees every precious thing.
[11]He binds up the streams so that they do not trickle,
  and the thing that is hid he brings forth to light.

[12]"But where shall wisdom be found?
  And where is the place of understanding?
[13]Man does not know the way to it,
  and it is not found in the land of the living.
[14]The deep says, 'It is not in me,'
  and the sea says, 'It is not with me.'
[15]It cannot be gotten for gold,
  and silver cannot be weighed as its price.

¹⁶It cannot be valued in the gold of Ophir,
　in precious onyx or sapphire.
¹⁷Gold and glass cannot equal it,
　nor can it be exchanged for jewels of fine gold.
¹⁸No mention shall be made of coral or of crystal;
　the price of wisdom is above pearls.
¹⁹The topaz of Ethiopia cannot compare with it,
　nor can it be valued in pure gold.

²⁰"Whence then comes wisdom?
　And where is the place of understanding?
²¹It is hid from the eyes of all living,
　and concealed from the birds of the air.
²²Abaddon and Death say,
　'We have heard a rumour of it with our ears.'

²³"God understands the way to it,
　and he knows its place.
²⁴For he looks to the ends of the earth,
　and sees everything under the heavens.
²⁵When he gave to the wind its weight,
　and meted out the waters by measure;
²⁶when he made a decree for the rain,
　and a way for the lightning of the thunder;
²⁷then he saw it and declared it;
　he established it, and searched it out.
²⁸And he said to man,
　'Behold, the fear of the Lord, that is wisdom;
　and to depart from evil is understanding.' "

Let us imagine a pause after the petering out of the long and
fractious disputation between Job and his three friends. Job has
silenced the friends; but he has still to settle his account with God
and, from his mood in chapter 23, Job seems to be as uncertain as
ever on how to go about it. A figure steps forward from the
surrounding audience and recites this magnificent poem whose
single thought is that true wisdom belongs to God alone and
cannot be found by men. We no longer know who he is, for the
introductory rubric containing his name has disappeared,
perhaps when the collection of fragments in chapters 24–27 was

added. Who does he represent and what is the point of his message at this juncture? These are the questions which face the interpreter of this beautifully crafted stretch of Hebrew verse. On its own it is relatively easy to follow; but how was a despairing but still defiant Job meant to take it? What did it say to the vanquished friends? And how does it help us to understand better where the author of the Book of Job is taking us?

(i)

In verses 1–11, the amazing ingenuity and technological skill of men are celebrated, and the example chosen as an illustration is the mining of metals and precious stones. In verse 1 the emphasis falls on the word *is*: there *is* a place where these valuable materials which sustain and enhance human life may be found and from which they may, although with great difficulty, be extracted. Men know where that place is and they know how to get the ore and precious stones out.

Verses 3–4 describe how men seek out valleys far from the centres of populations and penetrate the darkness under the ground, sinking shafts and opening galleries, descending in cages and swinging perilously from ropes in order to bring up the iron and copper for smelting. In verses 5–6 the subject is the finding of sapphires (or lapis lazuli) and gold dust; the earth yields grain almost of its own accord, but to get these, men have to dig under the earth creating devastation as they go. The falcon's keen eye cannot espy, nor does the fiercest beast dare to tread, the paths which they must take as they pierce through rock, overturn mountains, hew channels and dam streams, all with the purpose of carrying the hidden riches out into the light of day (vv. 7–11).

But then the poem asks the question (v. 12), "where shall wisdom be found?" The way to this men *cannot* discover, however far and wide they may explore the earth ("the land of the living"; v. 13). Nor do the vast oceans contain the place where wisdom dwells (v. 14). Furthermore, men cannot purchase wisdom, not even with the gold and silver and all the precious stones which they have acquired through their entrepreneurial dash and hard toil (vv. 15–19).

The question is repeated (v. 20), and so is the answer (v. 21): wisdom is hid from all creatures, including men. Not even when they die and reach the mysterious realms of Abaddon (*Sheol*) and death, will they be enlightened, for these places have caught only a rumour or faint echo of wisdom. Only God knows the way to wisdom and when he created the world in all its complexity, he sought wisdom out and gave it its name and made use of it (vv. 23–27).

But (v. 28) God did not impart this wisdom of his to men. The wisdom which belongs to mankind is of another kind, which is defined as "fearing God" (the Israelite name *Yahweh*, or "the Lord", is used, probably another slip by the author due to the familiarity of the phrase) and "departing from evil".

THE FEAR OF THE LORD, THAT IS WISDOM

Job 28:1–28 *cont'd*)

(ii)

In its quietly reflective, but thoroughly sceptical, tone this great poem seems to me the nearest bedfellow in the Old Testament to Ecclesiastes.

There is much in it with which, in their cooler moments, the friends might have agreed, notably the Eliphaz of chapters 4–5 and the Zophar of chapter 11; but it lacks the deeply ingrained suspicion of human motives and ability which mark these two speeches. It says nothing about human corruptibility and it does not, as its first verses clearly show, demean human knowledge. Rather, it puts human achievement and learning in their proper perspective.

The traditional teachers of the Book of Proverbs thought of wisdom, as this poem does, as the principle underlying the order and harmony of the universe; see in particular, Proverbs 8:22ff. But they did not doubt that they were in touch with that divine wisdom and that they could show, with some precision, how it was reflected both in the world of nature and in the lives of men. In that confidence lay the source of their exact analysis of human behaviour and its inevitable effects for good or ill, and of their dangerous division of mankind into only two classes; the wise (good) and the foolish (evil). There was, the speaker is implying, a direct line traceable from that older Wisdom teaching to the confusion evinced by the friends in their counselling of Job. Mostly they said the right things about God, but they did not grasp their significance. Perhaps they did not even mean them; for, driven by their own logic, they far too quickly classified Job among the wicked when it was obvious to anyone who had eyes to see that he did not belong there. They assumed too readily that they knew the mind of God and did not sufficiently distinguish God's wisdom from their own. As a result they had, not *no answer* (for there was none that men could work out unaided), but a cheap and false answer to the mystery of unmerited suffering. Instead of admitting honestly that there were matters which were beyond their comprehension, they had forced both God and Job through the mincer of their own small minds, and had in the process, not only diminished both, but put at risk ordinary decent morality.

But what of Job? He had dealt most effectively, if harshly, with the friends and made it abundantly obvious that he had a far greater respect for divinity than they had. But he too had refused to give God his freedom and, although he had himself shown that there was no evidence that God's providence operated in accordance with the rules of retribution, he still demanded from God open acquittal and vindication on the basis of these rules. He had accused God of putting him in the wrong, of being his enemy, of misgoverning the world, of ignoring the cries of oppressed and suffering humanity, of looking on the rich and powerful with favour, of protecting those who despised his very name.

To the man who spoke these verses, this was every whit as objectionable a stance to adopt as the attempts of the friends to explain God's actions by Job's sin. So there is implicit criticism of Job as well in his poem. To him, the Creator's ways were quite beyond explanation and thus beyond the ability of men to tie down with words either of approval or disapproval. Job had more of the fear of God in him than the friends, but he was too disposed to probe and remonstrate and blame and demand; he was constantly pushing his troubles, painful as they might be, to the centre of the argument, wanting to know what it was not his prerogative to know, and refusing therefore to bow before the wonder of God's providence. It can hardly be coincidental that the speaker chooses to describe the lesser wisdom, which is all that God allows men to attain, in terms taken almost word for word from the first verse of this Book. He is in effect chiding Job for not having remained as he was then, a man "who feared God, and turned away from evil" (1:1).

(iii)

The poet of chapter 28 thus tries, in his gentle and reasoned way, to calm the turbulent passions of the three men and the one man who had until recently been at each other's throats and had argued themselves to a standstill. Both sides had been battling with unseemly vigour to prove themselves right at the expense of the God whom they professed to worship but whom, in their different ways, they were in reality attempting to manipulate. His advice to both Job and the friends—and to us who read his poem today—is to cultivate what Dr Strahan in his commentary has well called a "reverent agnosticism". Let us not pry into problems which are too large for us and which will inevitably involve us in judgments that will be incomplete, if not spurious. We must not try to tell God how to do his job or pretend to others that we know how he does it. Let us instead leave creation in his safe hands and get on with the business of living as good lives as we can, enjoying prosperity gratefully, facing adversity bravely, solving the problems that are ours to solve, increasing the sum of human happiness as we are able, and avoiding the many temptations to do evil which are spread in our path. That is what God has placed men on earth to do, and there is enough there to occupy all their energies and abilities.

In the history of Israel's Wisdom movement, the man who speaks this poem marks, as surely as Eliphaz in chapters 4 and 5, or Job in chapter 21 (or indeed in his speeches as a whole), a turning away from an optimistic towards a pessimistic (or, as it might be better to term it, from a simplistic towards a realistic) view of God's ways with the world. The author of the book will give his own view (for what it is worth, we almost hear him saying) when we reach the speeches of *Yahweh* out of the whirlwind in chapters 38–41. But he obviously has some sympathy for Eliphaz's early message that all men are weak and ignorant and helpless and "born to trouble as the sparks fly upward" (5:7). And even more obviously, he has sympathy with many of the attacks which Job mounts on God's providence, at least in so far as they call into question the easy solutions which Israel's wise men had previously been wont to advance. So here, for a brief moment, he betrays his sympathy with an even more sceptical view than either Eliphaz's or Job's; that of a concerned onlooker who has listened attentively to all their speeches—and those of Bildad and Zophar as well—and has concluded that it is all "vanity", as the Preacher might have said. The voice comes out of the shadows, and it does not speak again; but it would be a rash person who judged that it was not worth paying attention to. We have, in studying this book, been immersed for a long time now in some of the most intractable problems that theology has to face, and we may even be feeling that we are getting somewhere. It is salutary to be reminded of the impossible task we are taking upon ourselves, and to be directed again (as in a different way we were directed by the folk tale in chapters 1 and 2) towards the simple life of faith and goodness which, at the last count, is what religion is all about.

The Preacher has at the end of his book (Eccl. 12:13) a very similar message to that of this peaceful and profound poem: "Fear God, and keep his commandments; for this is the whole duty of man".

OH, THAT I WERE AS IN THE MONTHS OF OLD!

Job 29:1–30:31

[1]And Job again took up his discourse, and said:

²"Oh, that I were as in the months of old,
　　as in the days when God watched over me;
³when his lamp shone upon my head,
　　and by his light I walked through darkness;
⁴as I was in my autumn days,
　　when the friendship of God was upon my tent;
⁵when the Almighty was yet with me,
　　when my children were about me;
⁶when my steps were washed with milk,
　　and the rock poured out for me streams of oil!
⁷When I went out to the gate of the city,
　　when I prepared my seat in the square,
⁸the young men saw me and withdrew,
　　and the aged rose and stood;
⁹the princes refrained from talking,
　　and laid their hand on their mouth;
¹⁰the voice of the nobles was hushed,
　　and their tongue cleaved to the roof of their mouth.
¹¹When the ear heard, it called me blessed,
　　and when the eye saw, it approved;
¹²because I delivered the poor who cried,
　　and the fatherless who had none to help him.
¹³The blessing of him who was about to perish came upon me,
　　and I caused the widow's heart to sing for joy.
¹⁴I put on righteousness, and it clothed me;
　　my justice was like a robe and a turban.
¹⁵I was eyes to the blind,
　　and feet to the lame.
¹⁶I was a father to the poor,
　　and I searched out the cause of him whom I did not know.
¹⁷I broke the fangs of the unrighteous,
　　and made him drop his prey from his teeth.
¹⁸Then I thought, 'I shall die in my nest,
　　and I shall multiply my days as the sand,
¹⁹my roots spread out to the waters,
　　with the dew all night on my branches,
²⁰my glory fresh with me,
　　and my bow ever new in my hand.'

²¹"Men listened to me, and waited,
　　and kept silence for my counsel.

²²After I spoke they did not speak again,
    and my word dropped upon them.
²³They waited for me as for the rain;
    and they opened their mouths as for the spring rain.
²⁴I smiled on them when they had no confidence;
    and the light of my countenance they did not cast down.
²⁵I chose their way, and sat as chief,
    and I dwelt like a king among his troops,
    like one who comforts mourners.

¹"But now they make sport of me,
    men who are younger than I,
    whose fathers I would have disdained
    to set with the dogs of my flock.
²What could I gain from the strength of their hands,
    men whose vigour is gone?
³Through want and hard hunger
    they gnaw the dry and desolate ground;
⁴they pick mallow and the leaves of bushes,
    and to warm themselves the roots of the broom.
⁵They are driven out from among men;
    they shout after them as after a thief.
⁶In the gullies of the torrents they must dwell,
    in holes of the earth and of the rocks.
⁷Among the bushes they bray;
    under the nettles they huddle together.
⁸A senseless, a disreputable brood,
    they have been whipped out of the land.
⁹And now I have become their song,
  I am a byword to them.
¹⁰They abhor me, they keep aloof from me;
    they do not hesitate to spit at the sight of me.
¹¹Because God has loosed my cord and humbled me,
    they have cast off restraint in my presence.
¹²On my right hand the rabble rise
    they drive me forth,
    they cast up against me their ways of destruction.
¹³They break up my path,
    they promote my calamity;
    no one restrains them.

¹⁴As through a wide breach they come;
    amid the crash they roll on.
¹⁵Terrors are turned upon me;
    my honour is pursued as by the wind,
    and my prosperity has passed away like a cloud.

¹⁶"And now my soul is poured out within me;
    days of affliction have taken hold of me.
¹⁷The night racks my bones,
    and the pain that gnaws me takes no rest.
¹⁸With violence it seizes my garment;
    it binds me about like the collar of my tunic.
¹⁹God has cast me into the mire,
    and I have become like dust and ashes.
²⁰I cry to thee and thou dost not answer me;
    I stand, and thou dost not heed me.
²¹Thou hast turned cruel to me;
    with the might of thy hand thou dost persecute me.
²²Thou liftest me up on the wind, thou makest me ride on it,
    and thou tossest me about in the roar of the storm.
²³Yea, I know that thou wilt bring me to death,
    and to the house appointed for all living.
²⁴"Yet does not one in a heap of ruins stretch out his hand,
    and in his disaster cry for help?
²⁵Did not I weep for him whose day was hard?
    Was not my soul grieved for the poor?
²⁶But when I looked for good, evil came;
    and when I waited for light, darkness came.
²⁷My heart is in turmoil, and is never still;
    days of affliction come to meet me.
²⁸I go about blackened, but not by the sun;
    I stand up in the assembly, and cry for help.
²⁹I am a brother of jackals,
    and a companion of ostriches.
³⁰My skin turns black and falls from me,
    and my bones burn with heat.
³¹My lyre is turned to mourning,
    and my pipe to the voice of those who weep."

The speech of Job in chapters 29–31 (it is, not counting the few verses (40:4–5; 42:2–6) where he responds to the divine speeches at the end of the book, his last) is not addressed to the friends, who have been unceremoniously dismissed by him and who are never mentioned in it. Apart from a small paragraph in chapter 30 (vv. 20ff.) in which Job speaks directly to God, the speech is technically a soliloquy like the one with which he began in chapter 3, (*ie* it is addressed to us in the audience). But that small paragraph gives the game away. Although Job may wish to have the favourable verdict of those listening to him, it is God's verdict above all that he seeks. So the speech is, in effect, a final appeal to God to break his long silence and say something to him. The first two chapters form a lengthy and emotional lament in which, like many a psalmist before and after him, Job deplores his miserable state and voices some bitter complaints against God. Then, in chapter 31, comes a dignified but defiant defence of Job's former way of life. But missing (or almost missing) throughout is any of the countervailing expressions of trust in God which we nearly always find in the laments in the Psalter, and which we got from Job himself in the glorious passages at the end of chapters 16 and 19. This is a cruel disappointment, and we shall have to ask, at the end of our study of these chapters, why it should be so. Certainly as Job begins to speak, it is not apparent that he has yet snapped out of the strange mixture of arrogance and gloom which characterized his reply to Eliphaz in chapter 23 and brought the debate with the friends to an abrupt conclusion. Nor is it apparent that he has paid much attention to the criticism of his stance, ever so gently hinted at by the sceptical voice from the shadows which has just recited the poem on divine and human wisdom in chapter 28. Indeed Job seems to be concentrating his mind with a renewed intensity on the quest which has been consuming him from at least chapter 13 onwards, namely how shall he get through to God and make him listen to him. Job is still taking his flesh in his hands, still waiting for God although he may slay him, still sure that he will be vindicated (see 13:13ff.).

MY LYRE IS TURNED TO MOURNING

Job 29:1–30:31 (*cont'd*)

(i)

Chapter 29 strikes a pensive note as Job meditates with infinite sadness and regret on how his life had been in the old days before tragedy ruined it all.

In my Genesis commentary (vol. II, p.160) I invited the reader to apply some well known words of Dante in the *Divina Commedia*, Book IV, to Rebekah as they thought on that resourceful, but embittered, woman having engineered the escape of her darling Jacob, waiting disconsolate at home for his return from Paddan-Aram, a return she did not live to see. But Dante's words, even more succinctly, fit a disconsolate Job at this poignant moment:

> *Nessun maggior dolore*
> *Che ricordarsi del tempo felice*
> *Nella miseria.*

> ("There is no greater sorrow than to recall a time of happiness in misery.")

It is not easy to find modern words to match the plaintive beauty of the Hebrew poetry which the author places in Job's mouth in this chapter, but perhaps these words of Dante suffice. And perhaps the words of Chaucer, cited by Dr Strahan from the poet's *Troilus and Criseyde*, are also fitting:

> For of fortunes sharpe adversitee,
> The worst kynde of infortune is this,
> A man to han ben in prosperitee,
> And it remembren, whan it passed is.

(ii)

But the chapter is invaluable not only for its insight into Job's bitter grief, but for the ideal of Hebrew morality it sets forth. It is a classic description of an old Hebrew community living in a small country town in the spacious days of the Israelite monarchy. The atmosphere it creates may be compared with that created in the novels of Jane Austen with their background in the rural England of the early 19th century. Job was the community's "squire" or leading citizen, and the light of God's friendship (v. 4) shone over his home. As a result Job was prosperous and happy, his family was around him, and he wanted for nothing. He was respected by everyone, young men moved out of his way to let him pass, old men stood when he entered the square by the gate where business was done. The poor and needy blessed him as he saw to their needs, he protected the orphan and caused the widow's heart to sing for joy, he searched out those who needed help, and he controlled and punished the selfish and the criminal. And basking in God's favour and in his own righteousness, he looked forward to a ripe old age and to dying, like Moses (Deut. 34:7), his vigour unabated, avoiding the onset of disease and senility, and leaving behind him an unsullied name to be his memorial.

The society of which Job speaks was one where righteousness mattered and justice was appreciated, and which was therefore integrated and whole. In Hebrew thinking, righteousness meant behaving appropriately, and justice meant giving every man his due. And what was appropriate and what was one's due depended on one's station in life. One recognized this, accepted life's appropriate rewards without resentment and discharged its appropriate duties without complaint. One was not jealous or envious of those whom God had called to a higher station, nor did one act superior to, or take advantage of, those whom he had called to a lower. It was this appropriateness, this harmony, that the Wisdom movement had tried in the Book of Proverbs to discern and commend, an appropriateness and harmony which was in tune with the way things were done in heaven. Where such appropriateness and harmony were present in a community, God would be bound to shower his blessings upon it; and where they were not present, where the commonality of men refused to acknowledge their place, and the rich and powerful indulged in exploitation of the poor for their own selfish ends, it was only to be expected that society's fabric should collapse and chaos reign.

We who live in a democratic and egalitarian age will not be overly impressed by Job's picture of the "good old days". To our ears it sounds rather smug and self-satisfied; an age which could offer no hope of change, no opportunity of advancement for anyone, and in which only *noblesse oblige* provided any barrier against the rich becoming richer and the poor poorer, an age whose motto could well have been;

> God bless the squire and his relations,
> And teach us all our proper stations.

There is truth in that assessment, but for all that, it is not an assessment which is particularly relevant to the interpretation of the Book of Job. For its day the ethic which the chapter outlines was an ethic that seems to have worked, and it produced a society better than any other in the ancient world of which Israel was a part. But what concerns us more is that it was in many ways the passing of the society which that ethic undergirded which gave rise to our book. Its author had been raised on the kind of teaching we find in the Book of Proverbs, and he was discovering to his horror that the answers it gave to so many of life's problems were no longer adequate in the generation to which he belonged. The various reactions that he makes his characters adopt to Job's dreadful suffering are sufficient proof of that. This chapter therefore enshrines his conviction, and that of many for whom he was writing, that things had once been better; and it encapsulates his and their bewilderment that God's will for their time should, by contrast to that time, be so difficult to discover. However different our world may be from theirs, that is a conviction we can understand and a bewilderment we can share; for we too live in an age when foundations are crumbling and old certainties are losing their grip and old ways are being overturned.

(iii)

Chapter 30 goes on to give the other side of Job's picture, how things are for him now—and the temperature immediately rises.

Longing and plaintiveness give way to shrillness, and there is
more than a touch of paranoia in his voice as he describes the
humiliation he has to suffer at the hands of the dregs of society,
whose fathers he would in the old days have scorned to house with
his sheepdogs. These outcasts, who had to retreat to the open
country and inhabit its ravines and caves, scraping a living where
they could, because decent folks had "whipped" them out (v. 8),
now mocked and spat at him as one beneath them. *They* avoided
him because God had put him in a position where they could do
so. He was in effect one of them as he sat alone on the rubbish
dump outside the village, and many of them could have been,
along with the relatives and neighbours mentioned in chapter 19,
among the shadowy circle of spectators of whose invisible
presence—at a safe distance!—we have from time to time been
reminded.

It is not certain whether verses 12ff., with their talk of attacks
by a rabble who make breaches in him and roll through
unopposed, refer exaggeratedly to the continuing insulting
treatment of him by these disreputable outcasts, or whether they
describe metaphorically the effects of his physical maladies on
him. But the language Job uses is wild in the extreme and reminds
us, with some of its phrases, of the incoherence he displayed in
chapter 16 where, in verses 7ff., it is almost impossible to know
whether it is God who is assailing him or whether it is those whom
he thinks of as his human enemies. Probably again both are in his
mind. But whatever the exact cause of his degradation, it is real
and it hurts cruelly. His honour is under threat and his erstwhile
prosperity has vanished (30:15).

And it is all ultimately God's doing. Pain racks Job's body,
choking him like a collar, and God has—it hardly matters whether
we take the phrase literally or figuratively—cast him into the mire
(v. 19). It is at this point that, patently in desperation, he turns to
address God directly—"thou dost not answer me", "thou dost not
heed me", "thou hast turned cruel to me", "thou dost persecute
me", and finally (and hopelessly, with one of the "I know"
passages mentioned in the commentary on 9:25–35) "I know that
thou wilt bring me to death, and to the house appointed for all

living" (v. 23). The old Job is back with us in full flow, or almost in full flow, as he describes his perilous condition; "blackened, but not by the sun", shunned in the village assembly when he goes there to appeal for help, and forced to resume his rôle as outcast with only the desert creatures who haunt the fringes of civilization for company. His lyre is truly "turned to mourning", and soon the only sound that will be heard will be the weeping of the professional women hired to do their keening as his body is carried to the grave.

(iv)

Shakespeare's *King Lear* is the closest parallel I can think of to these chapters of the Book of Job. In *King Lear*, as here, there is unbearable pathos as a great man falls and one who was accustomed to command has to beg for kindness and pity. There is also the common feeling that madness is not far away. And in both, if one is honest, there is a man hard to sympathize with, obstinate, suspicious, blustering and self-pitying. Both characters are redeemed in our eyes by the great poetry they utter; but that is a literary judgment, and it is not enough. The real link between Job and Shakespeare's most biblical hero is that both are in the end redeemed by humility. In Lear's case, it is by the recognition, as he is led off as a prisoner, that;

> Upon such sacrifices, my Cordelia,
> The gods themselves throw incense.

And we are content to let the "very foolish, fond old man" die, if not in peace, nor yet in sanity, at least in the dignity of painful self-knowledge.

In Job's case I have already given my opinion that it is, in the end, his faith that makes him whole (see the commentary on 23:1–17 (*cont'd*), *I am Hemmed in by Darkness*). But it is not easy at this moment to see much sign of that faith which led to the glorious outburst in the last verses of chapter 19. Only in the desperation of verse 24, "Yet does not one in a heap of ruins stretch out his hand?", is there any hint of it. Job is still, in these blistering chapters, on the heath with Lear, howling defiance at the elements, and the defiance will be joined with pride in the chapter still to come. But his endless talking will soon be over and his moment of catharsis will not now be long delayed.

IF MY STEP HAS TURNED ASIDE FROM THE WAY

Job 31:1–40

¹"I have made a covenant with my eyes;
  how then could I look upon a virgin?
²What would be my portion from God above,
  and my heritage from the Almighty on high?
³Does not calamity befall the unrighteous,
  and disaster the workers of iniquity?
⁴Does not he see my ways,
  and number all my steps?

⁵"If I have walked with falsehood,
  and my foot has hastened to deceit;
⁶(Let me be weighed in a just balance,
  and let God know my integrity!)
⁷if my step has turned aside from the way,
  and my heart has gone after my eyes,
  and if any spot has cleaved to my hands;
⁸then let me sow, and another eat;
  and let what grows for me be rooted out.

⁹"If my heart has been enticed to a woman,
  and I have lain in wait at my neighbour's door;
¹⁰then let my wife grind for another,
  and let others bow down upon her.
¹¹For that would be a heinous crime;
  that would be an iniquity to be punished by the judges;
¹²for that would be a fire which consumes unto Abaddon,
  and it would burn to the root all my increase.

¹³"If I have rejected the cause of my manservant or my maidservant,
  when they brought a complaint against me;
¹⁴what then shall I do when God rises up?

When he makes inquiry, what shall I answer him?
¹⁵Did not he who made me in the womb make him?
And did not one fashion us in the womb?

¹⁶"If I have withheld anything that the poor desired,
or have caused the eyes of the widow to fail,
¹⁷or have eaten my morsel alone,
and the fatherless has not eaten of it
¹⁸(for from his youth I reared him as a father,
and from his mother's womb I guided him);
¹⁹if I have seen any one perish for lack of clothing,
or a poor man without covering;
²⁰if his loins have not blessed me,
and if he was not warmed with the fleece of my sheep;
²¹if I have raised my hand against the fatherless,
because I saw help in the gate;
²²then let my shoulder blade fall from my shoulder,
and let my arm be broken from its socket.
²³For I was in terror of calamity from God,
and I could not have faced his majesty.

²⁴"If I have made gold my trust,
or called fine gold my confidence;
²⁵if I have rejoiced because my wealth was great,
or because my hand had gotten much;
²⁶if I have looked at the sun when it shone,
or the moon moving in splendour,
²⁷and my heart has been secretly enticed,
and my mouth has kissed my hand;
²⁸this also would be an iniquity to be punished by the judges,
for I should have been false to God above.

²⁹"If I have rejoiced at the ruin of him that hated me,
or exulted when evil overtook him
³⁰(I have not let my mouth sin
by asking for his life with a curse);
³¹if the men of my tent have not said,
'Who is there that has not been filled with his meat?'
³²(the sojourner has not lodged in the street;
I have opened my doors to the wayfarer);
³³if I have concealed my transgressions from men,
by hiding my iniquity in my bosom,

³⁴because I stood in great fear of the multitude,
  and the contempt of families terrified me,
   so that I kept silence, and did not go out of doors—
³⁵Oh, that I had one to hear me!
   (Here is my signature! let the Almighty answer me!)
   Oh, that I had the indictment written by my adversary!
³⁶Surely I would carry it on my shoulder;
   I would bind it on me as a crown;
³⁷I would give him an account of all my steps;
   like a prince I would approach him.

³⁸"If my land has cried out against me,
   and its furrows have wept together;
³⁹if I have eaten its yield without payment,
   and caused the death of its owners;
⁴⁰let thorns grow instead of wheat,
   and foul weeds instead of barley."

The words of Job are ended.

(v)

Chapter 31 contains Job's final *apologia pro vita sua*, summing up and enlarging upon the many previous passages (6:30; 9:20–21; 10:7; 12:4; 13:13ff.; 16:17; 23:10–12; and, if it belongs beside chapter 23, 27:5–6) in which he has maintained his innocence and boasted that he was blameless. It is both arrogant and moving, both self-centred and, for its age, very far-seeing. The device on which it is based is called the *oath of clearance*, which seems to have been a regular procedure in Hebrew law in trials, religious or secular, where the accused had difficulty in finding witnesses. In such cases he was put under a solemn oath by which he not only asserted his innocence but called down upon himself a fitting punishment should he be lying. We meet a variant of it in Numbers 5:19–22, in which a woman charged with adultery is made to swear by a priest that she has not lain with another man, and made to say "Amen" to a lurid curse that will bring about the miscarriage of any child she is carrying by that other man if she is not telling the truth. But rather more akin to Job's use of the procedure is Samuel's in his address to the people in 1 Samuel 12:1–5, in which, before castigating them for wanting a king like other nations, he denies that he had ever defrauded or oppressed or cheated any of them before. He invites anyone who is suspicious of his motives to testify before God that he has been guilty of such a crime, and he promises to make full restoration. But the invitation is rhetorical; his real intention is to emphasize his integrity and his right because of that to address them on the matter in hand.

As is his wont, Job speaks at some length, so that the chapter becomes, in effect, a roll-call of the vices which Hebrew ethics traditionally regarded as reprehensible in a man of substance such as Job had once been. It thus nicely balances chapter 29's picture of the virtues traditionally expected of a leading member of Hebrew society. There is undoubtedly about it something of the atmosphere of an "eye for [an] eye" (Exod. 21:23–25). But there is also an awareness of motive and attitude which lifts it out of its legalistic environment and allows us to compare it with the Book of Deuteronomy at its most incisive (see, *eg*, chapters 6 and 8) or even, in a few places, with the Sermon on the Mount. This should honestly be put down to Job's credit. He may still be much more strongly attached to the old Wisdom doctrine of retribution than, considering the arguments he has advanced against the friends, he ought to be. But he knows that virtue consists of more than doing the right thing and looking for the appropriate reward, and vice of more than doing the wrong thing and trying to avoid the inevitable punishment. As Professor Rowley expresses it succinctly, "he goes behind act to thought, and beneath conduct to the heart". We have not seen old Israelite Wisdom at its best in this book, and it is quite ironic that it should be the man who has by his insistent questioning undermined its chief *raison d'etre*, who also gives this most appealing presentation of it.

HERE IS MY SIGNATURE! LET THE ALMIGHTY ANSWER ME!

Job 31:1–40 (*cont'd*)

(vi)

The roll-call of vices begins with *lust* (vv. 1–4). To a man of Job's former station, female slaves would have been readily available, and he tells "the court" that he had made a "covenant" with his eyes not to interfere with them. However, there is probably more to Job's protestation than that. This particular vice may come at the head of the list because it reveals men at their most animal-like and, with its demotion of women to the status of objects, because it strikes at the most basic of human relationships, the one between the sexes. To Job, as to our Lord (Matt. 5:27), *lust* is worse than any actual sexual violence which ensues. That may be the reason, too, why no appropriate punishment for this archetypal lapse is suggested. Instead, we have a statement of the fundamental principle that God brings disaster on the "workers of iniquity", and a confident assertion by Job that the One who numbers all his steps will know that he has faithfully kept his "covenant". There is an element of sarcasm in Job's words which the attentive listener will not fail to appreciate; for it has, of course, been Job's complaint all along that God has been treating him as one of these "workers of iniquity", knowing that he was innocent. But he does not make too much of it. He means what he says here. Job believes passionately that God cannot allow himself to be mocked by men who, in such a basic matter, show themselves to be less than human.

The vices mentioned in verses. 5–8 are the equally basic ones of *lying* and *deceit* (v. 5) and *covetousness* (v. 7). No fair and equitable society can emerge where these go unchecked. Job has commercial malpractice chiefly in mind, as his invitation to God to weigh him in just balances and to find him innocent makes clear (in the parenthesis in v. 6, there is again irony and resentment present); compare Amos 8:4ff.; Psalm 24:4. The imprecation in verse 8 wishes upon himself, should he be guilty, the confiscation of his property by another, equally covetous.

Verses 9–12 are concerned with *adultery* in the narrower sense, and the fitting punishment is that his wife should become the slave of another man (cf. Exod. 11:5) and have to submit to his advances. Verses 11 and 12 underline in no uncertain terms the threat which, in Hebrew thinking, the disruption of the marriage bond posed to the stability of society; compare the phraseology in Deuteronomy 32:22. (Did Job at this juncture steal a glance at the wife he had so harshly upbraided all that time before, and ponder?)

In verses 13–15, Job denies that he has been *unjust to his slaves*, and follows his denial not with a curse but with a couple of questions which reveal significantly his own apprehension before *his* superior, and are also remarkable for their clear enunciation of the principle that all men are equal before God. Only Malachi 2:10 in the Old Testament is as forthright. There is no proposal here for the abolition of slavery, but Job subverts the institution from within in much the same way as St Paul does in Ephesians 6:5–9. Note again the irony of verse 14, more bitter this time perhaps, because it is for God to "rise up" (or "stand"; for the meaning of the verb see the comment at 19:25) and give him the justice that Job longs for more than anything else.

The crimes deplored in verse 16–23 are of *withholding kindness from the poor* and *disregarding the claims of widows and orphans*. These are the kind of crimes which the prophets were always accusing the idle rich in Israel of committing, particularly when they were accompanied by the scrupulous observance of outward religious duties; see Isaiah 1:16–17; Amos 5:21–24; Micah 6:6ff. And they are the kind of crimes which Eliphaz in the bitterness of defeat had tried viciously to lay at Job's door (22:5–9). Verse 18 probably means, in its rather exaggerated claim, that Job had from his earliest days regarded it as his duty to protect such weaker members of society, and doubtless he had (although it is only right to add that his humanitarianism does not seem to have extended to the wretched people he lampooned in chapter 30). The punishment in kind he calls down upon himself if he should fail in this duty (v. 22), is that the arm or hand that had refused help (v. 16) or had turned a beggar away (vv. 19–20), or that had been raised to vote against some unfortunate person "in the gate" (v. 21; cf. Amos 5:12), should be torn from its socket. For (v. 23) God had made his demands in this area of life crystal clear, and he, Job, should not in such a case be able to bring himself to face him (again there is a hint of irony; see 13:16).

In verses 24–28 *avarice* (*ie* making a god out of money; cf. Ps. 52:7; Matt. 6:24) and idolatrous practices like sun or moon worship are interestingly bracketed together. Being hauled to court seems a weak punishment until we recall that the sentence for idolatry in ancient Israel was death by stoning (Deut. 17:2ff.)!

In verses 29–34 three more vices are introduced by "if": *vindictiveness* (vv. 29–30), *meanness* and *inhospitality* (vv. 31–32), and *hypocrisy* (vv. 33–34). Each of these clauses identifies an attitude of which a true Hebrew "gentleman" like Job would almost automatically have been ashamed. This is particularly so of the second vice with its reminder of the prized values of the old tribal days, now gone; compare the ideal picture of Abraham welcoming the three visitors to his tent in Genesis 18 (see also Heb. 13:2). It should be noticed too that the third vice (*hypocrisy*) is given a sharper edge if we translate it with the RSV footnote "like Adam" (*ie* in the Garden; Gen. 3:8ff.) in preference to the colourless "from men" of the RSV text. But in none of the three cases is the "if" clause followed by a main clause giving the answering sanction. In the first two cases there is, in parenthesis, a vehement denial by Job that he could possibly have been guilty of such ignoble thoughts or deeds. Then in the third case there is a sudden break in the syntax and we find Job launching himself into his final powerful protestation of innocence. It is not difficult to sense the emotional turmoil in his mind as abruptly he stops his careful cataloguing. It is, needless to say, caused by the return, for the umpteenth time, of the paralysing thought that the only One who could do anything about all this may still be refusing to listen to him.

(vii)

There is a tingling tension in the air as another of the climaxes of the Book of Job is reached. In verses 35–37 the despairing intention Job first formed in 13:15–16 is at last, and unambiguously, put into effect as, formally addressing us in the audience but in reality addressing God, he wishes forlornly that he had someone to hear him; and then, banishing both his fears and his complaining, he announces boldly that he has signed his bit of paper affirming that in his own view he is in the right. His defence has been lodged with the court, and it is now up to God to do what he has hitherto inexplicably and remorselessly refused to do, which is to produce *his* bit of paper laying out the charges by virtue of which he has been so cruelly misusing him. When he does, as surely he must, he, Job, will lift up the Almighty's indictment and carry it proudly on his shoulders and wear it as a crown upon his head; for it will not in fact be an indictment. Finally compelled to tell the truth, God will have to produce an account of Job's life that will match Job's own record of it; and, with this, he, Job, will confront him like a prince, and win from God the verdict to which he is entitled.

In introducing this last speech of Job's, I tried to prepare the reader for the shock he should now be experiencing. The speech is full of nobility as a man driven to distraction by the most fearful physical sufferings, but above all by the interminable silence of unanswered prayer, declines to crawl before the God who had put him in the state he was now in and had abandoned him to it. It is the speech moreover of a man who is not given to self-deception and who holds his integrity precious for the best possible reasons. But for all that, it is selfish at its core. And it is unredeemed by any warmth or trust that one can detect. The God whom Job addresses is his adversary; one from whom concessions have to be squeezed, one who indeed has to be made out to be in the wrong if Job is to be in the right. Can it be that Job has forgotten the God whom he had once called his "witness" (16:19) and his *go-el* or kinsman (19:25)? Job claims to have observed all God's laws, all the conditions which God has laid down in order for men to be acceptable to him; and he claims to respect and fear him. But where is the evidence that Job *needs* God? Is it not his own doing of good and his own avoiding of evil that give meaning and dignity to this man's life? Could he not, if he had to, do without God?

This is hubris at its classic best—or should I say worst? The ruler of the universe is being asked to dance to Job's tune.

Yet I believe that there is one mitigating plea that we can enter on Job's behalf. His magnificent but Promethean protestation of innocence does not in fact conclude the speech. There is another "oath of clearance" in verses 38–40. On the surface it concerns the misappropriation of land, and the punishment to fit this crime is that his land will not yield its increase. However, if verse 39 refers to the murder of a previous owner, then we are forcibly reminded of the story of Naboth's vineyard in 1 Kings 21 with its dramatic encounter between Elijah and King Ahab. And even more so should the final verse remind us of the curse on the ground and the sentence on Adam pronounced in Genesis 3:17ff. Can we detect, in these subtle connections with other passages of Scripture inserted into Job's very last utterance, a reluctant realization on his part that he has gone over the score in his defiant defence, and a secret confession that, for all his vaunted perfection, he belongs to an arrogant humanity excluded from God's nearer presence? Has something of the querulousness and pessimism of the early Eliphaz of chapters 4 and 5, something indeed of the scepticism of the by-stander who recited the poem of chapter 28, crept, however surreptitiously, into Job's consciousness? My own impression is that we ought to answer these questions with *yes*. If the speech had closed with Job playing the "prince", I do not think I could have held out much hope for him. But Job seems to me to be steeling himself to be humble. He does not find it an easy thing to do. But as the divine thunder is heard faintly in the background, it is as creature that he will meet his Creator. I do not therefore withdraw my judgment that it will be in the end Job's faith that will save him.

A NOTE ON CHAPTERS 32–37: THE SPEECHES OF ELIHU

For the speeches of Elihu, which with many other scholars I do not regard as original to the Book of Job, see the *Appendix*, in which they are set forth with brief comments. It is my view that both *dramatically* and *theologically,* the speeches of the Lord from the whirlwind must follow at this point. Our patience has been stretched to breaking point and cannot be asked to endure another intrusion of human words.

WHO IS THIS THAT DARKENS COUNSEL BY WORDS WITHOUT KNOWLEDGE?

Job 38:1–3

[1]Then the Lord answered Job out of the whirlwind:
[2]"Who is this that darkens counsel
  by words without knowledge?
[3]Gird up your loins like a man,
  I will question you, and you shall declare to me."

We left Job at the end of his long and eloquent *apologia* in chapters 29–31 in a still defiant mood. Although by no means unaware of the danger in which he was putting himself by so recklessly provoking an all-powerful heaven, he was still insisting on interpreting his sufferings as a mark of God's displeasure and, because he knew that he was innocent, on interpreting God's displeasure as arbitrary and unjust, if not indeed motivated by animosity towards himself. He had not in so many words demanded that God restore him to his former prosperity; but he was still demanding, and vehemently demanding, that God acknowledge his, Job's, integrity, remove his shame, and reinstate his reputation in the eyes of all who had impugned it. Now at last—and how it has been delayed!—the divine voice speaks to him out of the whirlwind and he hears what God himself thinks of all that Job has been saying.

Within a very short time Job must have wondered—as we as readers still wonder today—what the long-awaited reply could have to do with his plea. Not once are the troubles of Job, which are what this book that we are studying is supposed to be about, as much as mentioned. Instead, we are regaled in a first speech in chapters 38 and 39, in the form of a long series of ironic questions directed at Job, with a survey of God's work in creation, his control of the various natural phenomena, and his providential concern with a number of animals and birds. There follows in 40:1–5 a short dialogue or argument between God and Job, after which we are treated for the rest of chapter 40 and throughout chapter 41 to a second divine speech which seems even more irrelevant to Job's sufferings than the first, being almost entirely devoted to the description of two very peculiar and rather frightening beasts called *Behemoth* and *Leviathan*.

It is, of course, patently obvious that Job is being put in his place. And at the beginning of chapter 42, Job duly submits, speaks of only having *heard* about God before, whereas now he *sees* him; and, despising himself, he repents in dust and ashes. But how is Job being put in his place; and how, in the larger context of the book, are we to interpret his submission? Is he told anything, if not explicitly then implicitly, in these two lengthy speeches, that enables him to understand his sufferings? Does he hear anything that allows him still to expect or even want an acquittal thereafter? Or, as quite a few commentators have suggested, do the pains and problems which have plagued him for so long, remain at the end unexplained and unresolved, as everything that has happened to him is taken up and has its sting drawn in the glow of what we might call a visionary experience? The answer to these questions are not so easy to ascertain.

One could even form the impression that we in the audience are being discouraged to ask them. And in a real sense this must be true. The author is in his imagination (and, we believe, under the inspiration of the divine spirit) putting words in God's mouth. He feels, therefore, that he must show due reverence as he writes, and that he is likewise entitled to look for due reverence from his audience. Yet in an equally real sense he knows that it is incumbent upon him to give *some* answers to the issues which he himself has raised in our minds in the inexorable chapters which have preceded this scene, even if the answers should turn out in the end to be chiefly negative. The way the author solves his dilemma is quite brilliant. He refuses to spell out his "solution" and so puts the onus on us to infer it for ourselves. Even as we are frustrated and uneasy in our search for something to infer, we cannot help but recognize that his approach is superbly right and fitting.

(i)

The scene is deliciously set by having God (who in the rubric can now be given his Israelite name of *Yahweh* or "the Lord") speak to Job out of a whirlwind or storm. It is not the kind of setting that would normally have been chosen by a Wisdom teacher or, for that matter, by one of Israel's prophets. The members of both these religious professions believed, although in different ways, that they had access to God's will and knowledge of his purposes. The wise men thought that through the cultivation of wisdom they could bring themselves into harmony with the divine wisdom that governed the universe (or let us say, with the sceptic of chapter 28 in mind, that most of them thought this). And the prophets were sure, if Elijah in 1 Kings 19 is to be believed, that God spoke to them not in the wind, nor in the earthquake, nor in the fire, but in the "still, small voice" (v. 12). Both professions looked askance at older Hebrew traditions which spoke of God's appearance to his people in terms of the clash of thunder and the flash of lightning. But it is exactly to these more venerable traditions that the author of the Book of Job has recourse, as he prepares Job—and us—for the book's last and greatest climax; to traditions like those preserved in the story of God's meeting with Israel at Mount Sinai (Exod. 19:16ff.), or in ancient poems such as the Song of Deborah (Judg. 5:4–5), or in Temple hymns such as Psalm 18:7–15 or Psalm 29 or Psalm 68:7ff. He wishes Job—and us—to be completely sure that an encounter with the Lord of Hosts is an awesome and humbling experience.

And so it turns out. Job must have thrilled with expectation when the divine thunder roared and the divine voice spoke. At last God was going to exonerate him, and his sour-faced friends (who were, it should be remembered, still there in the background) would be shown openly how wrong they had been. But what a shock lay in store for him! God's first words were words of sternest rebuke. Who was he, Job, to question providence? By "darkens counsel" in verse 2 God means not simply that Job, by what he had been saying, had been speaking unwisely but, specifically, that he had been misrepresenting the divine "counsel". For this sense of the word see Psalm 33:10–11, where God's "counsel" is contrasted with the "counsel" of the nations; or Proverbs 19:21, where his "purpose" (the same word) is contrasted with the "plans in the mind of a man".

It is not difficult to picture the friends nodding sagely and in self-satisfaction at each other at this juncture, particularly Zophar as he recalled his accusations of 11:5–6, 7ff. It looked as though God was going to support them! But of course he was not, although we can hardly blame them for thinking so. Their turn is still to come when to their consternation they will hear God approving of what Job had said and condemning them angrily for saying about him (God) that which was not right (42:7). For the moment, however, the consternation is Job's as he is told to rise up from the ash heap, brace himself like a man and cease his whining. He had flung his insolent questions at God. Now it was time for him to hear God's questions and answer them if he could.

There is irony flying in all directions in these initial verses— irony at the expense of the friends who may be laughing now but who will not have the last laugh; irony at the expense of Job who is himself being put into the dock where he would liked to have put God; and irony too at our expense. Or should I say potential irony at our expense? If we wish to avoid the charge, then we should see to it that we do not side too quickly with the friends and rejoice too readily at Job's discomfiture; for we know, as they do not, that Job will eventually—indeed, before very long— receive God's favourable verdict. At the same time we dare not make too much light of the divine lesson which Job is here being taught; for we know—or ought to know—that we and any who read these fork-tongued chapters are being judged along with him. Let us find out whether we have what it takes both to accept the rebuke which is now being addressed to Job and to escape the rebuke which will shortly be addressed to the friends.

WHERE WERE YOU WHEN I LAID THE FOUNDATION OF THE EARTH?

Job 38:4–24

4"Where were you when I laid the foundation of the earth?
Tell me, if you have understanding.
5Who determined its measurements—surely you know!
Or who stretched the line upon it?
6On what were its bases sunk,
or who laid its cornerstone,
7when the morning stars sang together,
and all the sons of God shouted for joy?

8"Or who shut in the sea with doors,
when it burst forth from the womb;
9when I made clouds its garment,
and thick darkness its swaddling band,
10and prescribed bounds for it,
and set bars and doors,
11and said, 'Thus far shall you come, and no farther,
and here shall your proud waves be stayed'?

12"Have you commanded the morning since your days began,
and caused the dawn to know its place,
13that it might take hold of the skirts of the earth,
and the wicked be shaken out of it?
14It is changed like clay under the seal,
and it is dyed like a garment.
15From the wicked their light is withheld,
and their uplifted arm is broken.

16"Have you entered into the springs of the sea,
or walked in the recesses of the deep?
17Have the gates of death been revealed to you,
or have you seen the gates of deep darkness?
18Have you comprehended the expanse of the earth?
Declare, if you know all this.

19"Where is the way to the dwelling of light,
and where is the place of darkness,
20that you may take it to its territory

and that you may discern the paths to its home?
²¹You know, for you were born then,
　　and the number of your days is great!

²²"Have you entered the storehouses of the snow,
　　or have you seen the storehouses of the hail,
²³which I have reserved for the time of trouble,
　　for the day of battle and war?
²⁴What is the way to the place where the light is distributed,
　　or where the east wind is scattered upon the earth?"

(ii)

The first division of the Lord's initial speech (38:4–15) contains three questions concerning the world's creation. To be able to comprehend God's "counsel" or purposes in their entirety, Job would have had to have been there at the beginning of things.

First (vv. 4–7) Job, not God, would have had to have decided the dimensions of the earth (cf. Isa. 40:12–13) and seen to it that it was set on sure foundations (cf. Pss. 24:2; 104:5); and he, not God, would have been the one to receive the plaudits of the heavenly beings as they cheered his accomplishments (cf. Ps. 29:1).

But *second*, more than that, Job, not God, would have had to deal with the dangerous waters of the sea (vv. 8–11), that lusty infant of the great deep of chaos whose swaddling bands were the primeval darkness itself and which had to be held back from overwhelming the earth. With the poet's word pictures, compare Psalms 93; 104:6–9; and, more prosaically, Genesis 1:6–10.

The *third* question (vv. 12–15) seems to have behind it a description of the coming of light into the darkness of the first chaos, and the distinguishing of the two as day and night (cf. Gen. 1:3–5). It is probable that the terms translated as "the wicked [ones]" and "the [not "their"] uplifted arm" in verses 13 and 15, are names of constellations, and that the primary reference is to their disappearance at dawn. But the names are suggestive and have clearly been chosen by the poet to enable him to make an additional point. In his imagination the two constellations stand also for wicked and arrogant people whose dark deeds are discovered by God's light and who will have to confront God's punishment. Translate the verses, therefore:

> Did you in all your born days issue orders to the morning
>   or assign the dawn its post,
> (tell them) to take hold of earth's skirts,
>   so that "the wicked [ones]" are shaken clear of it?
> It is transformed like clay under a seal
>   as they (*ie* morning and dawn) station themselves like a
>   cloak (around it);
> and light is withheld from "the wicked [ones]",
>   and "the uplifted arm" is broken.

The imagery is elusive, but the lesson is plain enough. Just as at the Creation God had to subdue the watery chaos of old, turning it into the seas we now know (and is by implication able to subdue today's powers of chaos and evil); so his light, which became the first day and limited the primeval darkness by turning it into night, is still today keeping in check the dark wickedness of men wherever it may be found: the Creator is still in charge of his creation.

(iii)

In verses 16–18 the subject is the underworld, that huge area beneath the sea and the earth where it was believed men's spirits went after death. But this time there is not any underlying thought of death as an enemy of God, as there was in verse 8ff. where the chaos waters were his enemy. The author has allowed Job once or twice to speculate a little about life beyond the grave, notably in chapter 14, and at the end of chapter 19, but it has not emerged as a major issue for him. He may be more than a little uneasy about death and God's relationship with it, but Job is still solidly rooted in an age when death marked the end of sentient existence for men and of their contact with the God of the living. We should not therefore look for hidden meanings in this paragraph. We have the underworld included briefly as a constituent part of creation and Job is ironically asked whether he has been there, and no more than that. (Probably we should retain the plaintive "shadow of death" of the AV in verse 17 instead of the RSV's "deep darkness"; and probably we should translate the Hebrew word for "earth" in verse 18 more precisely by "underworld", as suggested by Professor Dahood, otherwise the meaning of that verse could easily be misunderstood. The reference is to regions under the earth where a still living Job could not go, rather than to far-away places on the earth which, in theory, he could visit.)

In verses 19–21 there is another allusion to the creation of light and darkness at the beginning of time, as is clear from the cuttingly sarcastic verse 21, "You know, for you were born then!" But the poet is in fact moving on at this point to consider the heavens and the wonderful phenomena they contain. Job is asked by God whether he knows the way to where light and darkness dwell; and this leads, in verses 22–24, to further questions about the homes or "storehouses" of the snow, the hail, the mist or lightning (one of these was probably original to verse 24 rather than, for the third time, "light"; the three Hebrew words concerned are very similar) and, finally, the east wind (or *sirocco*). In ancient belief such phenomena were thought to inhabit remote chambers or quarters somewhere in the firmament when they were not required for their primary tasks (see, for the wind, Ps. 135:7). Verse 23 briefly mentions one such task: God reserves the hail for times of trouble. This too reflects a belief of the ancient world that the gods could and did use hail, storm, drought, *etc*, to punish or rebuke their people's enemies or even their own people; and passages like Exodus 9:19ff. and 10:21ff. (the plagues of hail and darkness) or Joshua 10:11 (the defeat of the five Amorite kings) or Amos 4:7ff. (the drought sent by God on Israel) show that Israel shared this belief.

There may be a hint of a suggestion here to Job (particularly since the *sirocco* has just been mentioned; see 1:19) that his "trouble" had been inflicted on him for a purpose. But I doubt it. As far as men are concerned, verse 23 is more likely to be reminding Job, and all of us, that what comes from the heavens is not always pleasant. But even that is but an aside. The chief lesson of this second division of the Lord's first speech (38:16–24) seems to me to be simply that the earth is not the only place in the

universe where God has business. He has vast regions under it
and beyond it to oversee, which only he has visited and where no
living creature has ever been.

WHO CAN TILT THE WATERSKINS OF THE HEAVENS?

Job 38:25–38

> 25"Who has cleft a channel for the torrents of rain,
>   and a way for the thunderbolt,
> 26to bring rain on a land where no man is,
>   on the desert in which there is no man;
> 27to satisfy the waste and desolate land,
>   and to make the ground put forth grass?
>
> 28"Has the rain a father,
>   or who has begotten the drops of dew?
> 29From whose womb did the ice come forth,
>   and who has given birth to the hoarfrost of heaven?
> 30The waters become hard like stone,
>   and the face of the deep is frozen.
>
> 31"Can you bind the chains of the Pleiades,
>   or loose the cords of Orion?
> 32Can you lead forth the Mazzaroth in their season,
>   or can you guide the Bear with its children?
> 33Do you know the ordinances of the heavens?
>   Can you establish their rule on the earth?
>
> 34"Can you lift up your voice to the clouds,
>   that a flood of waters may cover you?
> 35Can you send forth lightnings, that they may go
>   and say to you, 'Here we are'?
> 36Who has put wisdom in the clouds,
>   or given understanding to the mists?
> 37Who can number the clouds by wisdom?
>   Or who can tilt the waterskins of the heavens,
> 38when the dust runs into a mass
>   and the clods cleave fast together?"

(iv)

The third division of the speech (vv. 25–38) also contains questions about the phenomena of the heavens, but they concern not so much their remoteness from the earth as who controls and directs them. The theme then is God's government of his created world, a theme which we will find extended into the fourth section beginning at verse 39.

It was not Job who (vv. 25–27) constructed the sluices in the dome of heaven through which the "waters . . . above the firmament" (Gen. 1:7) fell as showers of rain or as thunderstorms (hardly "thunderbolt") on the earth; compare the reference to the "windows of the heavens" in Genesis 7:11. And they did not only fall where men lived (Professor Pope nicely renders it in verse 26 as "No-man's land"), but on the uninhabited desert, making (if briefly) the most desolate ground sprout with new grass!

The imagery in verses 28–29 is extremely daring. Old Testament writers usually avoid, obviously because of its pagan connotations, the idea that God is the father, far less the mother, of created things. But the author of the Book of Job is a poet, and here he prefers risky language to safe theology if it will help get his audience thinking. The rain (a gentler variety than in v. 25) and the dew, ice and frost (which like the rain were thought, in antiquity, to fall from heaven) originated with God, not with Job, and God alone decided what to do with them. Verse 30 describes the effect of the ice and frost on rivers and lakes as they are held fast by them, and their surfaces turned to stone.

In verse 31 the Authorized Version's wonderfully evocative "sweet influences of the Pleiades" is no more than a clever guess. It is thought that the translators had in mind the genial onset of spring associated with the appearance of the Pleiades preceding sunrise in the east. But although the influence of the stars on earth's weather is what verses 31–33 are about, we need a word denoting some physical feature of the constellation as seen from the earth. The Revised Version's "cluster" is more likely to be right, however, than the RSV's "chains". The Pleiades are a small group of stars in Taurus, and the term *Pleiad* can still be used metaphorically in English for a gathering of brilliant intellectuals.

Similarly Orion (the huntsman) does not have "cords" (RSV), but the three bright stars across its middle have, since ancient times, been referred to as its *belt*. Render the verse therefore;

> Can you bind the Pleiades into a cluster,
>   or loose Orion's belt?

"Mazzaroth" in verse 32 has escaped identification, unless it is a variant of a term used in 2 Kings 23:5 and thought to denote the signs of the Zodiac, *ie* the strip of the heavens containing all the main planets known to ancient peoples (RSV "the constellations"). The reference in that case would be to the appearance of each of these in their appropriate month. If the next constellation is "the [Great] Bear" (Ursa Major), as most scholars seem to agree, then its "children" (why not "cubs"?) will be the stars of the Little Bear (Ursa Minor). The New English Bible, however, has "Aldebaran and its train"; Aldebaran being a star in Taurus and its "train", the Hyades, a group of stars associated in Greek mythology (and therefore presumably in mythologies farther to the east) with both Orion and the Pleiades. It would be nice to know more about these constellations and the forgotten myths that grew up around them in antiquity. But fortunately we do not need to, since verse 33 makes it clear that the point of this paragraph is Job's inability to shift the stars about the skies, and have them in their right positions at the right times to inaugurate and end the changing seasons. It is highly unlikely that the poet is thinking of astrological influences. Genesis 1:14ff. supplies the only comment required.

Verses 34–38 sound a little repetitive, since the rain and the other phenomena linked with it have already been mentioned before. But in fact verse 36 may contain allusions not to clouds and mist, but to the ibis and the cock, birds believed by the ancients to be able to foretell when rain was coming, a skill which Job certainly did not possess. With the marvellous imagery of the second half of verse 37, compare Psalm 33:7 which speaks of God gathering the seas in goatskins. Verse 38 describes the dusty cracked earth before the rains fall and gives the final clue to the lesson of these verses. Job cannot summon the vital rains of spring and autumn on which life in the Biblical lands so depended. Only God can; see Psalms 65:9ff.; 104:10ff.

DO YOU GIVE THE HORSE HIS MIGHT?

Job 38:39–39:30

³⁹"Can you hunt the prey for the lion,
    or satisfy the appetite of the young lions,
⁴⁰when they crouch in their dens,
    or lie in wait in their covert?
⁴¹Who provides for the raven its prey,
    when its young ones cry to God,
    and wander about for lack of food?

¹"Do you know when the mountain goats bring forth?
    Do you observe the calving of the hinds?
²Can you number the months that they fulfil,
    and do you know the time when they bring forth,
³when they crouch, bring forth their offspring,
    and are delivered of their young?
⁴Their young ones become strong,
    they grow up in the open;
    they go forth, and do not return to them.

⁵"Who has let the wild ass go free?
    Who has loosed the bonds of the swift ass,
⁶to whom I have given the steppe for his home,
    and the salt land for his dwelling place?
⁷He scorns the tumult of the city;
    he hears not the shouts of the driver.
⁸He ranges the mountains as his pasture,
    and he searches after every green thing.

⁹"Is the wild ox willing to serve you?
    Will he spend the night at your crib?
¹⁰Can you bind him in the furrow with ropes,
    or will he harrow the valleys after you?

¹¹Will you depend on him because his strength is great,
    and will you leave to him your labour?
¹²Do you have faith in him that he will return,
    and bring your grain to your threshing floor?

¹³"The wings of the ostrich wave proudly;
    but are they the pinions and plumage of love?
¹⁴For she leaves her eggs to the earth,
    and lets them be warmed on the ground,
¹⁵forgetting that a foot may crush them,
    and that the wild beast may trample them.
¹⁶She deals cruelly with her young, as if they were not hers;
    though her labour be in vain, yet she has no fear;
¹⁷because God has made her forget wisdom,
    and given her no share in understanding.
¹⁸When she rouses herself to flee,
    she laughs at the horse and his rider.

¹⁹"Do you give the horse his might?
    Do you clothe his neck with strength?
²⁰Do you make him leap like the locust?
    His majestic snorting is terrible.
²¹He paws in the valley, and exults in his strength;
    he goes out to meet the weapons.
²²He laughs at fear, and is not dismayed;
    he does not turn back from the sword.
²³Upon him rattle the quiver,
    the flashing spear and the javelin.
²⁴With fierceness and rage he swallows the ground;
    he cannot stand still at the sound of the trumpet.
²⁵When the trumpet sounds, he says 'Aha!'
    He smells the battle from afar,
    the thunder of the captains, and the shouting.

²⁶"Is it by your wisdom that the hawk soars,
    and spreads his wings toward the south?
²⁷Is it at your command that the eagle mounts up
    and makes his nest on high?
²⁸On the rock he dwells and makes his home
    in the fastness of the rocky crag.
²⁹Thence he spies out the prey;

his eyes behold it afar off.
[30]His young ones suck up blood;
    and where the slain are, there is he."

(v)

The fourth and final division of the Lord's first speech also comes under the heading of God's rule or providence over his creation, although the scene has moved back to the earth again. It was with the creation and establishing of the earth that the speech began, and it returns to it for its long ending, the subject of which is the animals that inhabit it and the birds that fly above it. All the creatures, but one, are wild creatures, and it (the battle-horse) can hardly be called tame! No domestic animals appear in the list and, most significantly of all, men, who according to Genesis chapter 1 are the crown of creation, and the God-appointed rulers of nature and of the "lower" creatures, are not mentioned except insofar as, in the person of Job, they are contrasted to their discredit not only with their Creator, but with many of these "lower" creatures.

The first two paragraphs (38:39–41 and 39:1–4) celebrate God's care for the animals he has made. Job cannot provide prey for the lions and the ravens, and probably never spares them a thought; but God sees the cubs crouching in their dens and hears the chicks squawking in their nests, and he arranges for their hunger to be satisfied. In the same way he oversees the labour of the mountain goats and the calving of the hinds. He knows how long they should carry their young and when it is time for them to give birth; and it is under his protection that the kids and fawns grow strong and finally leave their parents to make their own way in the world. Does Job know or care anything about all this?

The next two paragraphs (vv. 5–8 and 9–12) are splendidly sarcastic as they describe two creatures notoriously unbiddable by men. Does the wild ass have, like his domesticated cousin, to ask their permission to roam free in the steppes? God has already given him permission; and it is with his approval that he scorns the noise of the city and is heedless to the cries of anyone who would harness him. The empty mountains are his domain as he runs endlessly on, searching for pasture. For the wild ox (the now extinct *aurochs*, a huge beast) the Authorized Version has the "unicorn", which was apparently thought in 1611 to have had a real existence. This fierce creature was not made by God to serve men. He would not, like the domestic ox, stay quiet in a stall or consent to be yoked to a plough. His strength was not available to do men's heavy work for them, nor could they put their faith in him to pull their carts at harvest home.

The ostrich (vv. 13–18) was in antiquity renowned for her stupidity and her cruelty to her young, leaving her eggs uncovered in the dust and her chicks, when hatched, to fend for themselves. That this may not be in fact the case is neither here nor there. The author of the Book of Job patently thought it was, and he includes her as the most peculiar and most unlikeable creature he could imagine—yet she too was created by God. Verse 13 is almost impossible to translate. It was probably the allusion to finely plumaged wings that led the Authorized Version to suppose that·the "peacock" was being described. But the ostrich's wings are mere stumps. The first half of the verse should therefore be treated as a question: "Are the wings of the ostrich worth singing about?" There is probably also a reference in the second line to the heron or stork, a bird well known for her motherly qualities: "Or are her pinions and feathers motherly like the stork's?" But this stupid and selfish bird, which could not even fly, had one supreme ability, and this is touchingly emphasized in the last verse of the paragraph:

> But when she rears herself up,
>   she laughingly outdistances the horse and its rider.

Verses 19–25 are a justly famous eulogy of the battle-horse, the glory of ancient armies, striking terror into the enemy's heart, richly equipped and heavily armoured, a truly noble beast. Could he really be said to do his rider's bidding? When the trumpet sounded, he was his own master, pawing the ground, sniffing the battle, galloping to the fray on his own accord, desperate to be at the foe, exulting in his own strength. For "aha" as a cry of joy or satisfaction see Isaiah 44:16. We smile at the thought of the ostrich as God's creature, a clown among birds; we stand in awe that he should have created the mighty battle-horse to lead men to war and to be the monarch of all he surveys.

Finally, as if to take us away from the earth once more, verses 26–30 portray first the hawk spreading its wings to the wind; and then the eagle as it soars aloft in the sky, builds its nest on the inaccessible cliff face, catches sight of its prey on the ground and swoops down for the kill, and, more ignobly, as it gathers with its young around the carrion. They too are God's creatures and their marvellous *and* repellent ways reflect God's wise and all-seeing providence. And on this characteristically ambivalent note the Lord's first speech to Job closes.

(vi)

How fitting it is that the author of the Book of Job, whose ability as a poet has enthralled us on so many occasions, should pour the richest gifts of his genius into this long and lovely and magnificent and perturbing poem, and should then humbly offer it to God to be his own! In the truest sense he is giving back to God what is already his. Do we get a tiny glimpse here of what divine inspiration at its gloriest best means? And another question: have we any right to lard these incomparable words with our prosaic comment? Of course we have not. Writers of Scripture commentaries are an arrogant breed of men who rarely have recourse to few words if many will do. I only hope that it may be said of me that in this commentary I was aware of what I was doing and knew well that I was playing with fire.

I LAY MY HAND ON MY MOUTH

Job 40:1–5

> [1]And the Lord said to Job:
> [2]"Shall a faultfinder contend with the Almighty?
>   He who argues with God, let him answer it."
>
> [3]Then Job answered the Lord:
> [4]"Behold, I am of small account; what shall I answer thee?
>   I lay my hand on my mouth.
> [5]I have spoken once, and I will not answer;
>   twice, but I will proceed no further."

Let us imagine a pause as the Lord waits for Job to respond, after which, when he says nothing, the Lord asks him (I translate verse 2 rather freely):

> Has the man who argued with the Almighty any more
>   instructions for him?
> Do I hear the man who found fault with God answering
>   him back now?

This sarcastic taunt draws a brief reply from Job; but before we consider his reply, perhaps we should try a little inferring (and we can, of course, do no more than try), and try to tease out from the magnificent jumble of chapter 38 and 39 at least some of the lessons which the first speech from the storm may have been intended to teach Job and, through him, us.

(i)

There is *first* the lesson of what is involved in knowledge of God. In many ways the key words of the Book of Job are *knowledge* and cognates of it like *wisdom* and *understanding*. Job "knows" all sorts of things about God and about himself (*eg* that God is being unfair to him and that he, himself, is a righteous man) and he wants to know a lot more (*eg* why God is being unfair to him). The friends, on the contrary, argue that Job does not "know", that only God knows; yet, when it comes to the crunch, they themselves seem to know as much as God knows: for example, that Job is a guilty sinner. Then, over against them both, there is the urbane voice which speaks from the shadows in chapter 28 and whose owner is sure that neither Job or the friends "know" anything of God's purposes at all; the knowledge which is given to men is of an altogether more mundane and practical kind.

I do not believe that Job is being browbeaten in these chapters into dropping his quest for God and accepting that he is an ignorant mortal who has no right to criticize his Maker. That is far too simple, and it is far too near the positions adopted by the friends and by the poet of chapter 28 to be convincing. Nor, as I have already pointed out, does it square with the verdict soon to be pronounced by God (42:7), that Job's knowledge of him is superior to that of the friends. Of course, the chapters contrast—and vividly contrast—Job's limited knowledge with the full and comprehensive knowledge that God alone possesses. Job is undoubtedly wrong in many of the conclusions he has reached about God's motives, if not so wrong as the friends. But that does not mean that he ought not to have probed. There is even an implication that God prefers Job's probing to the "reverent agnosticism" commended in chapter 28; for his speech contains numerous hints as to how Job might, if he probed more sensibly, detect his divine providence at work in the world around him.

Perhaps the words "more sensibly" give us our clue. Could it be not so much his knowledge as the use to which Job insists on putting it, which angers God? It will be recalled how concerned the opening chapters of Genesis are with the sinister links between knowledge and power. When they ate of the tree of the "knowledge of good and evil", men became God's rivals; ambition consumed them as they sought to usurp his rôle and control their own lives. It is to this insatiable thirst for knowledge, and the thrill of power that it brings, that the stories of the Garden of Eden and the Tower of Babel trace (more than to any other single cause) what we call the "fall" of man. (For a fuller discussion see my *Genesis* commentary in this series, volume I, pp.108ff., 128ff.) I suggest that the thrust of God's speech in chapters 38 and 39 is along similar lines. In God's eyes, Job, when he claims to know so much about God and insistently demands to know so much more, is in effect attempting to manipulate him and to force him to do what he, Job, wishes him to do. And that, the chapters made abundantly clear, cannot be tolerated. God must defend his freedom of action, his right as Creator to plan and dispose of his creation as he, not one of his creatures, thinks fit.

A *second* lesson of these two chapters is not unconnected with this theme of man's desire for knowledge. It is the obvious lesson: the universe does not revolve around man. There is no doubt that one of the reasons why so much of the speech is devoted to a description of the depth and height and vast extent of the created world, and of the marvellous phenomena and animals that fill and inhabit it, is to underscore the complexity of the task which, as Creator and Preserver, God has to perform. Job is being told, tangentially but bluntly, that God has more to think about than him and his little troubles. But with that lesson there comes through loudly and unmistakeably, the wider message that mankind as a whole is but one of God's concerns, and not necessarily the most important of them. He has the chaos waters to keep at bay, otherwise the whole universe—and mankind with it—will collapse. Men only occupy a tiny portion of that universe, so how can it all be for their benefit? God sends his rain on areas of the earth which no human foot treads. Storm and frost may cause discomfort or worse to men, but is that any reason why they should not exist? God has huge planets to haul about the firmament, otherwise the seasons of the year will not arrive when they should. He has the lions and the ravens to feed, not just his human creatures. And there are hosts of animals and birds, with which men have little or nothing to do, on which they cannot impose their will, and whose ways are inexplicable, even distasteful and frightening, to men yet they too are God's creatures. Wild animals have their rights with God as well as men do, and as well as the domesticated cows and sheep and donkeys which so liberally bespatter the pages of Scripture elsewhere, illustrating the interdependence of man and domestic animals.

Could there be a more salutary message for this humanist age in which we live or, for that matter, a severer reprimand to those devout people who believe in God but think he is there only to procure their miserable salvation? Who says we know nothing about God? Not these chapters at any rate. We only require to open our eyes and look around us at his immense creation and use a modicum of imagination, and we will learn scores of *facts* about him—and about ourselves as well, although we should also add that not all of these *facts* will always be to our liking.

(ii)

But behind these two relatively transparent lessons of the Lord's first speech—the one which spoke to Job's arrogance and hubris and the other which spoke to his self-centredness—there are, I believe, two other major lessons which are not so easy for us in this modern age to grasp. This is because they have to do with an apprehension of divinity which belongs more to the ancient world than to ours.

The first of these—it is our *third* lesson all told—is the lesson, not merely of God's great power and unsurpassed knowledge (attributes of divinity which are, if the truth be told, simply human attributes writ large), but of his transcendence, his otherness, his utter distance as Creator from any of his creatures; the lesson of all those qualities which go to make up the *mysterium tremendum* of which Rudolf Otto speaks in his famous book *The Idea of the Holy*. There is something about God which is beyond our capacity to explain rationally, but which can be sensed and which, when it is sensed, engenders in us feelings of awe and dread, and of excitement and expectancy. If it is to be described at all, it has to be in poetry and imagery; and rarely can Scripture have caught that elusive something so well as in these two chapters. Not even the sixth chapter of Isaiah, or the first of Ezekiel in the Old Testament, or the final verses of Hebrews (ch. 12), or the last two chapters of the Book of Revelation in the New

Testament can match them. Quite apart from any meaning the
chapters may have on an intellectual level, they create an
atmosphere. Job and his friends, and all the group around them,
being people of their age, would be bound to feel it. I am not so
sure that we today are on the required wavelength. We ought to
be. We ought as we read to imagine ourselves beside Moses as he
hears the divine voice out, not of the tempest, but of the equally
awesome burning bush, saying to him: "Do not come near; put
off your shoes from your feet, for the place on which you are
standing is holy ground" (Exod. 3:5).

The other lesson hidden in these chapters—and now our
fourth—is the lesson which, with remarkable perspicacity, the
Scottish Shorter Catachism encapsulates in its first question and
answer:

What is man's chief end?
Man's chief end is to glorify God and enjoy him for ever.

If we examine the language which the Lord uses in this speech
(chapters 38–39) we will find that (the surface form of a series of
questions being disregarded) it is in fact the language of the great
hymns of praise in the Psalter: like Psalms 19 or 29 or 33 or 93 or
98 or 104 or 148. Particularly germane here may be the early
allusion to the joyous singing of the sons of God on creation's
morning (38:7). Why else is this marvellous picture brought
before us if it is not to serve as a model to his earthly creatures?
We may, as human beings, have to submit in ignorance and
trembling, as Job will have to, before a Being infinitely wiser and
mightier than we. But it should be a willing submission, not one
into which we are shamed or forced. And that kind of submission
is best made through the language of worship and praise which
directs us beyond our own weakness and unworthiness to him in
whom alone our yearning and puzzled souls can find peace.

We can see now where the praise of God earlier in this book has
gone wrong—the praise of God by the friends (like Eliphaz's in
5:8ff., or Zophar's in 11:7ff.) went wrong because they were
using it to get at Job; the praise of God by Job (as in 9:4ff. or

12:13ff.) went wrong because he was using it to get at God; the praise of God by the poet of chapter 28 went wrong because he was using it to get at Job and the friends both. But here in God's own mouth is *authentic* praise, a praise which puts men in their place, yes, but which soon makes them forget themselves, as it rises to him who is the source of all life and blessing, and a praise which, contemplating him for his own sake, strangely gives meaning to everything else as well.

(iii)

It is to be taken for granted that Job would get some of the points made in this glorious speech, just as we have been able to get some of them. It is all the more galling, therefore, to have to admit that his reply is almost totally lacking in graciousness. Job is of small account, he states, compared to such a great God; and he confesses that he has nothing more to say and had better shut up. How in the light of our comments on chapters 38 and 39 can this possibly be called an adequate response? There is acknow ledgment of his ignorance and "creatureliness", and of God's power, even of God's freedom to do what he thinks best. But it is a reluctant acknowledgment. And where are the signs of gratitude that he has finally found the God whom he has sought so long and so hard, or the signs of any disposition to praise and adore him? Will this man ever be satisfied? Will he ever bow in contrition before his Maker? Not, it seems, until he has heard more, until he has received a word from God which bears more closely on *his* life and *his* problems. (Note how in vv. 4 and 5, "I" or "my" are mentioned no less than eight times, in comparison to a single mention of "thee".)

What are we to say? I suggest at this juncture, the less the better. For, whatever he thinks of the partially deflated, but still sulking, man on the ash heap in front of him, God does condescend to speak to him again. Caution dictates that, until we have carefully listened to the second speech out of the whirlwind, we do not rush either to condemn or to excuse.

WILL YOU CONDEMN ME THAT YOU MAY BE JUSTIFIED?

Job 40:6–14

> ⁶Then the Lord answered Job out of the whirlwind:
> ⁷"Gird up your loins like a man;
>   I will question you, and you declare to me.
> ⁸Will you even put me in the wrong?
>   Will you condemn me that you may be justified?
> ⁹Have you an arm like God,
>   and can you thunder with a voice like his?
>
> ¹⁰"Deck yourself with majesty and dignity;
>   clothe yourself with glory and splendour.
> ¹¹Pour forth the overflowings of your anger,
>   and look on every one that is proud, and abase him.
> ¹²Look on every one that is proud, and bring him low;
>   and tread down the wicked where they stand.
> ¹³Hide them all in the dust together;
>   bind their faces in the world below.
> ¹⁴Then will I also acknowledge to you,
>   that your own right hand can give you victory."

Job has been duly silenced, but it is a silence that speaks volumes; and it issues in a second divine speech from the same stormy quarter. Does this speech, as its almost identical opening to the first speech might seem to indicate, turn the knife again in Job's wounds and obtain by more of the same kind of pressure, the desired collapse of Prometheus which the first speech had not been able to obtain? Or does it, by the imparting of some further piece of information, bring Job to his knees, not in reluctant, but in willing, surrender? I believe that the second answer is the one we ought to give.

(i)

There are no more crucial verses in the whole of the Book of Job than those which begin this second speech of the Lord's. God does not betray any sympathy with the sufferer, perhaps because

Job's outrageous and incessant self-pity has, for the moment, rendered him incapable of accepting any genuine sympathy; any sympathy, that is, which is based on the truth. Rather, God repeats his cruel command to Job to stop scratching his sores, stand on his feet like a man, and answer some further questions straight. If he wants to argue with God, he will have to snap out of his huffiness and cease behaving like a disgruntled child whose father has withheld his pocket money.

But for all that, God's first question *does* touch upon the matters that perturb Job. He is asked whether he has to deny that God is just, and pass the sentence of guilty on him in order that he himself may feel innocent? It is a question which Job ought to have considered before, as I tried to indicate in my comments on chapter 21. At that stage in the confrontation between him and his friends, Job had finally lost patience with them, and grounding himself solidly in the hard facts of life, had in a quite savage speech demolished the neat equations which they drew between a man's behaviour and his prosperity or lack of it. Yet not long before this, in chapter 19, Job had won through to his vision of God as his redeemer, a kinsman no less, who would see to it that he got the vindication he merited. Was this not a "fact" too? Job ought there and then to have been able to put these two precious insights together, and to reach the only possible conclusion, namely that *in spite of* all the anomalies, real or apparent, of arrogant sinners prospering and good men being overwhelmed by adversity, the God with whom human beings had to deal, was a just and caring God.

What a pity, the question implies, that Job had instead allowed the vision to dim, and had himself fallen back on the line of argument he had so devastatingly ridiculed in the friends! They had argued from God's justice, via Job's suffering, to Job's guilt, and so demeaned the character of a good man. Why did he have to mimic their perverse logic and argue from his own innocence, via his suffering, to God's guilt, and so impugn God's providential concern for his creatures? Job's line of argument should, considering his boasted respect for the facts, have been from his own integrity to God's integrity *in spite of* his suffering.

The more we ponder God's first question to Job in his second speech, the more we marvel at how, in its pellucid brevity, it pierces to the core both of Job's problem and, if we may say so, of God's. That core is the *in spite of* which lurks behind it. It is the existence of evil in God's world, and God's relationship to it.

(ii)

In the rest of his second speech, it seems to me that God is turning his attention, as directly as he dares permit himself when explaining his ways to a mere mortal, to impressing it upon Job's consciousness that he, God, is able to deal with evil, and therefore, by implication, with the real and ultimate cause of Job's predicament. His second question, "Have you an arm like God, and can you thunder with a voice like his?", shows how God has been hurt and incensed by Job's sarcastic and insolent accusation that he, God, was misruling the world, destroying both the righteous and the wicked, blindfolding the earth's judges, taking away the discernment of counsellors, pouring contempt on princes, removing the hopes of mankind and prevailing for ever against them, withdrawing his rod from the wicked (see 9:22–24; 12:13ff.; 14:18ff.; 21:7ff., *etc*). And sarcastic and contemptuous in his turn, God summons Job to take over his job and see whether he could do it better. Let Job assume the robes of divinity and kingship (cf. Ps. 104:1), let him signal to all around the violence of his wrath (cf. Hos. 5:10), let him seek out the proud and wicked and abase and humiliate them (cf. Isa. 2:12–17), let him round them up and see them on their way to Sheol's eternal prison, and rid us all of them. Then he, God, would acknowledge to Job that his own right hand could win him victory, that is, could bring about the triumph of right over wrong that he so earnestly desired to see both in his own life and throughout the world (cf. Judg. 7:2; Isa. 63:5–6).

But God is not simply satirizing Job in this passage. As I read it, it conceals an admission on God's part that Job has been right to be so passionately concerned about justice, and indeed to pester God about it, even if in so doing, he more often than not transgressed the bounds of proper address to divinity. What God is now beginning to say has already been hinted at, and quite sharply, at the start of chapter 38, in the passage about the control of the chaos waters. There, the lesson was that the Creator is in charge of his creation and cannot permit such unruly and sinister forces to overturn what he has so lovingly and carefully made. But it was only one lesson among many, and most of the lessons in that first speech had been concerned to emphasize the contrast between God's knowledge and Job's, and to remind Job that he had other matters to attend to beyond his petty pains and complaints. Here God, in effect, confesses that Job's complaints may not have been so petty after all, and that he had not said enough about the problem of evil. The glorious panorama of chapters 38 and 39 was to that extent deficient. If I am correct in this interpretation, the author is here allowing his petulant and resentful hero to achieve a quite remarkable success over the Lord of all. Job has got more out of God than God at first had meant to part with.

And there may, again as I read it, be a still more vital admission on God's part hidden in this passage. By being apprized in the most pointed terms how little he can do to roll back both the tide of tragedy and evil that seek to engulf him and many like him, Job is not being commanded simply to leave the salvation of the world to a God who *is* able to defeat evil. He is not being told to give up his own fight against evil and turn the whole problem of suffering and injustice over to God. No Old Testament writer would ever narrow the question of salvation to such an "either . . . or . . ." choice, particularly one who belonged, as the author of this book did, to Israel's Wisdom movement. There was a law, a way for men to follow, and Job had followed it, he had fought well and he was shortly to be commended by God for doing so. There is no "saved *only* by faith" in this passage or in this book. No, the information which I believe that God is trying stealthily to get over to Job here is that the ultimate defeat of evil, which was an impossible task for Job, was, if not impossible, by no means an easy task for him.

Job and his friends believed, and most of the Old Testament

with them, that God was himself responsible for the presence of evil in his creation; and God accepts that this is so. But it is not, he suggests to Job, a simple matter of him doing something nasty one day and undoing it the next, all at the drop of a hat. When God built evil and darkness and chaos into the fabric of the universe, and thus into the lives of men and all his other creatures, he took a fearful risk. He was unleashing forces of whose menace and threat and ability to ruin and disrupt, he himself could scarcely have been aware. It is this which, in my view, Job is being given an intimation of in this second divine speech: he is being given a hint of the terrible reality of evil and the dangers it presents to men, but above all, of the frightening problem it poses to the One who allowed it entry into his world in the first place. Take no account of evil, God is saying in essence, and my creation is awesome, wonderful, immensely complicated, beyond men's power to understand, far less turn to their advantage. Take realistic account of evil, and it becomes, for all its goodness and blessing, a fallen world which even I, God, must battle hard to save, not to mention superintend well.

BEHOLD, BEHEMOTH, WHICH I MADE AS I MADE YOU

Job 40:15–41:34

15"Behold, Behemoth,
    which I made as I made you;
    he eats grass like an ox.
16Behold, his strength in his loins,
    and his power in the muscles of his belly.
17He makes his tail stiff like a cedar;
    the sinews of his thighs are knit together.
18His bones are tubes of bronze,
    his limbs like bars of iron.

19"He is the first of the works of God;
    let him who made him bring near his sword!
20For the mountains yield food for him

where all the wild beasts play.
²¹Under the lotus plants he lies,
in the covert of the reeds and in the marsh.
²²For his shade the lotus trees cover him;
the willows of the brook surround him.
²³Behold, if the river is turbulent he is not frightened;
he is confident though Jordan rushes against his mouth.
²⁴Can one take him with hooks,
or pierce his nose with a snare?

¹"Can you draw out Leviathan with a fishhook,
or press down his tongue with a cord?
²Can you put a rope in his nose,
or pierce his jaw with a hook?
³Will he make many supplications to you?
Will he speak to you soft words?
⁴Will he make a covenant with you
to take him for your servant for ever?
⁵Will you play with him as with a bird,
or will you put him on leash for your maidens?
⁶Will traders bargain over him?
Will they divide him up among the merchants?
⁷Can you fill his skin with harpoons,
or his head with fishing spears?
⁸Lay hands on him;
think of the battle; you will not do it again!
⁹Behold, the hope of a man is disappointed;
he is laid low even at the sight of him.
¹⁰No one is so fierce that he dares to stir him up.
Who then is he that can stand before me?
¹¹Who has given to me, that I should repay him?
Whatever is under the whole heaven is mine.

¹²"I will not keep silence concerning his limbs,
or his mighty strength, or his goodly frame.
¹³Who can strip off his outer garment?
Who can penetrate his double coat of mail?
¹⁴Who can open the doors of his face?
Round about his teeth is terror.
¹⁵His back is made of rows of shields,
shut up closely as with a seal.

¹⁶One is so near to another
   that no air can come between them.
¹⁷They are joined one to another;
   they clasp each other and cannot be separated.
¹⁸His sneezings flash forth light,
   and his eyes are like the eyelids of the dawn.
¹⁹Out of his mouth go flaming torches;
   sparks of fire leap forth.
²⁰Out of his nostrils comes forth smoke,
   as from a boiling pot and burning rushes.
²¹His breath kindles coals,
   and a flame comes forth from his mouth.
²²In his neck abides strength,
   and terror dances before him.
²³The folds of his flesh cleave together,
   firmly cast upon him and immovable.
²⁴His heart is hard as a stone,
   hard as the nether millstone.
²⁵When he raises himself up the mighty are afraid;
   at the crashing they are beside themselves.
²⁶Though the sword reaches him, it does not avail;
   nor the spear, the dart, or the javelin.
²⁷He counts iron as straw,
   and bronze as rotten wood.
²⁸The arrow cannot make him flee;
   for him slingstones are turned to stubble.
²⁹Clubs are counted as stubble;
   he laughs at the rattle of javelins.
³⁰His underparts are like sharp potsherds;
   he spreads himself like a threshing sledge on the mire.
³¹He makes the deep boil like a pot;
   he makes the sea like a pot of ointment.
³²Behind him he leaves a shining wake;
   one would think the deep to be hoary.
³³Upon earth there is not his like,
   a creature without fear.
³⁴He beholds everything that is high;
   he is king over all the sons of pride."

(iii)

It is against the background of verses 7–14, as just interpreted, that I would find a reason for the incorporation into this speech of descriptions—and lengthy and involved descriptions at that—of the two amazing and exceedingly odd creatures called "Behemoth" (a name meaning "the beast" *ie the* Beast *par excellence*) and "Leviathan". If they are merely to be identified with the hippopotamus and the crocodile, as the footnotes in the RSV at 40:15 and 41:1 propose, it is difficult to see why so much is made of them. The descriptions could in that case hardly do more than re-emphasize the lessons already sufficiently taught by the pictures of the wild ass, or the wild ox, or the battle-horse in chapter 39. (Dr F.I. Andersen uses the phrase "artistic over-kill"). But if we see in them two different embodiments of the fabled chaos monster of old, well known from many other passages in the Old Testament, we are immediately transported into a much more sinister atmosphere and one in which the author (who is, it should again be stressed, using his poetry to speak for God) may appropriately ask us to linger as he attempts to mark out a route for us into the divine heart and mind.

It is the atmosphere of Genesis 1:2 with its formless and disordered "earth", and the darkness that blanketed the face of the deep; that chaos which God had to bend to his will before he could create the cosmos; it is the atmosphere of the story of Noah and the Flood (Gen. 6–8), which spoke of a fair earth being returned by God, because of the wickedness of its inhabitants, to the chaos from which it had emerged; it is the atmosphere of Psalm 74:12ff. where the heads of Leviathan, and of Psalm 89:10 where the carcass of Rahab, both had to be crushed by God at time's beginning; it is the atmosphere of Isaiah 27:1 with its Leviathan, the fleeing and twisting serpent, the dragon in the sea, which God would have to punish with his hard and great and strong sword, at the close of the age; it is the atmosphere of Psalm 93:3–4 and the mighty floods which lift up their voice, but than which the Lord on high is mightier yet. Finally, (from earlier in this book) it is the atmosphere of 7:12, and the sea monster over which a guard had to be set; of 9:13 and the Rahab whose

helpers had to bow before God; and (a passage already
mentioned in our comments on 40:6–14) of 38:8ff. and its
primaeval sea, which had to be shut in with doors and for which
God had to prescribe; "Thus far . . . and no farther!".

CAN YOU DRAW OUT LEVIATHAN
WITH A FISHHOOK?

Job 40:15–41:34 (*cont'd*)

(iv)

It is interesting to note that of the popular modern English
translations, the New International Version follows the
naturalistic identifications favoured by the RSV, although it adds
"or elephant" to its footnote on Behemoth. The New English
Bible takes the same line, but conflates most of the two
descriptions into one, which it takes to be of the crocodile,
leaving only a few verses (41:1–6) for a second creature, which it
thinks is the whale. The Good News Bible also accepts the RSV's
identifications, but it adds significantly "or legendary creature" in
both of its footnotes. However, only the Jerusalem Bible, by
having no footnotes explaining the names and by heading the
whole of the Lord's second speech, "God is master of the forces
of evil", unambiguously directs its readers towards the mythical
interpretation which I am here espousing.

The various Job commentaries are similarly divided, a majority
taking the view that the creatures are natural, if perhaps most
unusual and exceptionally formidable beasts; a minority arguing,
as I do, that they are creatures drawn from the old myths of the
Bible lands to symbolize the forces of evil which God may have
created but which, having done so, he then had to oppose. As an
example of the latter, we may mention Professor Pope's theory,
cogently presented, that "Behemoth" is a Hebrew counterpart of
the Mesopotamian "bull of heaven", slain by Gilgamesh and his
companion Enkidu in the Gilgamesh Epic, and of a number of

fierce bovine creatures which stand in Baal's way in a passage from one of the more difficult Ugaritic myths. Finally, we should record that some scholars would omit the two descriptions altogether as not original to the Book of Job; this certainly gets rid of all the problems of interpretation, but it means admitting that the scribe who added them later was as good a poet as the book's author!

We are therefore, in studying this penultimate section of the Book of Job, trying to pick our way through a veritable minefield. I can only give my own opinion with circumspection, and for what it is worth.

It is my assumption that the author bases his description of his two mythical monsters on the hippopotamus and the crocodile, creatures of the Nile which would be well enough known (but not too well known) to his audience, so that he does not feel at all obliged to be zoologically accurate in every particular. He is probably following an ancient custom of describing the chaos monster in semi-naturalistic terms (in the other biblical passages we have cited, it is a snake—although with several heads!—which seems to have been the favourite model). His *hippopotamus* is thus, like the real hippopotamus, hideously thick and powerful: it slinks in the water near the river bank with only its eyes protruding sinisterly above the surface; it stands immovable even when the river is in headlong spate (40:16ff.). His *crocodile* likewise is clothed with a double coat of mail, there is terror round its teeth, the scales on its back are disposed in menacing rows, it squats like a threshing sledge on the mud flats, it churns up the water as it moves and leaves behind a spectacular wake (41:12–17, 30–32). But what real crocodile ever spat forth flame and smoke from its mouth, as Leviathan is said to do in 41:18–21? Does this not come straight from the imaginative world which gave us, in another cultural milieu, the old English tale of St George and the Dragon?

The end result is shudderingly impressive and the aura created—of superhuman strength, of invincible weaponry, of impregnable defences—is quite overpowering.

(v)

But it is the paragraphs containing the two descriptions where "Behemoth" and "Leviathan" are brought into contact with human beings that are the most obviously instructive. The basis of these is the hippopotamus and crocodile hunts which are so vividly and yet ironically portrayed on many ancient Egyptian murals. In one which I have in front of me as I write (it is one of many in a book in German by Professor Othmar Keel on the Lord's speeches from the whirlwind) a tiny little hippopotamus, in the bottom right hand corner, is festooned with darts and lances to which ropes are attached, and it has more ropes around its nostrils, and its front and back legs. The rest of the mural is taken up with men who are drawn much larger than the hippopotamus, and who are pulling with might and main on the ropes, but do not seem to be making much headway. Who says that the Egyptians and the other peoples of the ancient world had no sense of humour?

In our chapters of Job there are many signs of the same macabre humour. Only 40:24 describes the hippopotamus hunt, but in 41:1–2, 7–10 and 41:25ff. ("he counts iron [weapons] as straw", "he laughs at the rattle of javelins") the chances of taking the crocodile, "Leviathan", with fishhooks and harpoons are mockingly weighed, and the huntsmen are counselled (41:8ff.);

> Lay your hand on him;
> remembering the battle, you will not do it again!
> The hope of such a one is gone;
> he is hurled headlong at the very sight of him.
> and who is he who can stand before him?
> "Who" [he says] "can anticipate me? I will reward him!
> For everything under the whole heavens is mine".

The last two verses in this passage are very obscure. As rendered in the RSV they seem to be an aside by God in which he claims that he is even fiercer than Leviathan. I prefer to read "stand before *him*" in verse 10 (thus maintaining the balance of the verse), and also to make verse 11 a boast uttered by Leviathan. In

Romans 11:35, St Paul cites the first half of verse 11 according to the *Septuagint* (Greek) version, and clearly regards the words as God's. I suspect that the Authorized Version (which the RSV follows) has been unduly influenced by this. I have been more influenced in my rendering by the Devil's words to Jesus during his temptation in the wilderness (Matt. 4:8–9):

> Again, the devil took him to a very high mountain, and showed him all the kingdoms of the world and the glory of them; and he said to him, "All these I will give you, if you will fall down and worship me."

And what of the superb sarcasm of 41:3ff.? It probably reflects the crocodile's defiant demeanour even when, as they think, the huntsmen have him captured:

> Will he plead long with you for mercy,
>   or address you with cajoling words?
> Will he make a pact with you
>   so that you may take him as a slave for life?
> Can you play with him as with a pet canary,
>   or put him on a string for your little girls?
> Will traders haggle over him
>   ard parcel him out among the shopkeepers?

(With the reference to a slave for life, cf. Deut. 15:12–17.)

The inference is clear. The hippopotamus and crocodile both may be caught and subdued by men, although only with the utmost difficulty and at fearful cost. But Behemoth and Leviathan cannot be snared and put out of action by them at all.

(vi)

Yet, as we are reminded more than once, they too are God's creatures. God made Behemoth, as he made Job (40:15). But (and this Job was not) Behemoth was the first of God's works (40:19*a*). This latter statement seems to be putting Behemoth on a par with wisdom as a kind of primordial force or principle: see

Proverbs 8:22, where Lady Wisdom says of herself that "the Lord created me at the beginning of his work, the first of his acts of old". Both "evil" and "wisdom" were implicated in God's creation of the universe. I am sure that this is the meaning we are meant to take out of the similar wording of the two verses. But verse 19*b* may be even more revealing. The Hebrew is highly cryptic but, as I read it, there is an undoubted suggestion that the Creator has to be more than usually wary of this particular creature of his. I would render it with more bite than the RSV: "let him that made him keep his sword unsheathed!"

There is no such direct allusion to Leviathan's creation by God unless, as some scholars propose, we give the half-verse 41:11 to God ("Whatever is under the whole heaven is mine"). I have preferred to give it to Leviathan (see above). But there is a mention slipped in right at the end of the speech (v. 33*b*) to Leviathan as a "creature" (the Hebrew is literally "he is made") without fear. And if we translate 41:25 literally ("When he raises himself up the [very] gods are afraid") there is the necessary hint that Leviathan too can strike terror in the ranks of heaven. Verse 33*a* ("Upon earth there is not his like") is equally suggestive, if we recall how it is taken up in Luther's hymn *Ein' Feste Burg* (in Thomas Carlyle's rendering):

> The ancient prince of hell
> Hath risen with purpose fell;
> Strong mail of craft and power
> He weareth in this hour;
> On earth is not his fellow

The famous Reformer knew better than many a modern scholar what this long and, on the surface, so non-theological portrait of Leviathan is all about, although I doubt whether even he could quite have appreciated the appalling danger the author is intent on having Behemoth and Leviathan represent to the One who let them loose in the world. God must often have questioned why he made them.

(vii)

What message Job may have got from this magnificent second divine speech, and how he may have applied it to his personal predicament, we had better not yet ask. We will need his seemingly abject words of response at the beginning of the book's last chapter to guide us. But there is a wider message, other than for Job alone, in it, and this we can perhaps attempt to summarize. The poetry and the metaphors and, as we should not forget, the irony and the humour, are glorious, and they fittingly veil that message. But it does come through. These legendary beasts, whose very names conjure up the menace of chaos and evil, are worthy opponents of their Creator. They are quite beyond the reach of men to take on and bring under control. Indeed, they treat men with scorn and derision, delighting to tease and humiliate and terrorize them. But even God has to watch out for them and handle them with kid gloves. It takes all his "craft and power" to keep them in subjection and prevent them from bringing to naught all he has achieved.

(viii)

A final word is necessary here on the Satan who is also, in his different way, a personification of evil. But he was, at the time the Book of Job was written, too closely linked with God (indeed, the Satan was one of God's "sons", and a member of his heavenly retinue) for the author to make use of him in this second speech of the Lord's. And, as we saw when considering his rôle in the Prologue, the Satan operated chiefly in the human sphere, causing havoc in human lives, but not throughout the universe. He went "to and fro on the earth" (1:7) working his mischief, but he did not invade other spheres of the divine providence. He was not yet the "ancient prince of hell" of Luther's hymn, and he did not yet have the power which his successor—the Devil—had, to offer Jesus the world's glory in return for worshipping him. This explains why the author of the Book of Job had to have recourse to the chaos monster of ancient Eastern mythology—and indeed to turn him into twins—in order to make the points he wished to make. Only such fabled creatures of limitless destructive power could have carried sufficient imaginative clout with his audience and could have raised them to the necessary pitch of concern and horror. Of course, in an Old Testament context, the one God had to be their Creator, as he had to be the Satan's "father", and this is emphasized by the author in a way that no New Testament writer or, for that matter, no Reformer, would have done. But we should not get too bothered about that. It is the reality of the great beasts or, if you like, the reality which they stand for, and even more so, the reality of the terrible task which God has devolved upon himself (of subduing such recalcitrant and rebellious creatures of his) which the man who penned this breathtaking poem (and put it into God's mouth) above all wished to impress upon the mind of Job—and upon the minds of all, including ourselves, who may read it in time to come.

BUT NOW MY EYE SEES THEE; THEREFORE I DESPISE MYSELF

Job 42:1–6

[1]Then Job answered the Lord:
[2]"I know that thou canst do all things,
   and that no purpose of thine can be thwarted.
[3]'Who is this that hides counsel without knowledge?'
Therefore I have uttered what I did not understand,
   things too wonderful for me, which I did not know.
[4]'Hear, and I will speak;
   I will question you, and you declare to me.'
[5]I had heard of thee by the hearing of the ear,
   but now my eye sees thee;
[6]therefore I despise myself,
   and repent in dust and ashes."

Job was reduced to a surly silence by the marvellous and surpassing strange, but still natural, phenomena and creatures of God's universe paraded before him in chapters 38 and 39. He is completely bowled over by the thought of the two fantastic beasts so vividly portrayed for him in chapters 40 and 41; and at long last Prometheus collapses—although, if we read these verses superficially, it seems with no great show of dignity but with a whimper.

(i)

But I do not believe that what we are witnessing is an abject collapse. Rather it is, like St Paul's on the Damascus Road, a willing surrender by a man whose eyes have been opened to the truth both about God and about himself. Yet this is a risky comparison; for I have warned my readers more than once not to interpret Job's experience in terms of Paul's. What then is the nature of the truth which opens Job's eyes and leads him to abhor himself and repent in dust and ashes; and how does his reaction differ from the conversion experience of the great apostle which has become the chief model for Christians describing how God has changed their lives?

There is on the part of both Job and Paul an intense self-loathing, and a full and honest act of submission. But Job's self-loathing is not that of a Paul feeling himself "sold under sin" (Rom. 7:14–24) because;

> I know that nothing good dwells within me, that is, in my flesh. I can will what is right, but I cannot do it. For I do not the good I want, but the evil I do not want is what I do . . . Wretched man that I am! Who will deliver me from this body of death?

Job is far more worried about maintaining his innocence than about unburdening himself of a guilt he does not own. His self-loathing is that of a man who, in the interests of that innocence, has tried to bend God's will to his own, and who now realizes the full horror of his arrogance. His submission, therefore, cannot be that of a Paul longing to be quit of sin, who gives up his reliance on his good works and flings himself in faith on the grace of God. It is that of a man who has been wronged and wants justice, but who ceases to demand it as his right, and entrusts himself to a divine providence which he had previously impugned. Both have been, to use St Paul's own words (Acts 26:14, AV), kicking against different pricks. It would be a pity if, in this climactic scene of the drama of Job, which we have for so long watched with a mixture of pain and hope and of anger and sympathy, we should be unable to profit from Job's vision of God because we cannot sufficiently distinguish it from St Paul's.

(ii)

When in verse 2, therefore, Job speaks of God being able to do all
things, he is neither making a trite theological point nor is he
cringingly confessing that he himself can do nothing and only God
can save him; instead, he is realistically concluding that only God
can make justice prevail throughout his creation. And the reason
he concludes this is because God has opened his eyes to the
massive presence of evil in that creation. There are many
tragedies other than Job's with which God has to deal; many
other things in the life of mankind, indeed in the very constitution
of the cosmos, which ought not to be. Job is aware that God as the
Creator is responsible for the presence of these tragedies and
anomalies; but God's second speech has turned Job's mind away
from brooding on how evil entered the world, to the more
practical question of how God is to get rid of it. He now knows
that God has a battle on his hands and is ready to admit that he is
even at this moment, while Job himself still suffers, engaging the
enemy. And Job's confidence is such that he cannot see God's
enemy, however strong and fierce he may be, eternally thwarting
God's purpose.

Verse 2, then, is a cry of faith out of deep distress; it could
legitimately be compared with our Lord's terrible words in
Gethsemane (Mark 14:36):

> Abba, Father, all things are possible to thee; remove this cup from me;
> yet not what I will, but what thou wilt.

Compare also Genesis 18:14; Jeremiah 32:17; Luke 1:37.

In verse 3 Job quotes God's first question to him in his first
speech (38:2) and gives his considered reply. Gone is the irony of
his "praise" of God's wisdom and might in 9:4, and the sarcastic
taunting of that verse: "who has hardened himself against him,
and succeeded?" But there is more than self-reproach in Job's
new tone. He does not only condemn himself for having pried
into matters beyond his capacity to understand. It would be a rash
person indeed who claimed that Job could ever aspire to the
simple contentment of the writer of Psalm 131:

I do not occupy myself with things
    too great and too marvellous for me.

But *some* of the psalmists's relief that he does not have to occupy himself thus must be Job's at this moment:

But I have calmed and quieted my soul,
    like a child quieted at its mother's breast.

And there is also wonder and gratitude that God's judgments are not simply unsearchable, his ways inscrutable, but are such in a manner which Job can grasp and appreciate. He is left amazed but not groping helplessly in the dark. See Romans 11:33ff.

(iii)

In verse 4 Job repeats the question that came second in the Lord's first speech (38:3) and first in his second (40:7); and it must be significant that he does not repeat the Lord's command to him in both these contexts—to gird up his loins "like a man". Job has finished with arguing. For, as he confesses in his reply of verse 5, all his prior information about God was no better than the friends'. *They* had based themselves on the hearsay of tradition; *he* had insisted that God behave in accordance with his own small apprehension of him which, compared with what he now knew of him, was not worthy to be called knowledge at all. For now he could actually *see* him.

There are two comments to be made on this *seeing* of God, as Job calls it. The *first* is the less obvious, but perhaps the more important, namely that it must be connected with 19:25–27. That earlier flight of hope when, in his imagination, Job had looked into the future and caught momentary sight of his "Redeemer" in Sheol after his, Job's, death, and heard him tell him that he had been vindicated, has been fulfilled in a totally unexpected way. God has appeared to him, not in Sheol but in this life, and he has appeared in storm and thunder, in all the majesty and glory of his being. Yet Job must sense that the two visions, the brief foretaste of chapter 19 and the full flood of chapters 38–41, are of the same

God. And this must mean that his vindication is secure. His kinsman has arrived to deliver him from shame and ignominy, and to redeem his reputation, to acknowledge his integrity and to pronounce the blessed verdict of *not guilty*.

The *second* comment to be made on this seeing of God is the more obvious one, that it is not only a vindication of Job, but a humbling of him. No-one walks away unscathed from such an encounter in the Old Testament: Isaiah is convicted by God's holiness, and confesses that he is "a man of unclean lips" (Isa. 6:5-6); Ezekiel falls flat on his face in awe (Ezek. 1:28); Daniel's radiant appearance is fearfully changed, and he has no strength left in him (Dan. 10:8). So (v. 6) Job, seeing the shape of God in the clouds of the whirlwind and hearing his words in the thunder, despises himself. The Hebrew text only has "despises", leaving the object unstated. But it matters little whether we supply "myself" with the RSV or "my words" with the Jerusalem Bible (*ie* "I retract all my words").

Job is both uplifted and cast down; uplifted because he has seen God his *go-el*, cast down because he has, with Isaiah, seen "the King, the Lord of Hosts". This sterner, holier side of God as well, he had hitherto known of only by hearsay. And now that Job is confronted with it, he can but weep bitter and regretful tears that he had made so much of his own righteousness and so little of God's; that he had harboured the thought that this God was more interested in might than right; or harboured the suspicion that this God was not concerned to see justice done in his world; that he, Job, had lacked the grace or imagination to grasp that this God was even now locked in deadly combat with mighty and evil forces which threatened to usurp his throne and return his creation to the chaos from which he had originally pulled it free. Job's own small balance sheet had been reckoned up and his tiny innocence was about to be made public; but before such a holy, just and moral God, what can Job in the last resort do but repent? What, in traditional eastern style, his friends had done in horror (2:12); what he had complained of God unjustly making him do in 30:19, Job now does himself in willing and appropriate contrition (cf. Gen. 18:27; Isa. 58:5).

(iv)

At the end of the commentary on chapter 23 I tried to encapsulate under six headings Job's state of mind as the controversy between him and his three friends ran out in bitter recrimination and failure to communicate. Can we, now that Job has met his God and knows him in a way which neither the friends nor he himself knew him then, encapsulate his very different state of mind as the wider controversy between him and heaven runs out in reconciliation and hope for the future? Let us try to do so, using the same six headings.

Job's *hubris* has been deflated and he has bowed in tears and humility as a creature before his Creator. His surrender comes suddenly and it is unconditional, something that this modern age of ours which so loves a rebel may regret; but to the age in which Job lived it had to come, and it would have been satisfied. The potter, and not his clay, has had the last word.

Job's *obsession with his own righteousness* has been lanced, and a mighty bubble burst. His virtue has been acknowledged and he has not been forced to confess sins he did not commit; but he has learned that no-one can presume on his virtue and that suffering can come to the best of men. God does not operate in the moral sphere with a slide-rule.

Job's *paranoia* has vanished. He has found that God has not been persecuting him arbitrarily and maliciously; and Job will soon (42:8) be able to make intercession even for the three friends who caused him so much distress. Just as he no longer feels the need to trumpet his integrity from the housetops, so he no longer has to be suspicious of everyone—even, may we say, his forgotten and sorely misjudged wife?—who as much as looks at him.

Job's *depression* has been wonderfully lifted, and a great burden of sadness and resentment removed from his shoulders. Not all of his problems have been solved, but they have been set in a larger and more hopeful perspective. A man who wanted to know everything is learning to live with indeterminacy and uncertainty and—dare we say it?—even to smile in the midst of continuing darkness.

Yet, in spite of Job being a creature of God's creation, which he now acknowledges, he is not asked to set aside his human *dignity*. He has, on behalf of mankind, won some successes over God; he has lured God into the open and even made him change his mind. On the whole, the Old Testament, used to letting God know of its complaints, would have been pleased with this; and all those who think that men have no power with God, are suitably rebuked.

Above all, Job's *faith* has been justified. It was always fitful and had to struggle with other less worthy attitudes in his soul; but he hung on, and he was rewarded with the fleeting insights of 9:33, of 13:15ff., and of 16:19ff., with the glorious vision of 19:25–27 and, in the end, with the yet more glorious face to face encounter of these last chapters. We should not exaggerate what Job learned of God intellectually in these visions, nor, on the other hand, should we speak too readily of a personal communion with God which he achieved and which rendered intellectual answers irrelevant. The God of the Old Testament has a disconcerting habit of denying the human mind too close an access to the mystery of his, God's, nature, and the human heart too sentimental an access to his friendship. No-one is allowed in its pages to know too much about God or to be too familiar with him.

I would interpret Job's victory of faith in this way. Like the importunate widow in our Lord's parable (Luke 18:1–8), Job battered at heaven's door until it was opened. God spoke to him and gave him a few answers; and he showed himself to Job for a few moments. The void between God and man was briefly crossed and the awful silence of heaven briefly broken—and that was enough for Job. Is this then what the Book of Job is chiefly saying? All the theological problems which gather around the presence, in God's creation, of evil things (like a good man suffering as Job did) are thoroughly aired, but none is completely solved. But to a desperate man, a vision is given which goes beyond theology and enables him to soldier on in a bleak and fearful world. Could it be because he strove long and hard to achieve this vision that Job is commended (as shortly he will be) for speaking of God "what is right"? Is the ultimate message of the Book of Job that the vision of God (and of course. in this Old

Testament book, this means a momentary vision of the Old Testament God, not the beatific and self-indulgent vision of the mystic absorbing himself in the universal All) comes not to the pious, but to the desperate; not to the assured, but to the drowning man; not to the defenders of the faith once delivered to the saints, but to the man at the end of his tether?

AND THE LORD BLESSED THE LATTER DAYS OF JOB

Job 42:7-17

[7]After the Lord had spoken these words to Job, the Lord said to Eliphaz the Temanite: "My wrath is kindled against you and against your two friends; for you have not spoken of me what is right, as my servant Job has. [8]Now therefore take seven bulls and seven rams, and go to my servant Job, and offer up for yourselves a burnt offering; and my servant Job shall pray for you, for I will accept his prayer not to deal with you according to your folly; for you have not spoken of me what is right, as my servant Job has." [9]So Eliphaz the Temanite and Bildad the Shuhite and Zophar the Naamathite went and did what the Lord had told them; and the Lord accepted Job's prayer.

[10]And the Lord restored the fortunes of Job, when he had prayed for his friends; and the Lord gave Job twice as much as he had before. [11]Then came to him all his brothers and sisters and all who had known him before, and ate bread with him in his house; and they showed him sympathy and comforted him for all the evil that the Lord had brought upon him; and each of them gave him a piece of money and a ring of gold. [12]And the Lord blessed the latter days of Job more than his beginning; and he had fourteen thousand sheep, six thousand camels, a thousand yoke of oxen, and a thousand she-asses. [13]He had also seven sons and three daughters. [14]And he called the name of the first Jemimah; and the name of the second Keziah; and the name of the third Keren-happuch. [15]And in all the land there were no women so fair as Job's daughters; and their father gave them inheritance among their brothers. [16]And after this Job lived a hundred and forty years, and saw his sons, and his sons' sons, four generations. [17]And Job died, an old man, and full of days.

We return in this short prose passage to the old folk tale of chapters 1 and 2. However, a lot has happened since the time of which these chapters told. In its present context the passage no longer simply rounds off the popular story of the good man Job who remained faithful under the severest trials, but also supplies an Epilogue to the whole poetic drama of the good man Job who lost his faith when tragedy struck him, and who could not bear the shame and disgrace of it. Or does it?

(i)

It is hard not to feel uneasy with the thought that the author intended his fractious and tempestuous drama to have a conventional "fairy tale" happy ending. Should he not have left Job in the mixed condition of sorrow and hope, contrition and assurance which was his, following the Lord's intervention from the whirlwind? Would that not have been truer to life as it is, as well as being a sturdier and more realistic model for the sad and resentful sufferers who, in later times, might read this book? Why raise people's expectations by having Job restored to health and prosperity, given a new family to replace the one he had lost, and allowed to pass his remaining days in contentment and peace?

Not surprisingly there are scholars who think that we should in effect ignore the Epilogue. In their view the author may have felt that having begun with excerpts from the folk tale, he ought to make things tidy by concluding with a final excerpt from it, but he was not using it to make any points of his own. I cannot agree. I believe that he had at least three supplementary messages for his readers to ponder, and that, by reproducing the last pious scene from the old popular story more or less unchanged, he has succeeded in getting these messages across not only very cleverly, but with an added dash of irony.

First, there had to be a public vindication of Job. Not only the folk tale which presents his sufferings as a test sent by God, but also the poetic debate in which his integrity has been under constant attack, demand such a vindication. God's commendation of him in verse 7 for saying of God "what is right" is an essential clearing of his reputation in both contexts. In the context of the folk tale it is in recognition of his staunch statements in 1:21 ("The Lord gave, and the Lord has taken away; blessed be the name of the Lord") and 2:10 ("Shall we receive good at the hand of God, and shall we not receive evil?"). In the larger context of the poetic debate it has God saying out loud, in the hearing of the friends and the wider company of onlookers, that Job is innocent of the charges laid against him by those who thought they were speaking in the divine name. Of course God did not approve of everything that his proud and litigious servant had said about him (his speeches from the whirlwind have made that abundantly clear), but he does wish it to be placed unambiguously on record that he infinitely preferred Job's attacks on him to the friends' defence of him. And if the reader wants to take from that that God loves a doughty fighter, he is probably quite right.

Second, the author wishes it to be understood beyond any shadow of doubt that the orthodox Wisdom teaching which the friends represented was inadequate and, if pressed too far, downright dangerous. In the folk tale the friends are condemned for having, like his wife, tried to tempt Job away from the path of virtue and loyalty. In the larger context of the poetic debate, they are condemned for "justifying the ways of God to men" and, in God's name, anathematizing a good man because he did not, in their judgment, measure up to the required standard of piety. Again it is only fair to say that God did not disapprove of everything that the friends had said about him (the fact that his speeches from the whirlwind have quite a few things in common with their speeches makes that also abundantly clear). But in case, having heard his speeches, they were secretly congratulating themselves on how right they had been, he had to tell them to their faces that they were not defenders of the faith but stumbling blocks to the faithful. And if the reader wants to take from this that God has a healthy mistrust for his most self-assured supporters, he is again probably right.

(It is a nice touch that, under God's prompting, the "sinner" in the person of Job makes intercession for the "saints"—how that must have rubbed salt into the friends' wounds! But it is also nice to notice that they took their humiliation bravely. It would have been even nicer if a kind word could have been spared for Job's wife at this point. If Job could be rewarded after having lost his faith, why not she? Perhaps her reward is implied in the mention of new sons and daughters for Job, of which presumably she was the mother. And perhaps in an even more roundabout way it is also implied in Job's granting to his three new daughters "inheritance among their brothers." It is an unusually positive pro-female statement for a Hebrew folk tale to make.)

Third—(and this message does not necessarily contradict the *second*) the author, having savaged it, wants also to put in a word on behalf of traditional Wisdom; and therefore he allows the blessings which in the old folk tale are bestowed on Job for his sterling loyalty to stand. The tight equations of orthodoxy between good works and prosperity and, even more, between suffering and sin, had to go. But the author has no desire to deny that over large areas of life such equations still operated. He also is a representative of Wisdom and it is far from his intention to throw morality out of the window. As I said in the first section of the commentary (on 1:1–5), the author of the Book of Job is not out to destroy the insights of the movement to which he belonged, but to reinstate them on a more mature and less naïve basis. So having (using Job as his exemplar) emphasized that there is no *necessary* correlation between a man's behaviour and a man's fate in this world, and that there is such a thing as unmerited suffering, and that it can strike good men anywhere and at any time and empty their lives of happiness and comfort and hope, the author reminds us, quietly and effectively, that this does not mean that there is no correlation at all between what a man sows and what he reaps. If the reader wishes to take from this that orthodox religion and piety can survive onslaughts upon them as long as they avoid rigidity, and treat with sympathy and kindness the human beings they are guiding to the truth, he is probably right in that too.

(ii)

Many Jobs have stood before us in this book, which defeats all attempts at interpreting it too simply; and the reader, having now gone through it carefully, is entitled to identify with the one who speaks most closely to his or her heart and mind and experience. Is it the protester against injustice beloved of the world's radicals, the champion of the oppressed, the scourge of orthodoxy, the defender of mankind's dignity in the assize of heaven? Or is it the man who hangs onto his faith through thick and thin, the man who regrets his rebellion and prostrates himself in the dust, the man who learns the hard lesson that no-one is good enough to have any rights with God? Or again, is it the man who opens our eyes, as his were opened, to the majesty of God and our own creatureliness, to the wonders and complications of God's creation, and above all to the war which God is forever waging against all that would ruin his purposes and bring to nought his providential plan? Is it even the humbly acquiescent Job of the first two chapters before he went on the rampage against his Maker? Let each of us then choose our own Job; but let us also remember that there are other Jobs who may not be so much to our liking, but whom we ignore at our spiritual peril.

If I were to choose, it would be Job the sufferer *par excellence*. He does not win through to any idea of his suffering being on behalf of, or for the sake of, others. This is not a view of suffering that gets mentioned often in the Old Testament outside the magnificent fifty-third chapter of Isaiah. But no man, unless it was our Lord upon the Cross, has so plumbed the depths for us of what it means to be in pain, or what it feels like to be alienated from God, and to be the butt of human ridicule and scorn. He was a crusty and cantankerous sufferer, but he knew what old Eliphaz, in his better moments, suspected, but did not wait to make his own; that "man is born to trouble as the sparks fly upwards" (5:7). Is not suffering, the basic human condition? And can we not in our own small way suffer with Job, and with him come to the blessed discovery that life on this earth is only made bearable by the fleeting visions of a good and kindly God which, by his grace and pity, are ours from time to time?

APPENDIX: THE SPEECHES OF ELIHU (Chapters 32–37)

From the little piece of prose narrative which introduces Elihu we are obviously being given to understand that he was one of the *dramatis personae* of the old folk tale of Job, which the author of this book has used as his framework. Theoretically, this is not impossible, although his name is not mentioned in the final scene preserved for us in 42:7ff.; after all, Job's wife, who does have a rôle in the earlier part of the story, is not mentioned in that final scene either. What *is* impossible is that the first verses of chapter 32 as we have them could have belonged to such a tale. In the excerpts we possess, in chapters 1 and 2 and chapter 42, Job is blameless and upright and one who fears God at all times. Whatever may be said of him in the poetic debate, he could never have been described in the prose tale as a man who was righteous only in his own eyes, or who justified himself rather than God. It seems sensible to conclude that Elihu is an invented character brought into the debate by someone who thought he had a contribution to make, and furthermore that it was this *someone* who composed the prose introduction as well as the speeches which are given to Elihu.

But was that someone the author of the Book of Job or, as the majority of scholars today assume, a later writer who wished to place the orthodox Wisdom which Job assails in a better light and, indeed, to move it nearer the position which he considered is being adopted in the speeches of the Lord? By putting Elihu's speeches into this Appendix it is clear that I am agreeing with that majority.

The following considerations seem to me to speak decisively against the authenticity of the speeches (readers may test them against the annotated text which is given below):

(a) Chapter 32 tells of a new revelation given to a young man which was denied to his elderly predecessors; this is just the kind of tactic an editor, wishing to have the view of a later age considered, might adopt.

268

(b) Most of Elihu's arguments merely restate those of Eliphaz, Bildad and Zophar in more pointed and definitive terms; he agrees wholeheartedly with them and is, in effect, suggesting that the only reason they are condemned in the Epilogue is because they failed to silence Job.

(c) The writer steals, especially in his final two chapters, from the Lord's speeches, and obviously thinks that he and God are saying the same thing.

(d) There *are* some fresh insights in his speeches, notably in the second half of chapter 33 which speaks of mediating angels for every man, and expands on Eliphaz's brief and passing reference in 5:17 to suffering as a discipline leading men to repentance (see also the latter half of chapter 35 and the first half of chapter 36). We know that, in the Judaism of the post-Exilic period there was a great burgeoning of angelology and an increased emphasis on human corruptibility and the need to practise penance. What is new in Elihu's speeches accords well with the piety of that period, a period which would find (as indeed Christian piety still finds) Job's constant harping on about his innocence very hard to take.

(e) The poetry of the speeches is so inferior to what comes before (whether in the mouths of Job or his three friends) and to what comes after (the speeches of the Lord) that it is extremely difficult to conceive of a common authorship. It has been suggested by those who believe that the author of the Book of Job composed the speeches of Elihu that his purpose may have been the dramatic one of increasing the suspense before God finally spoke. I have already (in the short note following the second commentary on 31:1–40) given my opinion. It seems to me that not only dramatically, but theologically, another intrusion of human words at such a juncture is intolerable. I merely add here the observation that if the speeches *were* by the author and such was his purpose, their content can hardly be taken seriously. And where does that put the fresh insights we have been drawing attention to?

We have already found evidence in chapters 24–27 to reinforce the belief that the original Book of Job was subjected to later editing. Those chapters draw together a number of fragments which the author himself composed and which were probably being kept by him for a revision which, in the event, he never undertook. In the case of chapters 32–37, I cannot bring myself to accept that the author of the Book of Job composed them. I believe in fact that these bombastic and flatulent speeches have a sinister intent and were added to the book after the Exile to make it more palatable to a conforming age which could not stomach its radical theology. The man who wrote them is a worthy forerunner of the *Testament of Job* (see the commentary on 2:11–13).

(i) *Prose Introduction* (32:1–5)

[1]So these three men ceased to answer Job, because he was righteous in his own eyes. [2]Then Elihu the son of Barachel the Buzite, of the family of Ram, became angry. He was angry at Job because he justified himself rather than God; [3]he was angry also at Job's three friends because they had found no answer, although they had declared Job to be in the wrong. [4]Now Elihu had waited to speak to Job because they were older than he. [5]And when Elihu saw that there was no answer in the mouth of these three men, he became angry.

(ii) *Elihu's reasons for intervening* (32:6–22)

[6]And Elihu the son of Barachel the Buzite answered:
"I am young in years, and you are aged;
therefore I was timid and afraid to declare my opinion to you.
[7]I said, 'Let days speak,
and many years teach wisdom.'
[8]But it is the spirit in a man,
the breath of the Almighty, that makes him understand.
[9]It is not the old that are wise,
nor the aged that understand what is right.
[10]Therefore I say, 'Listen to me;
let me also declare my opinion.'

[11]"Behold, I waited for your words,
I listened for your wise sayings,
while you searched out what to say.
[12]I gave you my attention,
and, behold, there was none that confuted Job,

or that answered his words, among you.
¹³Beware lest you say, 'We have found wisdom;
    God may vanquish him, not man.'
¹⁴He has not directed his words against me,
    and I will not answer him with your speeches.

¹⁵"They are discomfited, they answer no more;
    they have not a word to say.
¹⁶And shall I wait, because they do not speak,
    because they stand there, and answer no more?
¹⁷I also will give my answer;
    I also will declare my opinion.
¹⁸For I am full of words,
    the spirit within me constrains me.
¹⁹Behold, my heart is like wine that has no vent;
    like new wineskins, it is ready to burst.
²⁰I must speak, that I may find relief;
    I must open my lips and answer.
²¹I will not show partiality to any person
    or use flattery toward any man.
²²For I do not know how to flatter,
    else would my Maker soon put an end to me."

These words are addressed first to the friends (vv. 6–14) and then to the wider circle of onlookers in the background (vv. 15–22). They reveal a man who is confident that he has a message, but who is in fact a self-righteous bore.

    (iii) *Elihu refutes Job's complaint that God will not
listen to him* (33:1–33)

¹"But now, hear my speech, O Job,
    and listen to all my words.
²Behold, I open my mouth;
    the tongue in my mouth speaks.
³My words declare the uprightness of my heart,
    and what my lips know they speak sincerely.
⁴The spirit of God has made me,
    and the breath of the Almighty gives me life.
⁵Answer me, if you can;

set your words in order before me; take your stand.
⁶Behold, I am toward God as you are;
  I too was formed from a piece of clay.
⁷Behold, no fear of me need terrify you;
  my pressure will not be heavy upon you.

⁸"Surely, you have spoken in my hearing,
  and I have heard the sound of your words.
⁹You say, 'I am clean, without transgression;
  I am pure, and there is no iniquity in me.
¹⁰Behold, he finds occasions against me,
  he counts me as his enemy;
¹¹he puts my feet in the stocks,
  and watches all my paths.'

¹²"Behold, in this you are not right. I will answer you.
  God is greater than man.
¹³Why do you contend against him,
  saying, 'He will answer none of my words'?
¹⁴For God speaks in one way,
  and in two, though man does not perceive it.
¹⁵In a dream, in a vision of the night,
  when deep sleep falls upon men,
  while they slumber on their beds,
¹⁶then he opens the ears of men,
  and terrifies them with warnings,
¹⁷that he may turn man aside from his deed,
  and cut off pride from man;
¹⁸he keeps back his soul from the Pit,
  his life from perishing by the sword.

¹⁹"Man is also chastened with pain upon his bed,
  and with continual strife in his bones;
²⁰so that his life loathes bread,
  and his appetite dainty food.
²¹His flesh is so wasted away that it cannot be seen;
  and his bones which were not seen stick out.
²²His soul draws near the Pit,
  and his life to those who bring death.
²³If there be for him an angel,
  a mediator, one of the thousand,
  to declare to man what is right for him;

²⁴and he is gracious to him, and says,
   'Deliver him from going down into the Pit,
   I have found a ransom;
²⁵let his flesh become fresh with youth;
   let him return to the days of his youthful vigour';
²⁶then man prays to God, and he accepts him,
   he comes into his presence with joy.
   He recounts to men his salvation,
²⁷   and he sings before men, and says:
   'I sinned, and perverted what was right,
   and it was not requited to me.
²⁸He has redeemed my soul from going down into the Pit,
   and my life shall see the light.'

²⁹"Behold, God does all these things,
   twice, three times, with a man,
³⁰to bring back his soul from the Pit,
   that he may see the light of life.
³¹Give heed, O Job, listen to me;
   be silent, and I will speak.
³²If you have anything to say, answer me;
   speak, for I desire to justify you.
³³If not, listen to me;
   be silent, and I will teach you wisdom."

Turning to Job, Elihu assures him (vv. 1–7) that he need not be perturbed at his intervention. He then goes over (vv. 8–11) what Job calls his case against God. Job is wrong in this, Elihu says, and wrong especially in suggesting that God refuses to answer him (vv. 12–13). God speaks in two ways to men: in warning dreams (vv. 14–18) and in the discipline of suffering (vv. 19–22). If Job repents, his personal angel will intercede for him with God and he will be restored (vv. 23–28). Job ought to pay attention (vv. 29–33). It is a pity no-one has found an opportunity to let Job reply; the author of the book would certainly have given him something devastatingly sharp to say.

(iv) *Elihu defends God's justice* (34:1-37)

[1]Then Elihu said:
[2]"Hear my words, you wise men,
    and give ear to me, you who know;
[3]for the ear tests words
    as the palate tastes food.
[4]Let us choose what is right;
    let us determine among ourselves what is good.
[5]For Job has said, 'I am innocent,
    and God has taken away my right;
[6]in spite of my right I am counted a liar;
    my wound is incurable, though I am without transgression.'
[7]What man is like Job,
    who drinks up scoffing like water,
[8]who goes in company with evildoers
    and walks with wicked men?
[9]For he has said, 'It profits a man nothing
    that he should take delight in God.'

[10]"Therefore, hear me, you men of understanding,
    far be it from God that he should do wickedness,
    and from the Almighty that he should do wrong.
[11]For according to the work of a man he will requite him,
    and according to his ways he will make it befall him.
[12]Of a truth, God will not do wickedly,
    and the Almighty will not pervert justice.
[13]Who gave him charge over the earth
    and who laid on him the whole world?
[14]If he should take back his spirit to himself,
    and gather to himself his breath,
[15]all flesh would perish together,
    and man would return to dust.

[16]"If you have understanding, hear this;
    listen to what I say.
[17]Shall one who hates justice govern?
    Will you condemn him who is righteous and mighty,
[18]who says to a king, 'Worthless one,'
    and to nobles, 'Wicked man';
[19]who shows no partiality to princes,
    nor regards the rich more than the poor,

for they are all the work of his hands?

²⁰In a moment they die;
at midnight the people are shaken and pass away,
and the mighty are taken away by no human hand

²¹"For his eyes are upon the ways of man,
and he sees all his steps.
²²There is no gloom or deep darkness
where evildoers may hide themselves.
²³For he has not appointed a time for any man
to go before God in judgment.
²⁴He shatters the mighty without investigation,
and sets others in their place.
²⁵Thus, knowing their works,
he overturns them in the night, and they are crushed.
²⁶He strikes them for their wickedness
in the sight of men,
²⁷because they turned aside from following him,
and had no regard for any of his ways,
²⁸so that they caused the cry of the poor to come to him,
and he heard the cry of the afflicted—
²⁹When he is quiet, who can condemn?
When he hides his face, who can behold him,
whether it be a nation or a man?—
³⁰that a godless man should not reign,
that he should not ensnare the people.

³¹"For has any one said to God,
'I have borne chastisement; I will not offend any more,
³²teach me what I do not see;
if I have done iniquity, I will do it no more?'
³³Will he then make requital to suit you,
because you reject it?
For you must choose, and not I;
therefore declare what you know.
³⁴Men of understanding will say to me,
and the wise man who hears me will say:
³⁵'Job speaks without knowledge,
his words are without insight.'
³⁶Would that Job were tried to the end,
because he answers like wicked men.

[37]For he adds rebellion to his sin;
he claps his hands among us,
and multiplies his words against God."

These words are addressed by Elihu to the friends and are little more than an attempt to preach to the converted. Job is not innocent (vv. 2–9), God cannot do wrong (vv. 10–15); he is ominpotent and impartial in his justice (vv. 16–20), he is omniscient and his judgments are infallible (vv. 21–30), whereas Job speaks without knowledge and is a rebel (vv. 31–37).

(v) *Elihu refutes Job's claim to be innocent* (35:1–16)

[1]And Elihu said:
[2]"Do you think this to be just?
Do you say, 'It is my right before God,'
[3]that you ask, 'What advantage have I?
How am I better off than if I had sinned?'
[4]I will answer you
and your friends with you.
[5]Look at the heavens, and see;
and behold the clouds, which are higher than you.
[6]If you have sinned, what do you accomplish against him?
And if your transgressions are multiplied, what do you do to him?
[7]If you are righteous, what do you give to him;
or what does he receive from your hand?
[8]Your wickedness concerns a man like yourself,
and your righteousness a son of man.

[9]"Because of the multitude of oppressions people cry out;
they call for help because of the arm of the mighty.
[10]But none says, 'Where is God my Maker,
who gives songs in the night,
[11]who teaches us more than the beasts of the earth,
and makes us wiser than the birds of the air?'
[12]There they cry out, but he does not answer,
because of the pride of evil men.
[13]Surely God does not hear an empty cry,
nor does the Almighty regard it.

¹⁴How much less when you say that you do not see him,
   that the case is before him, and you are waiting for him!
¹⁵And now, because his anger does not punish,
   and he does not greatly heed transgression,
¹⁶Job opens his mouth in empty talk,
   he multiplies words without knowledge."

This speech is addressed to Job. Neither a man's virtues nor his sins can affect God, but they can affect the man himself (vv. 2–8). Oppressed people who cry to God and are not answered have not fully learned their lesson (vv. 9–16). The lack of the milk of human kindness in this chapter speaks loudly of the writer's fervid, but essentially warped, mind.

(vi) *Elihu's explanation of the purpose of suffering* (36:1–23)

¹And Elihu continued, and said:
²"Bear with me a little, and I will show you,
   for I have yet something to say on God's behalf.
³I will fetch my knowledge from afar,
   and ascribe righteousness to my Maker.
⁴For truly my words are not false;
   one who is perfect in knowledge is with you.

⁵"Behold, God is mighty, and does not despise any;
   he is mighty in strength of understanding.
⁶He does not keep the wicked alive,
   but gives the afflicted their right.
⁷He does not withdraw his eyes from the righteous,
   but with kings upon the throne
   he sets them for ever, and they are exalted.
⁸And if they are bound in fetters
   and caught in the cords of affliction,
⁹then he declares to them their work
   and their transgressions, that they are behaving arrogantly.
¹⁰He opens their ears to instruction,
   and commands that they return from iniquity.
¹¹If they hearken and serve him,
   they complete their days in prosperity,
   and their years in pleasantness.

¹²But if they do not hearken, they perish by the sword,
    and die without knowledge.

¹³"The godless in heart cherish anger;
    they do not cry for help when he binds them.
¹⁴They die in youth,
    and their life ends in shame.
¹⁵He delivers the afflicted by their affliction,
    and opens their ear by adversity.
¹⁶He also allured you out of distress
    into a broad place where there was no cramping.
    and what was set on your table was full of fatness.

¹⁷"But you are full of the judgment on the wicked;
    judgment and justice seize you.
¹⁸Beware lest wrath entice you into scoffing;
    and let not the greatness of the ransom turn you aside.
¹⁹Will your cry avail to keep you from distress,
    or all the force of your strength?
²⁰Do not long for the night,
    when peoples are cut off in their place.
²¹Take heed, do not turn to iniquity,
    for this you have chosen rather than affliction.
²²Behold, God is exalted in his power;
    who is a teacher like him?
²³Who has prescribed for him his way,
    or who can say, 'Thou hast done wrong'?"

Having (or so he thinks) refuted Job's arguments, Elihu proceeds to teach him "on God's behalf" (v. 2). God destroys the wicked, but the righteous are those who learn from their afflictions and turn to him. Job should, instead of whining to God, take to heart what God, the supreme teacher, is telling him through his suffering. It seems to me that Elihu regards all men as depraved, and the difference between the wicked and the righteous as one of degree only; and his claim to speak for God is nauseating.

(vii) *Elihu's praise of God's wisdom and might* (36:24–37:13)

²⁴"Remember to extol his work,
    of which men have sung.

[25]All men have looked on it;
　　man beholds it from afar.
[26]Behold, God is great, and we know him not;
　　the number of his years is unsearchable.
[27]For he draws up the drops of water,
　　he distils his mist in rain
[28]which the skies pour down,
　　and drop upon man abundantly.
[29]Can any one understand the spreading of the clouds,
　　the thunderings of his pavilion?
[30]Behold, he scatters his lightning about him,
　　and covers the roots of the sea.
[31]For by these he judges peoples;
　　he gives food in abundance.
[32]He covers his hands with the lightning,
　　and commands it to strike the mark.
[33]Its crashing declares concerning him,
　　who is jealous with anger against iniquity.

[1]"At this also my heart trembles,
　　and leaps out of its place.
[2]Hearken to the thunder of his voice
　　and the rumbling that comes from his mouth.
[3]Under the whole heaven he lets it go,
　　and his lightning to the corners of the earth.
[4]After it his voice roars;
　　he thunders with his majestic voice
　　and he does not restrain the lightnings when his voice is heard.
[5]God thunders wondrously with his voice;
　　he does great things which we cannot comprehend.
[6]For to the snow he says, 'Fall on the earth';
　　and to the shower and the rain, 'Be strong.'
[7]He seals up the hand of every man,
　　that all men may know his work.
[8]Then the beasts go into their lairs,
　　and remain in their dens.
[9]From its chamber comes the whirlwind,
　　and cold from the scattering winds.
[10]By the breath of God ice is given,
　　and the broad waters are frozen fast.
[11]He loads the thick cloud with moisture;

the clouds scatter his lightning.
[12]They turn round and round by his guidance,
to accomplish all that he commands them
on the face of the habitable world.
[13]Whether for correction, or for his land,
or for love, he causes it to happen."

The last verse sums up the purpose of this powerful but conventional, and obviously angled, poem. This is "preaching praise" with a vengeance.

(viii) *Elihu's praise of God's mystery and inscrutability* (37:14–24)

[14]"Hear this, O Job;
stop and consider the wondrous works of God.
[15]Do you know how God lays his command upon them,
and causes the lightning of his cloud to shine?
[16]Do you know the balancings of the clouds,
the wondrous works of him who is perfect in knowledge,
[17]you whose garments are hot
when the earth is still because of the south wind?
[18]Can you, like him, spread out the skies,
hard as a molten mirror?
[19]Teach us what we shall say to him;
we cannot draw up our case because of darkness.
[20]Shall it be told him that I would speak?
Did a man ever wish that he would be swallowed up?

[21]"And now men cannot look on the light
when it is bright in the skies,
when the wind has passed and cleared them.
[22]Out of the north comes golden splendour;
God is clothed with terrible majesty.
[23]The Almighty—we cannot find him;
he is great in power and justice,
and abundant righteousness he will not violate.
[24]Therefore men fear him;
he does not regard any who are wise in their own conceit."

This eloquent poem would have been more impressive if we had not just been exposed to five and a half chapters in which Elihu had explained in considerable detail what God's providence was all about. I find the man insufferable. His speeches do not deserve to be mentioned in the same breath as the speeches of the three friends he chides for not doing their job well enough, far less the speeches of Job and the Lord. The author of the book is of course skilled enough to have penned so obnoxious a portrait and to have given a pretentious man suitably pretentious words to mouth; but I cannot see what reason he could have had. I get the impression that the writer of these chapters is putting himself into Elihu's place and that, sad to say, he means every word of them.

FURTHER READING

Books marked * are more suitable for initial study.

Commentaries

*F. I. Andersen, *Job* (Tyndale Old Testament Commentaries) (Inter-Varsity Press, 1976)

*D. Bergant, *Job, Ecclesiastes* (Old Testament Message) (Gill and Macmillan and Michael Glazier, 1982)

A. B. Davidson, *The Book of Job* (The Cambridge Bible for Schools and Colleges) (Cambridge University Press, 1884, and many subsequent editions)

E. Dhorme, *A Commentary on the Book of Job*, English translation (Thomas Nelson, 1967)

S. R. Driver and G. B. Gray, *A Critical and Exegetical Commentary on the Book of Job* (International Critical Commentary) (T. & T. Clark, 1921)

R. Gordis, *The Book of Job* (The Jewish Theological Seminary of America, distributed by KTAV, 1978)

*N. C. Habel, *The Book of Job* (The Cambridge Bible Commentary on the New English Bible) (Cambridge University Press, 1975)

M. H. Pope, *Job* (The Anchor Bible) (Doubleday, Third Edition, 1973)

H. H. Rowley, *The Book of Job* (The New Century Bible Commentary) (Marshall, Morgan and Scott, Second Edition, 1980)

J. Strahan, *The Book of Job Interpreted* (T. & T. Clark, 1913)

*S. Terrien, "The Book of Job" in *The Interpreter's Bible*, Volume III (Abingdon Press, 1954)

Studies

D. Cox, *The Triumph of Impotence: Job and the Tradition of the*

Absurd (Analecta Gregoriana) (Università Gregoriana Editrice, 1978)

*R. Davidson, *The Courage to Doubt: Exploring an Old Testament Theme* (SCM Press, 1983), Chapter 9

C. Duquoc and C. Floristán (editors), *Job and the Silence of God* (Concilium, No. 169) (The Seabury Press and T. & T. Clark, 1983)

*J. H. Eaton, *Job* (Old Testament Guides) (Journal for the Study of the Old Testament Press, 1985)

*N. Glatzer (editor), *The Dimensions of Job: A Study and Selected Readings* (Schocken Books, 1969)

E. M. Good, *Irony in the Old Testament* (The Westminster Press, 1965; The Almond Press, 1981), Chapter VII

R. Otto, *The Idea of the Holy*, English translation (Oxford University Press, 1925), Chapter X

H. W. Robinson, "The Cross of Job" in *The Cross in the Old Testament* (SCM Press, 1955)

*P. S. Sanders (editor), *Twentieth Century Interpretations of the Book of Job* (Prentice-Hall, 1968)

C. Westermann, *The Structure of the Book of Job* (Fortress Press, 1981)

*J. Wood, *Job and the Human Situation* (Geoffrey Bles, 1966)

Interest

William Blake, *Illustrations of the Book of Job 1820-25* (frequently reproduced in Fine Art publications)

Carl Gustav Jung, *Answer to Job*, English translation (Routledge and Kegan Paul, 1954)

J. H. Kahn, *Job's Illness: Loss, Grief and Integration, A Psychological Interpretation* (Pergamon Press, 1975)

Archibald MacLeish, *J. B., A Play in Verse* (Samuel French, Inc., 1956)